THE SMOKE OF SATAN IN THE TEMPLE OF GOD

The Church in the United States since the Second Vatican Council

By Timothy Wallace

D1065865

PRESS

For Mary Jane —

May you always read
from this in a time of great
joy!   Under the Mercy

Jim

For Marcy, the first girl who liked me back. May we grow old together in faith, hope, and love under the Mercy until we see God in the face.

For God created man for incorruption,
and made him in the image of his own eternity,
but through the devil's envy death entered the world,
and those who belong to his party experience it.

Wisdom 2:23–24

Contents

Foreword

*L*ike many of the twenty-five percent or so of the American people who would respond with "Roman Catholic" when asked their religion in an emergency room, I am a "cradle Catholic," born into an Irish-American family in Detroit as a baby boomer in 1952 and baptized at St. Gabriel's on the southwest side in the same year. I first received the body, blood, soul, and divinity of Our Lord and Savior Jesus Christ in second grade at St. Eugene's parish in northwest Detroit, for which the Sisters of Notre Dame DeNamur admirably prepared me. I still stand amazed at the reverence instilled in the second-graders in the black-and-white photos shot by my father, Don, that day. I was also confirmed at St. Eugene's parish in the fourth grade, after which my mother, Ann, took me out for my favorite breakfast, strawberry pancakes, where I played "Fun, Fun, Fun" by the Beach Boys at least twice. Since my return and faithful assent to all that the

Catholic Church teaches in 1995, I have been a regular communicant and penitent.

My first memory on this earth is as a baby less than a year old, being driven by my parents to a funeral in Pennsylvania, an event my mother corroborated years later as I described it. My favorite memory from childhood is one I frequently think back on. It is one of observing from my pew prior to the 6:30 a.m. Mass in 1958 the Sisters entering St. Eugene's from the front-side entrance of the Church, special to them for access from their one-room convent in the adjoining school. It was winter, and the church was dimly lit. They entered with awe-inspiring reverence, processing in their full habits, the beads of their waist-draped rosaries colliding gently, genuflecting and kneeling in silent preparation for the soon to occur reenactment in a non-bloody manner of Our Lord's eternal sacrifice first offered on Calvary for our salvation, the Holy Sacrifice of the Mass. The latent aroma of incense and the sight of fresh beeswax candles flickering on the altar, together with the sisters' silent reverence and obvious practice of what they taught their first graders — *the importance of reverence in the House of God* — is an impression which not only convinced me that Jesus lived there in the Tabernacle, but was also an actual grace which I believe, together with my baptismal grace and my Mom's faith witness, was instrumental in eventually leading me back into the fullness of Catholic teaching.

I do not know now what became of each Sister, but I am sure that whatever their relationship with Our Lord today, they had no idea that one of their first-graders was so inspired by their witness to the real Presence they gave that winter morn.

In the years prior to the Second Vatican Council, I also remember attending daily Mass before elementary school, which, because we had fasted for three hours, allowed us to eat breakfast in math class. I remember singing *Tantum Ergo* at Wednesday Evening Benediction, which I was in the habit of attending with my Mom, siblings, and "Gramp," (her Dad, John). I also remember looking forward to participating in the praying of that most sublime form of prayer, the Holy Sacrifice of the Mass, with my St. Joseph's Daily Missal.

With Pope Benedict's having granted permission for priests to offer the Extraordinary form of the Roman Rite, we hear much ado in the form of reaction against this from Catholic "progressives," and about how the Council placed a new emphasis on the laity's participation at Mass, the implication being that Catholics did not actively participate at Mass prior to Vatican II, opting for such devotions as the praying of the Rosary or Holy Cards. To such persons I say, not only did I pray along with the priest in the Latin Missal, but I was a better-than-average singer of Gregorian chant, thanks to convert and organist Mrs. Crowley's daily faithful rendering of the chanted antiphons and propers in Latin. Having failed to become an altar server by stumbling over one Latin syllable in my tryout test, (Sr. Isabelle must have had a bad habit day that day), I also remember telling my younger brother John, who passed, that he forgot the proper order in covering the communion rails before Holy Communion.

St. Eugene's eventually closed in the Year of Our Lord 1989 due to "white flight" and demographic changes after the 1967 riots in Detroit, and with this the demise of the place where I spent some of the holiest years of my life, years in which neither I nor my classmates were ashamed to *publicly* give witness to our faith in Christ (yes, I too dressed in sheets and played the priest in acting out the Mass with my siblings). My memories of participation at Mass are glorious ones. There was a *sense of the sacred* that has since, through misimplementation of *Sacrosanctum Concilium*, long since evaporated at Mass.

I graduated from St. Eugene's in 1966, when the liturgical changes after the close of the council promulgated in *Sacrosanctum Concilium* to the best of my memory had not yet been thoroughly implemented. I journeyed off to Detroit Cathedral High School downtown, where my experience of the presence of Christ in the Eucharist began to fade, as I no longer was required to attend daily Mass, and cannot remember one thing taught to me in high school religion class by my teacher, who was also the Business Ed. and Typing teacher and track coach. A rumination of the yearbooks for these years reveals photo captions such as "DC Sodality Men Reach Out," and "Fr. Trainor Celebrates Mass Facing the Seniors as he Closes the Senior Retreat." To be sure, in my adolescent years I hadn't the foggiest idea of what was happening in the Church in the United States after the Council, and, after seeing a pretty, red-headed sophomore on the bus on her way to Immaculata High one day (in the end I proved too shy to sit next to her on the DSR bus . . .), I confess I really never paid it much attention.

In the ensuing college years I drifted further and further away from the Church in true "prodigal son" fashion, often arguing with my mother over matters of faith. In college, I was approached by evangelicals asking, "Are you saved, brother?" something they did not believe of me as long as I was Catholic. The norm would have been for this now-lukewarm Catholic to have been lured away from the Church, but baptismal grace proved me an exception. Though I was not all that holy, I wasn't about to become a Pentecostal! How Our Lord led me home is outside the scope of this endeavor; suffice it to say that there are rough parallels with St. Augustine.

Upon returning to the Faith I was unable to find employment in my undergraduate field, history, and so volunteered to teach CCD in my parish, hoping eventually to land a job there, teaching history. This required me to earn catechist certification offered by the Archdiocese of Detroit, which I did in 1978. No sooner had I completed the requirements, when a combination Religion/History opening occurred at a co-ed Catholic High school in inner-city Detroit. I taught there for one year, after which I landed a job teaching Scripture (for which I, by true Catholic standards, was woefully unprepared to do) in my parish high school, where I remained for one year. I then took a position at a Catholic high school in a suburb of Detroit, where I have been ever since. Since 1995, however, and my "reversion" to the fullness of Catholic teaching, I began an extensive study of the post-conciliar years in the United States, for which my training in history and as a catechist at the St. John Bosco Institute for Catechetics, as well as twenty-five years as a catechist in the Archdiocese of Detroit amply prepared me.

Since 1965 there has been no shortage of books written on the Second Vatican Council, and for a single author to offer an account of these years perhaps requires greater *chutzpah* than anyone should possess. Indeed, there is very little that is original in the book. I merely offer a synthesis of much that I have read about and experienced in the Church in the United States in the decades following the Second Vatican Council in my experience as a catechist (1978–2000) and history teacher. What I believe is original in my synthesis is a look at these events in the context of the oft-ignored Church teaching on the reality of spiritual warfare.

After an analysis in chapter one of the neomodernist heresy which emerged as the dominant influence in theology after Vatican II, subsequent chapters outline the influence and effects of theological error in sexual moral teaching, the Mass, religious life, catechesis, and the role of the bishop in the face of this error, concluding with a reflection on Vatican II's universal call to holiness. Lack of space, and competence, has necessitated passing over a discussion of the priesthood and higher education after Vatican II. On these subjects the reader can do no better than Monsignor George A. Kelly's classic *The Battle for the American Church.*

I have written for those Catholics born and perhaps catechized before Vatican II or immediately thereafter who as yet are unaware of the true teaching of the Council. It should not surprise the reader that there are Catholics whose lifestyles do not differentiate them all that much from those who are not Catholic and/or Christian. Moreover, many Catholics of the "baby-boom" generation are alienated from the Church all together because their only exposure has been to a superficial, cultural Catholicism, impotent in the face of an American culture increasingly without faith. Conversely, many others have left the Church—hungrier, as they say, for a more "biblically-based church." The book is also intended for young people of the "JP II" generation of Catholics, born long after the council but perhaps not fully aware of the turmoil spawned by dissent in the Church which, though on the wane, is still with us today. These young people, especially those in authentically Catholic colleges (Franciscan, Christendom, Aquinas, *Ave Maria,* etc.) will be the Church of the twenty-first century, and in my experience have an interest in this recent history of the Church.

I owe a debt of gratitude to author and friend, Elizabeth Heiter, who read and edited the manuscript and much improved the writing. Matthew Hill reviewed the early chapters and provided much-needed theological and historical criticism. In addition to his endorsement, Fr. Michael Wilkes read the manuscript and offered incisive criticism on the papacy of Paul VI. Any errors in the text are the sole responsibility of the author, who remains first and foremost a layman who loves Our Lord and His One, Holy, Catholic, and Apostolic Church.

CHAPTER ONE

The "Smoke of Satan" in Context

"And he said to them, 'I saw Satan fall like lightning from heaven.'"

Luke 10:18

"Put on the whole armor of God, that you may be able to stand against the wiles of the devil. For we are not contending against flesh and blood, but against the principalities, against the powers, against the world rulers of this present darkness, against the spiritual hosts of wickedness in the heavenly places."

Ephesians 6:11–12

"It is clear that the Church is facing a grave crisis. Under the name of 'the new Church,' 'the post-conciliar Church,' a different Church from that of Jesus Christ is now trying to establish itself; an anthropocentric society threatened with immanentist apostasy which is allowing itself to be swept along in a movement of general abdication under the pretext of renewal, ecumenism, or adaptation."

-Cardinal Henri de Lubac, S.J., Christian Witness (1967)

I.

ctor Mel Gibson, when filming his now classic *The Passion of the Christ*, was interviewed on the set by *Time* in January, 2003. As far as Gibson was concerned, Vatican II "corrupted the institution of the Church. Look at the main fruits: dwindling numbers and pedophilia." In this Gibson misrepresents the moral crisis which faced the Church in 2003, which was not "pedophilia" but an inordinate amount of active homosexuals ordained as priests and some inattentive bishops who ran interference for them, all consequences of a failure to uphold and live the Church's sexual moral teaching. Accolades to Gibson are in order, though, for his perception of Catholic demographics. The chart which follows gives us the tip of the iceberg regarding a few indicators since 1965 (the underwater portion is the subject of the remainder of the book): [1]

	1965	Today
Priests	58,000	45,000
Ordinations	1,575	450
Priestless Parishes	1%	15%
Seminarians	600	200
Sisters	180,000	75,000
Catholic High School Enrollment	700,000	386,000
Catholic Elementary Enrollment	4.5 million	Less than 2 million
Attendance at Mass	3 out of 4	1 out of 4

An interesting contrast to Mr. Gibson's view is Temple University professor Leonard Swidler's assessment in his introduction to *The Church in Anguish: Has the Vatican Betrayed Vatican II?* Swidler writes of:

" . . . the anguish engendered in the Catholic church during the past decade[2] through what appears to many Catholics, and non-Catholics, as an attempt by the present leadership in the Vatican to reverse the momentous gains in maturity that were made at the Second Vatican Council (1961–65) . . . Vatican II was clearly a peak experience. Today we seem to be going through "the valley of the shadow . . ."[3]

Neither Mr. Gibson, who in common parlance is a traditionalist Catholic, nor Swidler have it just right. Mr. Gibson's "dwindling numbers and pedophilia" are not the fruits of the actual reforms set down in the documents of Vatican II any more than is Professor Swidler's claim of "momentous gains in maturity" prior to 1978. The evidence reveals that the true fruits of Vatican Council II are only *today* beginning to be realized in each of the four main areas addressed by the Council documents, which brings to mind one final assessment of the Council's fruits I discovered which, when I began understand *why* it was offered, inspired me to write this book.

At the close of Vatican II, Pope Paul VI remarked that Christianity, the religion of God-Incarnate, had encountered the religion of man-made God. He was of the opinion that much of the Council was given over to demonstrating the compatibility of Enlightenment belief with Catholicism. [4] Several years hence, on June 29, 1972, Paul delivered another assessment of the state of the Roman Catholic Church since the close of Vatican II. As Cardinal Silvio Oddi recalled it (in an article first published on March 17, 1990, in *Il Sabato* magazine in Rome) the Holy Father told a congregation:

> We have the impression that through some cracks in the wall the smoke of Satan has entered the temple of God: it is doubt, uncertainty, questioning, dissatisfaction, confrontation. And how did this come about? We will confide to you the thought that may be, we ourselves admit in free discussion, that may be unfounded, and that is that there has been a power, an adversary power. Let us call him by his name: the devil. We thought that after the Council a day of sunshine would have dawned for the history of the Church. What dawned instead was a day of clouds and storms, of darkness, of searching and uncertainties.[5]

His fears of demonic penetration of the Church were even stronger in a later statement:

> The opening to the world [*aggiornamento* or "updating"] became *a veritable invasion of the Church by worldly thinking.* . . . We have perhaps been too weak and imprudent.[6]

Following these remarks we have a further address given by the Pope to a general audience in November, 1972 which sheds much light on what the Holy Father had in mind and heart in referring to "the smoke of Satan." It deserves careful reflection, and so is quoted at length. The Holy Father began:

What are the Church's greatest needs at the present time? Don't be surprised at Our answer and don't write it off as simplistic or even superstitious: one of the Church's greatest needs is to be defended against the evil we call the Devil.

After discussing the goodness of God's creation, the fall, and the problem of evil in a world created good, and man's capacity to do evil, he continued:

We come face to face with sin which is a perversion of human freedom and the profound cause of death because it involves detachment from God, the source of life. And then sin in its turn becomes the occasion and the effect of interference in us and our work by a dark, hostile agent, the Devil. Evil is not merely an absence of something but an active force, a living, spiritual being that is perverted and that perverts others. It is a terrible reality, mysterious and frightening.

It is a departure from the picture provided by biblical Church teaching to refuse to acknowledge the Devil's existence; to regard him as a self-sustaining principle who, unlike other creatures, does not owe his origin to God; or to explain the Devil as a pseudo-reality, a conceptual, fanciful personification of the unknown causes of our misfortunes. When the problem of evil is seen in all its complexity and in its absurdity from the point of view of our limited minds, it becomes an obsession. It poses the greatest single obstacle to our religious understanding of the universe. It is no accident that St. Augustine was bothered by this for years: "I sought the source of evil, and I found no explanation."

The Pope then reminded his listeners of references in Scripture and the Mass to the aggressive and oppressive "power of darkness," adding:

So we know that this dark disturbing being exists and that he is still at work with his treacherous cunning; he is the hidden enemy who sows errors and misfortunes in human history. It is worth recalling the revealing Gospel parable of the good seed and the cockle, for it synthesizes and explains the lack of logic that seems to preside over our contradictory experiences: "An enemy has done this." He is "a murderer from the beginning . . . and the father of lies,"[Jn 8:44] as Christ defines him. He undermines man's moral equilibrium with his sophistry. He is the malign, clever seducer who knows how to make his way into us through the senses, the imagination and the libido, through utopian logic, or through disordered social contacts in the give and take of our activities, so that he can bring about in us deviations that are all the more harmful because they seem to conform to our physical or mental makeup, or to our profound, instinctive aspirations.

This matter of the Devil and of the influence he can exert on individuals as well as on communities, entire societies or events, is a very important chapter of Catholic doctrine which should be studied again, although it is given little attention today. Some think a sufficient compensation can be found in psychoanalytic and psychiatric studies or in spiritualistic experiences, which are unfortunately so widespread in some countries today.

People are afraid of falling back into old Manichean theories, or into frightening deviations of fancy and superstition. Nowadays they prefer to appear strong and unprejudiced to pose as positivists,[7] while at the same time lending faith to many unfounded magical or popular superstitions or, worse still, exposing their souls—their baptized souls, visited so often by the Eucharistic Presence and inhabited by the Holy Spirit!—to licentious sensual experiences and to harmful drugs, as well as to the ideological seductions of fashionable errors. *These are cracks* [emphasis added] through which the evil one can easily penetrate and change the human mind.

This is not to say that every sin is directly due to diabolical action; but it is true that those who do not keep watch over themselves with a certain moral rigor are exposed to the influence of the 'mystery of iniquity' cited by St. Paul which raises serious questions about our salvation.

Our doctrine becomes uncertain, darkness obscured as it is by the darkness surrounding the Devil. But our curiosity, excited by the certainty of his multiple existence, has a right to raise two questions. Are there signs, and what are they, of the presence of diabolical action? And what means of defense do we have against such an insidious danger? . . . We have to be cautious about answering the first question, even though the signs of the Evil One seem to be very obvious at times. We can presume that his sinister action is at work where the denial of God becomes radical, subtle, and absurd; where lies become powerful and hypocritical in the face of evident truth; where love is smothered by cold, cruel selfishness; where Christ's name is attacked with conscious, rebellious hatred, where the spirit of the Gospel is watered down and rejected where despair is affirmed as the last word; and so forth. . . . It is easier to formulate an answer to the other question — what defense, what remedy should we use against the Devil's action? — even though it remains difficult to put into practice. We could say: everything that defends us from sin strengthens us by that very fact against the invisible enemy. Grace is the decisive defense. Innocence takes on the aspect of strength. Everyone recalls how often the apostolic method of teaching used the armor of a soldier as a symbol for the virtues that can make a Christian invulnerable. The Christian must be a militant; he must be vigilant and strong; and he must at times make use of special ascetical practices to escape from certain diabolical attacks. Jesus teaches us this by pointing to "prayer and fasting" as the remedy. And the Apostle suggests the main line we should follow: "Be not overcome by evil, but overcome evil with good. "

With an awareness, therefore, of the opposition that individual souls, the Church and the world must face at the present time, we will try to give both meaning and, effectiveness to the familiar invocation in our principal prayer: "Our Father . . . deliver us from evil!" [8]

During the course of my research for this book, Cardinal Virgilio Noe, the chief Vatican liturgist during the pontificate of Paul VI, in an interview with the Roman *Petrus* website, related that when Paul spoke of the "smoke of Satan" entering the Catholic Church, he was referring to liturgical abuses. In that denunciation, he said, the Pope "meant to include all those priests or bishops and cardinals who didn't render proper worship to the Lord, celebrating Holy Mass badly because of an errant interpretation of the implementation of the Second Vatican Council." While I agree this was indeed a concern, I believe that the Holy Father's subsequent remarks on this subject discussed above do not take away from the book's argument, and, were the Pope alive, he would agree with his former master of ceremonies when in the same interview he stated, "Now it is necessary to recover — and in a hurry — the sense of the sacred in the *ars celebrandi*, before the smoke of Satan completely pervades the whole Church." [9]

And so it was that Paul VI became of a mind that by 1972 an "adversary power" which he called by his name — the Devil — had entered the Church. (*cf.* Job 1:6; *Satan* means "the opponent" or "adversary"[10]) How so? For starters, Bishop Fulton Sheen warned us in his popular retelling of the life of Christ, *The Eternal Galilean:* "Do not mock the Gospels and say there is no Satan. Evil is too real in the world to say that. Do not say the idea of Satan is dead and gone. Satan never gains so many cohorts as when, in his shrewdness, he spreads the rumor that he is long since dead." Such an attitude only leaves the devil freer than he would otherwise be to work to gain souls for hell. "I am who am not."

A 1997 survey of beliefs about Satan revealed that 69 percent of Catholics believe that "Satan is only a symbol of evil," only 26% believing that "Satan is a living being."[11] Pope Paul instructs us that the former position is "a departure from the picture provided by biblical Church teaching. . . ." This appears as one little "crack in the wall" through which the smoke could enter: belief in the Devil makes for bad cosmology![12] Priests, catechists and religious who take the Devil lightly are indeed the easiest target for what St. Paul termed "the mystery of iniquity."[13] What the Sisters of Notre Dame De Namur taught me regarding the reality of the Devil prior to Vatican II proved no different from what the *Catechism of the Catholic Church* teaches us today:

> The doctrine of original sin, closely connected with that of redemption by Christ, provides lucid discernment of man's situation and activity in the world. By our first parents' sin, *the devil has acquired a certain domination over man, even though man remains free* [emphasis added]. Original sin entails 'captivity under the power of him who thenceforth had the power of death, that is, the devil. Ignorance of the fact that man has a wounded nature inclined to evil gives rise to serious errors in the areas of education, politics, social action and morals.[14]

This originally good angel, the Devil, is a powerful spiritual creature whose goal is to destroy us by turning us against the Father. Christians refer to him every time they pray the Lord's Prayer—"deliver us from evil" refers to the Evil One, of and to whom Jesus spoke regularly in the Gospels, the angel who opposes his Father. The Catechism broadens this teaching, noting that "heresy, apostasy, and schism — do not occur without human sin: Where there are sins, there are also divisions, schisms, heresies, and disputes."[15] Thirty years of teaching in Catholic schools, all of them since the time of Vatican II, has taught me that the Church has witnessed the aforementioned errors in the Sacred Liturgy, religious life, catechesis, social action, and morals, all of which have divided the People of God.

Satan, called in Sacred Scripture "the father of lies" had also entered the Church, Paul warned us, by making his "way into us through the senses, the imagination and the *libido*, through utopian logic, or through disordered social contacts in the give and take of our activities, so that he can bring about in us deviations that are all the more harmful because they *seem* to conform to our physical or mental makeup, or to our profound, instinctive aspirations." It thus should not surprise us that the majority of Catholics who believe you can disagree with the fundamentals of the Catholic faith and still remain a Catholic in good standing dissent on issues of gender or sexual morality. Or, if not sexual morality, one might think the Church's priorities skewed, desiring to prioritize "building God's Kingdom on earth" through the establishment of justice and peace, believing this to be the target of Vatican II's "updating" of the Church. When divorced from the *totality* of the deposit of the faith this is reminiscent of Paul's VI's phrase "utopian logic" as an opening to the diabolic.

While these are just a few instances of what Paul VI warned the faithful against as he neared the end of his life, I hope I have been clear in suggesting at least a *context* for what was on the Holy Father's mind in reference to the smoke of Satan entering the temple of God.[16] As we know, Our Lord, when he commissioned Peter "the rock" upon which He would build his Church, also said that the gates of Hell would not prevail against it. He never said Hell would not *try* to prevail.

In St. John's gospel, Our Lord calls Satan "ruler of this world,"[17] teaching that the salvation he would bring us as God's gift involved the destruction of Satan's power in this world. Just before His passion, Jesus told the apostles that an eternal fire awaited Satan and his angels. Sacred Scripture teaches that the Prince of Darkness will be allowed by God to test us for a time, but in the end will be "thrown into the lake of fire and sulphur where the beast and the false prophet were, and they will be tormented day and night for ever and ever."[18] Thus, in Catholic teaching, the reality of spiritual warfare, though often dismissed, is something the Church Militant here on earth must be prepared for.

It is consistent with Catholic teaching to describe the "worldly thinking" alluded to by Paul VI and Fr. De Lu Bac as "ideological seductions of fashionable errors" through which the Evil One may penetrate the human mind. Today this ideology has been labeled "neomodernist," and understands the Church not as a supernatural institution but as a social one, intended to advance human civilization. As I hope to show, we would do well to consider that the neomodernist phenomenon underlies the heresy, apostasy, and schism evident in the Church, a means by which the 'ruler of this world" is "testing" us.

II.

The French, as Jacques Maritain has written, have a saying: "When a fish corrupts, the rot begins in the head." Thus we begin our study of the causes of the crisis of faith in the Catholic Church by looking to the realm of the mind, the intellectual order. In so doing we are well-disposed in taking a closer look at the collection of theological, philosophical, and Scriptural errors termed neomodernism by the Church.

My reading of the documents of the Council cleared up for me Fr. De Lu Bac's use of the phrase "new church" as "*post-conciliar;*"[19] there is little of what we hear emphasized today as "the spirit of Vatican II" Church actually *in* the documents of Vatican II. But how many of the faithful today read and study them? I certainly did not before 1995.

Prior to that time my habit as a catechist had been to read the writings of the scholars on what the Council taught or had changed, often trusting the word of diocesan personnel under whom I trained as a catechist in the late 1970s. Unwisely, I never read the council documents in their *entirety* for myself; my paperback Flannery edition yellowed on the shelf. This is a crucial point, because many priests and religious trained in "the spirit of Vatican II" have used their particular positions in the Church to educate the faithful as to what Vatican II taught, as we shall see. Both theologians seduced by neomodernist thought and religious education "consultants" who studied their works did nothing less, I was to discover, than attempt to implement an ecumenical council whose documents were not widely read nor studied, which afforded them ample opportunity to misimplement authentic conciliar teaching.

Were one to ask, for example, an adult Catholic whom one perceived to be a "liberal"Catholic the following: "does the Church still see herself as hierarchical?" My bet is the person would respond something like this: "Oh, no, that is pre-Vatican II. The Council teaches that the Church is the People of God." If, then one were to procur a copy of the Documents of Vatican II, one could reference *Lumen Gentium,* Chapter II, entitled "The Church Is Hierarchical." This section teaches that a hierarchical structure is necessary to best shepherd "the People of God." Many baptized Catholics today have thus come under the influence of dissenting theologians, priests or sisters, or DREs, or seminary or university professors, or whomever. These individuals are responsible for the error which has exploited true conciliar teaching. These brethren often label Catholics such as myself who study what the Council Fathers actually taught as "pre-Vatican" or "traditionalist," or "fundamentalist."

So, if Fr. De Lu Bac is correct, the real question we must explore is how to account for inadequate interpretations of the Council which coalesced as "the spirit of Vatican II." One other question naturally follows from this—have a majority of the Bishops in the United States since 1965 failed to exercise responsibly the role of bishop in exercising the authority granted them (in union with the successor of St. Peter) by Jesus to teach and discipline those who, under the guise of *aggiornamento,* and ecumenism have worked to make what is something other than Christ's Church a reality?[20]

Historically, modernism was a philosophical school which aimed at a radical transformation of human thought in relation to God, man, the world, and life, this and the next. Space allows us only a brief overview of the roots of modernism, which lay in the development of historical consciousness during the Renaissance (1300–1600), which by the nineteenth century had produced in the European mind the conviction that everything is so conditioned by its historical age or epoch that no absolute truth could possibly transcend historical change. Additionally the humanists of the Renaissance in their exaltation of the individual laid the groundwork for the later, more secular humanism of the nineteenth and twentieth centuries.[21] Western civilization's contact with other civilizations during the fifteenth and sixteenth century voyages of discovery fashioned a relativization of culture and religious beliefs, which, coupled with the dissolution of Christian unity after the Reformation, further weakened Christianity's moral and spiritual authority. The Scientific Revolution, in its assertion that the new science alone could produce certain knowledge over time relegated the validity of Christian belief, so contrary to human reason, to the individual's subjective experience.

Modernism's philosophical origin is generally traced to the philosophy of Rene Descartes (1596–1650), often styled modern philosophy's founding father in light of his methodical exaltation of human reason as the true source of knowledge. Though a philosopher inspired by the new science, as a devout Catholic Descartes took pains to protect religious belief from skeptical attack, in effect "protecting" it by putting it off to one side. His epistemology centered on the "thinking self" as the point of departure for what one can truly know. Such knowledge Descartes thought was innate, merely awaiting the self's discovery.[22] His dualistic anthropology asserted that the human person was made up of antithetical essences, that is, mind and body, spirit and flesh, and space-occupying corporeality and "thought thinking thought."

The French philosopher took great pride in his argument for the existence of God from human reason alone, set down in his *Discourse on Method*. This was an astounding development, for since the emergence of the European universities in the twelfth century, theology had served as the "queen of the sciences," and religion was regarded as at the epicenter of reality. Now philosophers like Descartes regarded mathematics as the most perfect of disciplines, the one which provided a hope of certitude in other areas of inquiry. His rationalist disciples, the Cartesians, asserted that man could know things with certainty only through the use of reason. The Cartesian approach to epistemology disseminated throughout continental Europe during the "Age of Reason" (the 17th and 18th centuries), the age when many traditional attitudes of the "Age of Faith" were being undermined.[23] In reaction to Cartesian rationalism other thinkers turned to empiricism, another strand of modernist thought which argued that man could know things with certainty only through his senses; that it is sensory data and not innate cognition that creates certain knowledge. Spearheaded by the English thinker John Locke's *Essay Concerning Human Understanding*, empiricists argued that as our thoughts cannot be sensed, measured, weighed, in short—subjected to the scientific method—they are fundamentally unknowable.[24]

It should be clear that from the perspective of Catholic philosophy that in their understanding of the human person both rationalists and empiricists were looking at only part of and not the whole man, as a unity of body *and* soul. When applied to theology, rationalism separated faith from objective biblical history, focusing on how man conceives of God rather than on how one can know Him through creation and revelation. This is best seen in the thought of Benedict Spinoza (1632–1677), a Jewish philosopher and disciple of Descartes who, while arguing for the necessity of seeking the truth in one's own mind, departed from Descartes in abandoning belief in traditional theology wholesale. Spinoza regarded the biblical miracle stories as nothing more than misinterpreted natural phenomena; for him the Bible provided no incontrovertible evidence for metaphysical phenomena, that is, belief in angels, the immortality of the soul, and so forth. His religion too was one of the mind, independent of historical events, institutions, and dogma.

This "religion of the mind," in its denial of God's absolute otherness and self-revelation planted the seeds of modernist thinking. They began to sprout in the eighteenth-century Deists' argument that the essence of Christianity was morality or "natural religion," man's awareness of the natural moral law knowable by reason and precluding any need for institutional religion. Thus for the modernist God does not reveal what is moral to man—man's morality dictates his understanding of God. This should sound familiar to the Catholic Christian: "But the serpent said to the woman, 'You will not die. For God knows that when you eat of it your eyes will be opened, and you will be like God, knowing good and evil.'"[25]

These basic ideas of what Pope St. Pius X branded "Modernism" were also present in the philosophy of Immanuel Kant and George W.F. Hegel, in Darwinian biological science, and in liberal political movements in post-French-Revolutionary Europe. A summary of the ideas which gave rise to Modernism prior to Vatican II reads as follows:

- The existence of God, the immortality of the soul, the existence of revelation, in fact all that is not a matter of personal experience, cannot be known with certainty by our reason (thus, reducing the reality of God to the way the autonomous individual conceives of him).
- Sacred Scripture and tradition do not contain revelation from God to men, but merely feelings and experiences of highly-gifted religious persons.
- Christ did not found a Church with a divine constitution and unchangeable dogmas and moral standards; these are the result of a gradual evolution and must continue to develop and give place to others as times change.

I hope it is clear that the phenomenon of modernism in effect was the endgame of the subjective thinking, blossoming as the twentieth century opened. Space will not allow a thorough discussion of Catholic modernism—I propose only to highlight its most notorious personages. Its initial wave appeared in the Church in the writings of Fr. Anton Guenther (1783–1863), who as a young man had his Catholic faith badly shaken through exposure to the philosophy of Kant and Johann Gottlieb Fichte, though his parish priest restored his faith. Upon entering the priesthood Gunther attempted a refutation of the Hegelian pantheism of modernist thought in his *Introduction to the Speculative Theology of Positive Christianity*, a task for which Guenther thought scholastic theology was wholly inadequate. In short, he sought a scientific demonstration of the fundamentals of Christianity, regarding them as necessary truths in light of reason alone. Though a devout priest with many followers, Guenther's speculative thought proved unduly influenced by the very thinkers he endeavored to refute; thus his writing was found unacceptable by Pius IX in 1857.[26]

Modernism's second, more infamous wave found expression in the works of Catholic theologians George Tyrell (1861–1909) and Alfred Loisy (1857–1940). Loisy was perhaps the most influential of the Catholic modernists. He proved susceptible to the nineteenth century German "Higher Criticism" of Sacred Scripture, which sowed doubt as to the Bible's historicity and the possibility of reaching the "historical Jesus" in the Gospels under the influence of Ernest Renan. Loisy also introduced the notion of "vital immanence," arguing that religious truth subsists in the heart and mind of the believer, not in an immutable, objective reality exterior to him. In other words, "God" originates in mankind's universal need for the divine. He submitted that Jesus never viewed himself as God—only as a prophet, and so never intended to found an institutional Church nor institute the Sacraments.[27]

This lent itself to a subjective faith without the constraints of institutions and creeds, which proved seductive to younger clergy who found it hard to reconcile Catholic teaching with the new scientific theory. Correlative to my thesis we see also modernism's denial of a religious understanding of creation (for Paul VI a sign of the diabolical) in Loisy's rejection of three Catholic teachings as unscientific:

- Old Testament teaching on God and revelation.
- Old Testament foreshadowing of Christ and the Church.
- Christ's direct institution of the Catholic Church with its doctrines and hierarchy.[28]

All things considered, modernism aimed at a synthesis of Church doctrine and science through a reinterpretation of revelation, faith, Sacred Scripture, and the teaching authority of the Church. Here are key errors from the "Syllabus" of Errors condemned by Pope Pius IX (I have included only those which directly concern my thesis):

1. There exists no Supreme, all-wise, all-provident Divine Being, distinct from the universe, and God is identical with the nature of things, and is, therefore, subject to changes. In effect, God is produced in man and in the world, and all things are God and have the very substance of God, and God is one and the same thing with the world, and, therefore, spirit with matter, necessity with liberty, good with evil, justice with injustice. — Allocution "Maxima quidem," June 9, 1862.

3. Human reason, without any reference whatsoever to God, is the sole arbiter of truth and falsehood, and of good and evil; it is law to itself, and suffices, by its natural force, to secure the welfare of men and of nations. — Ibid.

5. Divine revelation is imperfect, and therefore subject to a continual and indefinite progress, corresponding with the advancement of human reason. — Ibid.

8. As human reason is placed on a level with religion itself, so theological must be treated in the same manner as philosophical sciences. — Allocution "Singulari quadam," Dec. 9, 1854.

9. All the dogmas of the Christian religion are indiscriminately the object of natural science or philosophy, and human reason, enlightened solely in an historical way, is able, by its own natural

strength and principles, to attain to the true science of even the most abstruse dogmas; provided only that such dogmas be proposed to reason itself as its object. — Letters to the Archbishop of Munich, "Gravissimas inter," Dec. 11, 1862, and "Tuas libenter," Dec. 21, 1863.

14. Philosophy is to be treated without taking any account of supernatural revelation. — Ibid.

16. Man may, in the observance of any religion whatever, find the way of eternal salvation, and arrive at eternal salvation. — Encyclical "Qui pluribus," Nov. 9, 1846.

17. Good hope at least is to be entertained of the eternal salvation of all those who are not at all in the true Church of Christ. — Encyclical "Quanto conficiamur," Aug. 10, 1863, etc.

18. Protestantism is nothing more than another form of the same true Christian religion, in which form it is given to please God equally as in the Catholic Church. — Encyclical "Noscitis," Dec. 8, 1849.

19. The Church is not a true and perfect society, entirely free— nor is she endowed with proper and perpetual rights of her own, conferred upon her by her Divine Founder; but it appertains to the civil power to define what are the rights of the Church, and the limits within which she may exercise those rights. — Allocution "Singulari quadam," Dec. 9, 1854, etc.

79. Moreover, it is false that the civil liberty of every form of worship, and the full power, given to all, of overtly and publicly manifesting any opinions whatsoever and thoughts, conduce more easily to corrupt the morals and minds of the people, and to propagate the pest of indifferentism. — Allocution "Nunquam fore," Dec. 15, 1856.

80. The Roman Pontiff can, and ought to, reconcile himself, and come to terms with progress, liberalism and modern civilization. Allocution "Jamdudum cernimus," March 18, 1861.[29]

The movement was also condemned by Vatican Council I in 1870, though not surprisingly the modernists challenged Vatican I's censure, necessitating further action by Pius X, who in his Encyclical *Pascendi Dominici Gregis* (September, 1907), presented a more systematic exposé of modernism directed particularly at the writings of Loisy. This action against what the Pope termed the "synthesis of all heresies" and his subsequent institution of an oath against modernism, required of all clergy prior to ordination, checked the movement for a time. However, Pope Pius XII found the writings of Fr. Pierre Teilhard De Chardin reflective enough of modernist sentiment to issue his encyclical *Humani Generis* ("Warnings against Attempts to Distort Catholic Truths," 1950).[30] My use of the term *neo*modernism will from here on refer to the third strand of modernism which emerged after the Church did away with both the *Index* and the *Oath Against Modernism* shortly after Vatican II. The term describes principally those Catholic intellectual thinkers who retrospectively regarded the modernists as heroes in their unabashed willingness to do away with Church traditions which contravened modernity. The Church followed this neomodernist influence with great interest in France and Germany.[31] It was most evident at the time of the Council in the writings of Jesuit Frs. De Chardin and Karl Rahner,[32] Frs. Hans Kung, Dominican Fr. Edward Schillebeeckx,[33] and Frs. Hans Kung and Charles Curran.

To pursue a little deeper, the facade in neomodernism is evident in three areas, the first of which is its argument that because the dogmas of the Church do not possess indisputable knowledge of the supernatural, they are relative to how they impact one's imagination, and may be believed or disbelieved accordingly. Theologians susceptible to this argument believe dogma to be changeable over time and that dogma may be disregarded when no longer fruitful for the individual or reinterpreted to better meet with individual experience. This is a blatant misunderstanding of development of doctrine, and is most famously demonstrated in the dissent of many American theologians to *Humanae Vitae* so soon after its promulgation.[34]

In addition, a careful reading of the aforementioned syllabus reveals that neomodernists do not think real objective knowledge of God possible, despite arguments from reason, fulfilled prophecies, and documented miracles. For them knowledge of God comes only from subjective religious experience, "from the heart." The fruits of such religious experience are binding only on the one undergoing the experience. Neomodernists refer to this as *"on-going* revelation," and its theological interpretation as *"process theology."* Neomodernism's subjectivism has also given rise to a confused notion of the Catholic teaching on divine immanence, which is that we are in God (He made us, gives us grace) and God is in us (sanctifying grace in our souls). Modernists prior to Vatican I, influenced by Spinoza, thought that human beings were emanations from the divine, which leaned toward the pantheistic cosmology of the eastern religions, where God is identical with the world or a part of it. The Church has always taught the *transcendence* of God, even when God lives in us. Since for the neomodernist all revelation comes from subjective personal experience, it is only fitting that the "people of God" be the final authors of what should be believed and done. This means that they favor reforming the Church along the lines of a modern, popular democracy.[35]

Secondly, in neomodernist thought, theology, incapable of knowledge of the Divine, reduced Sacred Scripture to little more than an expression of the religious experience of the biblical authors, not a tried and true lamp for guiding our feet on the road to Heaven. In the Bible, they argued, were to be found errors, an untrustworthy historical record, and quite a bit of symbol and myth. The result for the neomodernist was a huge gap between what was recorded in the Bible and what in fact actually took place.

When I began training as a catechist at an archdiocesan conference in the 1970s, one noted catechetical author informed those present (paraphrased), "Traditionally we Catholics have allowed the Christ of Faith to dominate our faith expression, but after Vatican II it is important to give equal emphasis to the 'Jesus of history.'" Pope Benedict XVI has decried the impact of this dichotomy as "tragic" for Christian faith, for he has written that the Gospels do present the real, historical Jesus.[36] Neomodernists also raised questions, as we have seen, as to whether Jesus intended to found a Church, since they understand his mission as concerned only with inaugurating the Kingdom of God, that is, delivering people from spiritual and physical suffering in this world, which is how neomodernists understand salvation. The *Syllabus* also cites their rejection of Christ's conferring the keys of the Kingdom on St. Peter, and with this grant of divine authority Peter's earthly leadership of His Church, and His institution of the sacraments, all except Baptism and the Eucharist.

Lastly, in the neomodernist movement, believing all dogma to be relative, all Christian denominations (now over 30,000) were to be regarded as equal with the Catholic

Church. Indeed, Tyrell came to view Christianity as merely an intermediary stage in the evolution of a new "universal religion."[37] Neomodernists declared that the ecumenism taught by Vatican II required that Catholics see non-Christian religions as *equally* valid expressions of man's search for truth.

My reading of the literature on the Church since Vatican II has persuaded me that Fr. De Lu Bac in the epigraph is dead on—the crisis currently facing the Church (and crises are nothing new to the Church) after 1965 originated in a neomodernist-led attempt at reform toward what in reality would indeed be "a different Church from that of Jesus Christ," the result of apostasy, the total rejection by a baptized Catholic of the Catholic faith he or she once possessed. Fr. De Lu Bac described this "other church" as an "anthropocentric society" in which "man is the measure of all things," more commonly recognized as the philosophy of secular humanism.

Thus, as neomodernist thinking became preponderant after the Council's close, traditional Church teaching on man's nature began to be challenged. In summary, as rationalism— which does not accept knowledge gained by the senses as valid—rejected revelation as source for human knowledge, and its antithesis, empiricism, developed, ultimate meaning was sought in "the now."[38] The past, including tradition, was to be distrusted and would lead neomodernists to reject any

45

appeal to Sacred Scripture and Tradition as interpreted by Church as a basis for knowledge of God.

As a corollary there emerged a rising immanentism, the philosophy which argued that anything of ultimate importance was contained within the individual, the standard for judgment. Objective, exterior reality became unimportant except to the extent the individual could express himself in it, and religion came to be understood as an expression of individual emotion. Carried to its logical conclusion, immanentism eliminated the role played by reason in religion in favor of the purely emotional.

We have ended our brief overview of the humanist cosmology strongly ingrained in both theology and philosophy at the opening of the Second Vatican Council. Pope John Paul II has said of this theological liberalism that "by exchanging relevance for truth, this form of modernism shows itself incapable of satisfying the demands of truth to which theology is called to respond."[39] Nevertheless, it remains among prominent laity, religious, and priests today, in effect a rejection of Catholic teaching on divine revelation, human nature, and God's gift of reason as capable of leading us to Him. Fr. De Lu Bac noted that the apostasy of this man-centered society developed under the pretext of renewal, ecumenism, or adaptation to modernity. These topics will be taken up in turn—here I wish to stress that we as Catholics should be attentive to Church teaching in acknowledging the reality of and the need to combat evil in the world through our adherence to the teachings of the Second Vatican Council and its primary message, the universal call to holiness.

III.

I conclude this overview of Catholic teaching on Satan and Pope Paul VI's belief that the Church needed to defend herself from Him with a little-known event in his life that occurred in March, 1976. The Holy Father, now nearly 80, melancholic and in poor health, invited a priest to preach the annual papal household retreat. The homilist began the retreat with a meditation on the infinite majesty of God, and then moved to the topic of the "God of the covenant," in Genesis, chapters 1–3, before the onset of original sin, succinctly described in Eucharistic Prayer IV. How many times we have heard this, but perhaps have taken for granted its truth:

> We give you praise, Father most holy, for you are great, and you have fashioned all your works in wisdom and in love. You formed man in your own image and entrusted the whole world to his care, so that in serving you alone, the Creator, he might have dominion over all creatures.

He noted here that love was the motive for God the Creator becoming the God of the covenant, commanding only that on his part, man must not eat of the tree of knowledge of good and evil, a symbol for human nature, as creatures in the proper order of creation cannot decide the moral law for themselves. And this tree was linked with another — the tree of life, linking the obedience of the creature to the covenant with the fulfillment of man's destiny. The homilist applied catechesis on Genesis to the signs of the times in 1976, suggesting that an understanding of these chapters is basic to any discussion of the relationship between the Church and the world. To discern this relationship it was necessary to return to the creation of the world and of man — and the first covenant — the foundation for the New Covenant, which rebuilt the original by God's offer of redemption to man through His Son, of which the Church is a sign. This was taken up in the fourth conference of the retreat, "The Ways of Denial," beginning with Vatican II's *Gaudium et Spes* ("Joy and Hope") and its analysis of the relationship between the world and Christ's Church. The preacher outlined the diverse psychological and moral conditions typical of the times, and then quoted from the conciliar document:

> Finally, these new conditions have their impact on religion. On the one hand a more critical ability to distinguish religion from a magical view of the world and from the superstitions which still

circulate purifies it and exacts day by day a more personal and explicit adherence to faith. As a result many persons are achieving a more vivid sense of God. On the other hand, growing numbers of people are abandoning religion in practice. Unlike former days, the denial of God or of religion, or the abandonment of them, are no longer unusual and individual occurrences. For today it is not rare for such things to be presented as requirements of scientific progress or of a certain new humanism. In numerous places these views are voiced not only in the teachings of philosophers, but on every side they influence literature, the arts, the interpretation of the humanities and of history and civil laws themselves. As a consequence, many people are shaken. [40]

To explain this problem of the denial of God and his rights as Creator, the homilist returned to Genesis, in order to

... delve into the reality of Satan ... [for] *present-day anthropocentrism — even the Christian and theological variety — will have little or nothing to do with it.* We all remember the outcry when the Holy Father quite simply recalled the elementary truths of church teaching on the subject. [41]

In his preaching on original sin the homilist saw that the evil spirit was identifiable "solely from the content of his words," concluding that human history would thus be "subject to rule by the Word and the anti-Word." In Genesis 3 the "anti-Word," Satan articulates the temptation, for which his source is his own rebellion and denial: "Were you to eat

49

it your eyes would open and you would become like God, acquiring knowledge of good and evil."[42] What is this truth for man that is destroyed by Satan's words? The truth that his existence as a created being requires him to acknowledge this limitation—only God is the author of the moral law. Being created in God's image and likeness does not mean that we may assume His place! In brilliant fashion, the papal preacher said that what was occurring here was Satan's attempt "to transmit to man his own rebellion," that is, "the attitude with which he—Satan—has identified and by which he has, in consequence, placed himself outside the truth, outside the law of dependence on the Creator." Indeed, this original temptation of mankind marked the beginning of a long process which wound its devious ways throughout subsequent human history.

Noting the obvious relevance of the nature of the original temptation for the present day, the homilist noted that Satan had not succeeded in his attempt at sowing in man the seeds of total rebellion; but only in "inducing man to turn towards the world, and to stray progressively in a direction opposed to the destiny to which he has been called," in effect, making the world the "terrain of man's temptation." Here man rebels against God in diverse ways rather than cooperating with Him, "a terrain where human pride seeks not the glory of God but its own greater satisfaction." He recalled that *Gaudium et*

Spes called this secularism, the idea that created things in the end do not depend on God, and may be dealt with in a fashion unrelated to the Creator. "Without the Creator the creature vanishes," he said, quoting *Gaudium et S*pes: "When God is forgotten, however, the creature itself grows unintelligible.[43] The homilist concluded that day's conference as follows:

> We may now be wondering if this is the last lap along that way of denial which started out from around the tree of the knowledge of good and evil. To us, who know the whole Bible from Genesis to Revelation, no stretch of that route can come as a surprise. We accept with trepidation but also with trust the inspired words of the Apostle Paul: "Let no one deceive you in any way; because first it is necessary for the rebellion to come, and for the man of sin, the son of perdition, to reveal himself . . ." (2 Thess 2:3). Laicist anthropocentrism is even more opposed to admitting man's relationship with Satan than it is to acknowledging man's relationship with God. . . . Man is alone, and his greatness requires that he be so: . . . independent of good and evil, independent of God and Satan. . . . These are the perspectives of the third chapter of Genesis, *which are now becoming more understandable — not so much in their original expression as in the light of the signs of our times.*[44]

Recalling the years in the decade after the close of Vatican II through my research for this thesis, it was easy for me to discern the work of the guiding hand of the Holy Spirit in the Catholic Church. The preacher for the papal household for 1976 was Karol Cardinal Wojtyla, within a few years to be elected Pope John Paul II. What struck me in his meditations was his inference that "the signs of the times" might explain the denial of the truth of Church teaching which had infiltrated her like "the smoke of Satan."

Cardinal Wojtyla had warned in his conference of "rebellion," that is, the apostasy of the present age, the source for the present crisis of faith facing the Church.[45] I believe it is consistent with Church teaching on spiritual warfare to see in St. Paul's "son of perdition" one who would lead humanity away from the Church toward a humanist, man-centered world-view claiming the right of authorship of the moral law. This also explains why those who dissent from Church doctrine and the authority of the magisterium claim an amorphous "spirit of Vatican II" (an "anti-word?") as their authority for what amounts to unbelief. In our own time the reader perhaps has experienced the war for the soul of men waged between the authentic Christian humanism of the Gospel, which permeates the teaching of John Paul the Great, and the "new humanism" which violates the rights of God as true Author of all that is good. John Paul II had it just right: "Without the Creator, the creature vanishes."

Following his death on April 2, 2005, many of the eulogies in the mainstream media were diffuse in their praise and criticism of John Paul II's pontificate. Typical among them is the following:

> .... At the same time, however, he was a profoundly conservative leader whose moral opinions alienated many, and whose centralizing instincts stifled the move toward a more open, democratic church. ...

> Most conservatives proudly and happily claim the pontiff as one of their own, while too many liberals — upset by some doctrinal disagreement such as the Pope's total opposition to the ordination of women — overlook the legacy of the quarter-century commitment to social justice. ...

> .... What liberals — more than a few of whom while possibly agreeing with the Pope on abortion dissent from the Pope's teaching on birth control — fail to appreciate is that John Paul II's record on human rights, workers rights, the environment, the poor and more is truly remarkable. ...[46]

This routine use of the secular vocabulary of liberal and conservative in reference to the Supreme Shepherd of the Holy Catholic Church, the Servant of the Servants of God, and by implication, to Catholics in general shows how little modern society understands of the true nature of the Catholic Church, a topic to which we now turn in our study of "the smoke of Satan" in God's Temple.

CHAPTER TWO

Liberal Catholic? Conservative Catholic? Or Catholic?

But I, brethren, could not address you as spiritual men, but as men of the flesh, as babes in Christ. I fed you with milk, not solid food; for you were not ready for it; and even yet you are not ready, for you are still of the flesh. For while there is jealousy and strife among you, are you not of the flesh, and behaving like ordinary men? For when one says, "I belong to Paul," and another, "I belong to Apollos," are you not merely men?

1 Corinthians 3; 1–4

But false prophets also arose among the people, just as there will be false teachers among you, who will secretly bring in destructive heresies, even denying the Master who bought them, bringing upon themselves swift destruction. And many will follow their licentiousness, and because of them the way of truth will be reviled. And in their greed they will exploit you with false words; from of old their condemnation has not been idle, and their destruction has not been asleep.

2 Peter 2:1–3

And I will pray the Father, and he will give you another Counselor, to be with you for ever, even the Spirit of truth, whom the world cannot receive, because it neither sees him nor knows him; you know him, for he dwells with you, and will be in you. . . . But the Counselor, the Holy Spirit, whom the Father will send in my name, he will teach you all things, and bring to your remembrance all that I have said to you.

John 14:16–17; 26

I.

I do not recall a time when as a youngster I heard the word "Catholic" modified by anything other than "Irish," "devout," or "lapsed." Today a cursory awareness of media coverage of the Catholic Church makes necessary an understanding of the "liberal-progressive-left" and "conservative-traditional-right" schemas to modify "Catholic" in the United States. Most writers on Vatican II history attribute this phenomenon to Fr. Francis X. Murphy, C.SS.R., author of the pseudonymous "Xavier Rynne" briefings for the American public from Rome in *The New Yorker* magazine. His articles reporting from the Council sessions have been condensed into a book, two reviews of which give us the indispensable

55

setting for the subsequent "liberal/conservative division" within the Church.[47] The first:

> The Amazing True Story about the Legacy of Pope John XXIII. A shrewd, candid, wonderfully written insider's account of what actually happened at the Second Vatican Council, the decisive turning point in the history of modern Catholicism. The original version of these stories. . . . brought smiles to the faces and hope to the hearts of thoughtful Catholics all over the country and beyond. The desperate, dishonest, and sneering comments by industrious *Catholic rightists* [emphasis added], still huffing and puffing about the 1960s, the decade of Vatican II, the Civil Rights movement, the Catholic Peace movement, the efforts to re-energize movements to care about poor people, to secure the rights of women, and to take responsibility for the endangered natural environment, tell you all you will ever need to know about their version of Jesus' "Love one another. . . ." This particular sect of *reactionary Catholics* [emphasis added] has been spewing contempt on democratic values since the late 18th century, while cozying up to a long line of corrupt aristocrats, fascists, megalomaniacs, and cynical thugs. Being honest about history is the path with heart for Catholics today. Just telling the truth will re-activate the long-stalled renewal of our church. Trust Paul Lakeland, a distinguished Catholic theologian, and trust what the Holy Spirit is accomplishing even in these sad and painful times. And meanwhile—enjoy this terrific, heartening book.

And the second:

Blowing in the wind. Rynne offered the world a liberal fantasy of what 'the spirit of the Council' was all about. According to him, the council was pastoral, but not dogmatic. How then to explain those dogmatic constitutions on the church and on relevation, with all those troublesome endorsements of Trent and Vatican I? According to him, the council was about openness, freedom, and tolerance. But the Council's claim of the Catholic Church to be the true Church founded by Christ and of the duty for all Catholics to assent to the teaching of the magisterium on faith and morals somehow gets lost. The book has interest as a relic of mid '60's liberal dreams. But for those of us who have given up our love beads and our sandalwood incense, it's all a bit embarrassing. For a better take on the Council, read Wiltgen's *The Rhine Flows into the Tiber*.[48]

During the course of my prior catechetical career I spoke often with parents, colleagues, and parishioners about catechesis and the Church. Stereotypical remarks in these conversations ran as follows: "Oh, I hear the principal is a liberal Catholic," or "the teachers at my previous job were all from the Catholic Right," or "Isn't the new Pope a conservative?" The principal so-called "liberal" groups in the public square today are Call to Action, Voice of the Faithful, Women's Ordination Conference, the Catholic Theological Society of America, the Leadership Conference of Women Religious, and Catholics for a Free Choice. During the homosexual priest scandals in 2003, the American media sought out almost exclusively representatives of these groups and priests and religious sympathetic to their views as spokespersons for the Church. Among those (mis)labeled by the "liberal-progressive-leftists" as "conservative-traditional-rightist" are Catholics United for the Faith, *Regnum Christi,* Women for Faith and Family, the Fellowship of Catholic Scholars, *Opus Dei,* The Priestly Fraternity of St. Peter, the Conference of Major Superiors of Men, the Council of Major Superiors of Women Religious, Priests for Life, the Sisters of Life, and the Eternal Word Television Network.[49] As I hope to show, their terminology misses the mark; rather, it would more accurately fit the Society of Pius X. To see through this smokescreen we must look to the origins of this division among Catholics.

The Council Fathers and their *periti,* a few of whom are still with us (among them the present Holy Father), would no doubt recall that the council sessions took place in an atmosphere of contention on the part of a minority group of Fathers resistant to change and the reform-minded Fathers, inspired by Pope John XXIII's vision of a more effective proposal of the truths of the Catholic faith to the modern world. The three proposed targets of reform were pastoral practice, Catholic theology, and the Church's ecclesiastical structure. To the alarm of the minority, the reformist-minded council Fathers were able to secure majorities for their positions in each of these areas; this was the pattern emerging as John XXIII died and Paul VI was elected to oversee the Council.

Most importantly, what in reality was *not* in evidence during the council sessions was the ideological battle being reported in the United States by "Xavier Rynne," Robert Kaiser, et. al. As a result, Catholics in the United States were not given an objective account of what actually happened in the Eternal City. Be that as it may, once the sixteen official Council documents were voted upon and promulgated by Pope Paul VI in 1965, they became part of the Magisterium of the Catholic Church.[50] As such, faithful Catholics are called to view the documents as what they are: the product of the teaching office of the Church under the guidance of the Holy Spirit.

The first criticisms of the council were born of this disaffection with the documents of Vatican II and the changes in the aforementioned three areas of pastoral practice, theology, and ecclesiology on the part of those today who call themselves "traditionalists." Specific areas of concern were liturgical reform (*Sacrosanctum Concilium*), the Church's relation to modernity (*Gaudium et Spes*), and especially religious freedom (*Dignitatis Humanae*). A reading of their literature to date reveals no letup in such criticism, recent Vatican attempts at reconciliation notwithstanding. The writings of their spiritual descendants continue to foster doubt and confusion in some circles about the authenticity of Vatican II documents as binding on Catholics. These traditionalists are stereotyped in the first of the Xavier Rynne article reviews quoted above, though their numbers are negligible.[51]

We begin our examination of the emergence of the second group of Catholics under discussion by reading the words of a then self-proclaimed "progressive" shortly after Vatican II:

> There is no question . . . that Vatican II initiated almost every major reform which American progressives, prior to 1965, generally desired. . . . How then can the bitterness, the disappointment, the deep disillusionment, of post-conciliar American progressives be explained? . . . The official progressive myth continues to argue that it was not the reformers discovering the inadequacy of their own ideas and programs which brought disillusionment but rather the institutional Church, which refused calls for meaningful reform. . . . In the post-conciliar years the progressives have become increasingly radical and also increasingly paranoid. They manifest an extreme reluctance to examine honestly their own attitudes and their own history and a corresponding compulsion to blame all failures on "the establishment. . . ." The radicals implicitly repudiate the earlier reform movement as much as they repudiate the conservatives. They are not simply extending the moderate reform but are moving in *new and totally alien directions,* [emphasis added] and in many cases specifically negating much that was central to the spirit of conciliar reform.[52]

These "radicals" are the object of the rhetoric in the second of the Rynne article reviews; how their influence has impacted the Church in the United States is the focus of the remainder of this work. An accurate understanding of their worldview sheds much light on the remarks of Fr. De Lu Bac and Cardinal Wojtyla about the emergence of a different Church from that of Jesus Christ.

We must remember that the council documents offer guidelines for reform and renewal. The practical changes to implement these guiding principles,[53] which are properly the efforts of the Pope and bishops, have in numerous cases gone significantly further than what the decrees suggested or absolutely mandated.[54] Thus, rather ominously, a "spirit of reform" began to show itself in the implementation of the council. One began to observe innovations which were never intended by the Council Fathers.

Whenever documentation for such a specific innovation was not evident in the Council documents, an appeal was made by prominent theologians in the Church to a nebulous "spirit of Vatican II," that is, what the documents in *their* view intended, or what they *would* have said had they not been compromised in their view by those labeled "traditionalist" council Fathers. As discussed previously, those sympathetic to this "spirit" of the Council were given the bulk of media coverage at the time, a key means by which they furthered their interpretations (unto the present day).

A particularly pernicious alien direction of these radicals was their contention that due to traditional habits of thought, the Council Fathers in drafting the documents had expressed the meaning of Vatican II defectively. The task of correction and full expression of the council thus fell to the theologians,[55] who often felt no responsibility to cite the texts of the documents to sanction their new theological interpretation. This practice was evident, to cite one example, in their interpretation of *Gaudium et Spes* – namely, that the best way for the Church to dialogue with modernity was to forsake her role as sole depositor of Truth and adopt a more secularized, democratized institutional presence. This would in effect remove the Church as an independent authority in any dialogue with the modern world, whose lead she would in turn follow.

My advice to one confronted with doubt sown by those who make reference to "correct interpretations of Vatican II" is to reflect closely upon the words of John Paul II:

> With the Council, *the Church first had an experience of faith,* as she abandoned herself to God without reserve, as one who trusts and is certain of being loved. It is precisely this act of abandonment to God which stands out from an objective examination of the Acts. Anyone who wished to approach the Council without considering this interpretive key *would be unable to penetrate its depths.*

Only from a faith perspective can we see the Council event as a gift whose still hidden wealth we must know how to mine.[56]

It is this abandonment, this interpretive faith perspective that is woefully lacking in many who would offer to explain what the Council taught in "the spirit of Vatican II."

In sum, there emerged after Vatican II a minority of traditionalist Catholics who never believed reform necessary (in spite of the attention the Holy Spirit, working in the Church, wished be given to it), and more vocal radicals who demonstrated little to no sense of commitment to the traditional Church as she has existed since her founding by Our Lord. The latter have exercised a dominant influence on many in the American hierarchy, Catholic universities, diocesan offices and religious orders and thus on at least two generations of the Faithful since the close of Vatican II. It is my contention that it is this influence which has given rise to the present crisis of faith among Catholics.

Lest we forget, there were indeed reform-minded Council Fathers who responded to Pope John's vision of the Church growing in spiritual riches as a fruit of the Council under the guidance of the Holy Spirit in the hope that the faithful might through grace be aided in turning hearts and minds toward heavenly things. Given what has been said thus far, it should not surprise the reader that many "liberal Catholics" view the pontificate of John Paul II as too conservative, and out of touch with the modern world, while the traditionalists view the writings and teachings of the Holy Father as modernist!

Thus the schema of "liberal" (progressive, left) versus conservative (traditional, right) which followed upon the close of Vatican II is wholly inadequate for explaining the present-day crisis of faith within the Church of Jesus Christ, though it is most unfortunate that usage of these terms persist among many Catholics and in the media today. Division within Christ's Church is a clear attack by the evil one. Satan's strategy here is the time-honored one of *divide et impera* – divide and conquer. Remember, too, Jesus' words to the Pharisees: "Every kingdom divided against itself is laid waste, and no city or house divided against itself will stand."[57] Quite simply, no ideology, no matter how sincerely embraced, may substitute for personal conversion.

II.

In our attempt to get a clear understanding of how we arrived at the present crisis of faith, it is instructive to examine the experience of another council *peritus,* Joseph Cardinal Ratzinger, theologian, Prefect for the Congregation of the Doctrine of the Faith, gloriously elevated by the Holy Spirit to the Chair of St. Peter as Pope Benedict XVI in April, 2005. By way of background, from 1930–1950 in response to the pervasive secularism of these years in Europe, a broad intellectual and theological movement emerged among prominent European theologians, among them Frs. Romano Guardini, Karl Adam, Henri de Lubac, Jean Danielou, Yves Congar, Louis Boyer, and Hans Urs von Balthasar. The inspiration for this movement was a belief that the Catholic Faith had to speak more effectively to the modern world, and that to do this a rediscovery of all of the riches of the two-thousand year tradition of the Church was a crucial step.

These reform-minded theologians saw that the precursor to any *aggiornamento* (the famous "updating," one purpose for which John XXIII convened the Council) must be a *ressourcement,* a restoration of tradition, a return to the sources of the Catholic Faith. The writings of these reformers played a profound role in influencing the direction the Council was to take, and were a formative influence on Archbishop Wojtyla and Fr. Ratzinger. These priests hoped for a return to classical (patristic-medieval) sources, a renewed interpretation of Aquinas, and a dialogue with the major movements and thinkers of the twentieth century, with particular attention given to problems associated with the Enlightenment, modernity, and liberalism. Fr. Ratzinger in 1964 was included among the founders of a new international theological journal, *Concilium,* along with other notables Frs. Karl Rahner, Edward Schillebeeckx, Hans Kung, Johann Baptist Metz, Yves Congar and Gustavo Gutierrez — at the time, the elite of the more progressive Catholic theologians. At present *Concilium* exists

> . . . . to promote theological discussion in *the spirit of Vatican II* [emphasis added], out of which it was born. It is a catholic journal in the widest sense: rooted firmly in the Catholic heritage, open to other Christian traditions and the world's faiths. [58]

When asked by Vittorio Messori in his famous interview with Cardinal Ratzinger about the fact that he once was associated with some theologians who have since run afoul with the CDF, the Cardinal's reply sheds much light on this "spirit of Vatican II":

> It is not I who have changed, but others. At our very first meetings I pointed out two prerequisites to my colleagues. The first one: our group must not lapse into any kind of sectarianism or arrogance, as if we were the new, the true Church, an *alternative magisterium* [emphasis added] with a monopoly on the truth of Christianity. The second one: discussion has to be conducted without any individualistic flights forward, in confrontation with the reality of Vatican II with the true letter and the true spirit of the Council, not with an imaginary Vatican III. These prerequisites were increasingly less observed in the following period up to a turning point — which set in around 1973 — when someone began to assert that *the texts of Vatican II were no longer the point of reference for Catholic* theology. . . . that the Council still belonged to the traditional, clerical moment of the Church and *that it was not*

possible to move forward very much with such documents [emphasis added]. They must be surpassed.[59]

It is important to understand the part played by neomodernism in bringing about this division within the ranks of the "new theology." As I hope to show, it was the establishment of "an alternative magisterium" on the part of theologians who viewed the Vatican II documents as inadequate who demonstrated the pride warned against by Cardinal Ratzinger. I believe it consistent with Catholic teaching to see in the apostasy of this anthropocentric society the work, in Paul VI's words, of "the hidden enemy who sows errors and misfortune in human history."

As we have seen, *ressourcement* was to be the guidepost for the much-desired *aggiornamento,* or "updating." In its Dogmatic Constitution on the Church, the Council Fathers remind us of Christ's all-encompassing call to *personal holiness.*[60]

Looking back on my life from the close of the Council down to 1995, I admit to a huge gap between what I said I believed as a Catholic, and the thoughts, words, and deeds that encompassed how I was living this life. When I first began to actually read the texts of the Vatican II documents, I began to sense this was a major reason the Holy Spirit inspired Pope John to convene the council — to address this all-too-prevalent phenomenon in the lives of Catholics in the Church in the United States.

Sadly, during these years, due to sloth I remained deaf to the call to holiness. What I have learned from my study of Church history following the Council is that those transcendent elements which had drawn me to the Faith in my youth and made the Church so important in my life were in short supply. What the Council Fathers desired was a restoration of the balance between *ressourcement* emanating from the "new theology,"[61] and those elements in Church life that prior to the Council had received the lion's share of attention — devotional practices, Thomistic theology, and vocations.

Vatican II never intended to exclude the latter but to *reform* it, to make available a more attractive, easily understood presentation of the fundamentals and rich traditions of the Catholic faith to the world. This presentation was to serve as the foundation for the subsequent *aggiornamento* after 1965 in the following areas:

- the option for use of the vernacular in the Mass
- the revised Code of Canon Law
- ecumenism
- reform of religious life
- the emergence of synods and bishops' conferences
- changes in local Church administration

Unfortunately for me and undoubtedly for many Catholics, this was not what occurred. To make closing the gap between faith and life easier, the calling of Catholics to greater personal holiness, and giving them a fuller understanding of the whole of traditional Catholicism — *ressourcement* – the Fathers offered *aggiornamento,* "updating," the second purpose for the Council. While I think it a safe bet that many readers have never heard of *ressourcement,* I am confident that many Catholics at one time in their lives have either read of or heard of *aggiornamento* explained as the sole purpose and achievement of Vatican II.

The problematic element here was that "updating" was patently *not* reform! Let us take an example from Church history. We see *aggiornamento,* properly understood, in Church history when, after the Fall of the Roman Empire, the Church adapted and employed the best elements of the predominantly Greek culture of the Empire in the service of further evangelization. St. Augustine made use of the thought of Plato, and St. Thomas the use of Aristotelian logic in his *Summa Theologica.* It can also be witnessed in the adoption of Latin as the language for the liturgy when the bulk of the ever-increasing faithful no longer spoke Greek. In short, *aggiornamento* in Church History, while often necessary, has often been accompanied by the danger to the Church of an "impassioned love affair with the times."[62]

It must be emphasized that the Church's encountering new ideas and modes of thinking do not require changes in doctrine, but may involve the *development of doctrine.* This is the teaching of the Church that revelation is understood in the full depth of its meaning only in stages over time, made clearer by the Church, often in the form of defining doctrine. *This is not new doctrine or new revelation,* but rather a development, a magnification of doctrine toward a more profound understanding of truth. Development of doctrine serves to adapt Church teaching to the needs of the people of a particular culture.

There exists also one other false notion which has sown confusion among Catholics—Pope John XXIII's statement that the council was to be a "pastoral" council. We should not take this to mean that doctrine was henceforth to be unimportant—after all, Pope Paul VI promulgated two dogmatic constitutions (on the Church and on Divine Revelation), and there are numerous references to dogmatic teaching in the pastoral constitutions of Vatican II. To clear up this confusion it is best to read from the relevant portions of Pope John XXIII's address opening the council:

> In calling this vast assembly of bishops, the latest and humble successor to the Prince of the Apostles who is addressing you intended to assert once again the Magisterium (teaching authority), which is unfailing and perdures until the end of time, in order that this

Magisterium, taking into account the errors, the requirements, and the opportunities of our time, might be presented in exceptional form to all men throughout the world. . . .

The great problem confronting the world after almost two thousand years remains unchanged. Christ is ever resplendent as the center of history and of life. Men are either with Him and His Church, and then they enjoy light, goodness, order, and peace. Or else they are without Him, or against Him, and deliberately opposed to His Church, and then they give rise to confusion, to bitterness in human relations, and to the constant danger of fratricidal wars. . . .

Illuminated by the light of this Council, the Church—we confidently trust—will become greater in spiritual riches and gaining the strength of new energies therefrom, she will look to the future without fear. In fact, by bringing herself up to date where required, and by the wise organization of mutual co-operation, the Church will make men, families, and peoples really turn their minds to heavenly things. . . .

In the daily exercise of our pastoral office, we sometimes have to listen, much to our regret, to voices of persons who, though burning with zeal, are not endowed with too much sense of discretion or measure. In these modern times they can see nothing but prevarication and ruin. They say that our era, in comparison with past eras, is getting worse, and they behave as though they had learned nothing from history, which is, none the less, the teacher of life. They behave as though at the time of former

Councils everything was a full triumph for the Christian idea and life and for proper religious liberty. . . .

The greatest concern of the Ecumenical Council is this: that the sacred deposit of Christian doctrine should be guarded and taught more efficaciously. That doctrine embraces the whole of man, composed as he is of body and soul. And, since he is a pilgrim on this earth, it commands him to tend always toward heaven. . . .

In order, however, that this doctrine may influence the numerous fields of human activity, with reference to individuals, to families, and to social life, it is necessary first of all that the Church should never depart from the sacred patrimony of truth received from the Fathers. But at the same time she must ever look to the present, to the new conditions and new forms of life introduced into the modern world, which have opened new avenues to the Catholic apostolate.

The manner in which sacred doctrine is spread, this having been established, it becomes clear how much is expected from the Council in regard to doctrine. That is, the Twenty-first Ecumenical Council, which will draw upon the effective and important wealth of juridical, liturgical, apostolic, and administrative experiences, wishes to transmit the doctrine, pure and integral, without any attenuation or distortion, which throughout twenty centuries, notwithstanding difficulties and contrasts, has become the common patrimony of men. It is a patrimony not well received by all, but always a rich treasure available to men of good will.

The salient point of this Council is not, therefore, a discussion of one article or another of the fundamental doctrine of the Church which has repeatedly been taught by the Fathers and by ancient and modern theologians, and which is presumed to be well known and familiar to all.

For this a Council was not necessary. But from the renewed, serene, and tranquil adherence to all the teaching of the Church in its entirety and preciseness, as it still shines forth in the Acts of the Council of Trent and First Vatican Council, the Christian, Catholic, and apostolic spirit of the whole world expects a step forward toward a doctrinal penetration and a formation of consciousness in faithful and perfect conformity to the authentic doctrine, which, however, should be studied and expounded through the methods of research and through the literary forms of modern thought. The substance of the ancient doctrine of the deposit of faith is one thing, and the way in which it is presented is another. *And it is the latter that must be taken into great consideration with patience if necessary, everything being measured in the forms and proportions of a Magisterium which is predominantly pastoral in character* [emphasis added].[63]

Misunderstanding and misapplication of the final sentence of this excerpt has resulted in great confusion on the laity's part following the council. A major reason for such obfuscation was the "infelicities, not to say inaccuracies," and omissions in the Abbot-Gallagher translation of the conciliar documents.[64] A recent assessment is prescient; it was "by taking advantage of the Council's often looser terminology that, since the Council, theologians in rebellion against the Church have been able to introduce changes of meaning under cover of the Council's authority."[65] Here a close reading of the Pope's speech reveals that the Council was convened under the inspiration of the Holy Spirit not to put forth new definitions of doctrine,[66] (indeed Pope John called Catholics to be ever more faithful to authentic doctrine) but to present the timeless deposit of the Church's doctrinal truth more effectively through an active engagement with modernity, principally by imitating more closely her Master. In *this* sense it was to be a "pastoral" Council

As the "revolution" subjected more and more of traditional papal and doctrinal teaching to neomodernist skepticism and analysis, and as the Vatican refrained from taking a traditional disciplinary approach with such revolutionaries, allowing them to continue to write, teach, and preach, "an heretical movement devoted to altering the Church's beliefs developed like a cancer in the entrails of the movement for reform and *aggiornamento*."[67] Some of the side-effects of this malignancy appear on the first page of this book, which have given rise to our present crisis of faith. In my view, it is high time we label neomodernism what it really is, false *aggiornamento*. It is also high time that we remember that heresy is still part of Church teaching:

Those things are to be believed by divine and catholic faith which are contained in the word of God as it has been written or handed down by tradition, that is, in the single deposit of faith entrusted to the Church, and which are at the same time proposed as divinely revealed either by the solemn magisterium of the Church, or by its ordinary and universal magisterium, which is manifested by the common adherence of Christ's faithful under the guidance of the sacred magisterium. All are therefore bound to shun any contrary doctrines.

Heresy is the obstinate denial or doubt, after baptism, of a truth which must be believed by divine and catholic faith. Apostasy is the total repudiation of the Christian faith. Schism is the withdrawal of submission to the Supreme Pontiff or from communion with the members of the Church subject to him.[68]

Defined as such, heresy is rampant in parts of the Body of Christ today, the "weeds among the wheat." This should not surprise us. As believers in divine revelation, we cannot escape the historical existence of that which claims to be revealed, but in fact contradicts, distorts, or augments authentic revelation as taught by Christ's Church.

For this reason, Pope Paul VI made the Sacred Congregation for the Holy Office the first Congregation to be reformed following the close of Vatican II, renaming it the Congregation for the Doctrine of the Faith in his *motu proprio* of December 7, 1965. It was charged with the mandate "to promote sound doctrine in order to provide preachers of the gospel with new energies."[69]

Because it is true that man lives "on every word which comes forth from the mouth of God," His word must be preserved in its original meaning, safe from those who would distort it in the interests of living on "bread alone" — for example, emphasis on *orthopraxis,* or "right conduct, (love of neighbor) to the *exclusion* [emphasis mine] of orthodoxy, 'right belief.'" The Holy Father was aware of the presence in the Church of some who doubted that there is one truth, and viewed the Church as merely a human institution charged principally with ensuring love of neighbor on the part of Christians in this life, with no corresponding charge to preserve the Word of God and hence "right belief" to make possible our soul's salvation in the next.

An example from my experience as a catechist comes to mind — the emphasis given by certain thinkers to "liberation theology," (i.e., employing Marxist doctrine as a *sine qua non* in interpreting and applying the Gospel in Latin America). My point is that Catholics must not think it foolish to acknowledge that *heresy still exists.* Examples for the reader's consideration will be given in subsequent chapters.

Our main priority as faithful Catholics must be for "right belief" according to the authentic meaning of God's Word in Sacred Scripture. This is the preserve of the teaching office of the Church, to whom Jesus promised, "He who hears you hears me, and he who rejects you rejects me, and he who rejects me rejects him who sent me."[70] True *orthopraxis* is dependent upon the Church's search under the Holy Spirit's guidance for *orthodoxy*. Sage exegesis on this is the following:

It [neomodernist thought] is of course a revolution of ideas and therefore without unpleasant or frightening physical consequences. There are no bombs or firing squads. The wheels of diocesan and parish life continue to turn, while the revolutionaries themselves, and their now numerous sympathizers well entrenched in most Western ecclesiastical bureaucracies, are respectable professional men and women with, for the most part, friendly smiles, agreeable manners and what they regard as the highest intentions, who talk the language of religion and use catch-phrases and theories [*e.g.*, "process theology"] rather than dynamite. Now therefore that the first shocks and excitements are over, many Catholics find it fairly easy to persuade themselves that nothing all that important has happened, or if it has, whatever it was is over. But a revolution, or attempted revolution it still is even if the transformations are now mostly worked out of sight in the minds and hearts of the faithful without there being aware of it. . . . When we find numbers of bishops permitting, or even actively encouraging teaching at variance with that given by the Pope, and that given constantly by the Church through the centuries, one can only presume they have come to believe at least some of the doctrinal novelties. Inevitably many of the faithful have concluded either that heresy does not matter all that much, or that the Pope and a local hierarchy have equal authority and one can follow which teaching one pleases.[71]

Having been trained as a catechist in precisely this revolutionary atmosphere and, through grace and publication of the *Catechism of the Catholic Church* having been returned to the actual teachings of the Council in my attempt at responding to the call to holiness, I can corroborate the truth of this finding firsthand.

I have read much speculation about why the Pope and the Magisterium tolerate this rebellious activity in the Church. Philip Trower avers that it is because of the new conciliar emphasis on collegiality, ecumenism, and the dialogue with modernity. Collegiality came to be interpreted that decentralization was to take place such that it would be the responsibility of the local bishop rather than Rome to do any requisite disciplining of dissenting theologians. Added to this was the problem of how our "separated brethren," newly engaged in dialogue with the Church, would react if Rome was to discipline those in the Church who held "views similar to those of the separated brethren themselves."[72] Surely in the "dialogue with modernity," the bishops might be tempted to see disciplining wayward theologians as a violation of freedom of thought and expression. We shall examine the validity of these explanations in later chapters.

To conclude, the crisis facing the Catholic Church today is not that of liberal *versus* conservative interpretations of the Second Vatican Council; it is silly to argue that one may be liberal or conservative on the Apostles' Creed. No, the crisis is one that originated in an apostate rival magisterium successfully taking root within the Church in the United States, rebelliously asserting the right to teach heresy on the same level as the teaching of the successor of St. Peter and the bishops in union with him. It began in earnest with publication of Pope Paul VI's encyclical *Humanae Vitae* and the rebellion against Papal authority which emerged from this dissent. As we shall see shortly, this was to be the manner in which the gates of hell would attempt to prevail against Christ's Church at the time of the death of Paul VI. Here we must remember Paul's assertion that it is easier to form an answer to the question of the solution to employ against satanic action than it is to put the remedy into practice.

CHAPTER THREE

Libido

If then you have been raised with Christ, seek the things that are above, where Christ is, seated at the right hand of God. Set your minds on things that are above, not on things that are on earth. For you have died, and your life is hid with Christ in God. When Christ who is our life appears, then you also will appear with him in glory. Put to death therefore what is earthly in you: fornication, impurity, passion, evil desire, and covetousness, which is idolatry.

Colossians 3:1–5

I.

*T*hus far we have seen how a neomodernist second magisterium established itself in the Church shortly after the closing of the Second Vatican Council. It appealed to a "spirit of Vatican II" in support of its ideology, often in direct contradiction to the official teaching of the Catholic Church as set down in the conciliar documents, Sacred Scripture, and Sacred Tradition. The story of how this so-called faithful dissent began to wreak havoc among the faithful in the United States originates in the historical setting in which Paul VI issued his encyclical *Humanae Vitae* and the reception it received among theologians comprising this alternate magisterium. It is not my intention to retell this story in-depth, for it is all-too-well-known.[73] Rather, I shall focus only on those points of history and Catholic teaching which support Paul VI's vision of the "smoke of Satan" entering the Church.

We recall that among the Pope's telltale signs of a diabolic presence were doubt, uncertainty, questioning, dissatisfaction, and confrontation—all hallmarks in the story of the reception of *Humanae Vitae* in the United States. Contraceptive practice, taught from the beginning of the Church as serious sin, in Paul's thinking became the occasion and the effect of interference by what he called the "hidden enemy who sows errors," who undermines our moral equilibrium—the Devil. In Paul's teaching The Devil is the clever tempter who makes his way into man through the sensual, the libido, a "crack" through which the Evil One attempts to prevail against the Church.

Did you ever notice that when people take issue with Catholic teaching, rarely does it concern the Hypostatic Union, the Vatican's guidelines on road rage, or the Vatican Conference on Extraterrestrial Life? No, those things with which they take issue bear directly or vicariously on their sexual lives—homosexuality, same-sex "marriage," premarital sex, adultery, contraception, masturbation, population control, abortion, divorce, remarriage, *in vitro* fertilization, and so forth. It isn't as though Our Lord did not warn us of this: "What comes out of a man is what defiles a man. For from within, out of the heart of man, come evil thoughts, fornication, theft, murder, adultery, coveting, wickedness, deceit, licentiousness, envy, slander, pride, foolishness. All these evil things come from within, and they defile a man."[74] As Fr. Curran has pointed out, dissent from *Humanae Vitae* "was paradigmatic of the dissent in all specific moral questions."[75] My advice to those desiring to make sense of our sexually-befuddled world is to understand that it is a fatal not to observe "how Lucifer actually works and *why* he is so intent on perverting our sexuality." Indeed, a Catholic understanding of human sexuality gives us "a glimpse of the 'great mystery' of God's plan to unite all things in Christ."[76]

Close study of her history shows that *aggiornamento* has often been accompanied by the danger to the Church of an "impassioned love affair with the times," an invasion of "worldly thinking" as Paul VI termed it. The danger to souls here is the reality that some succumb to using the world's categories to judge the Church instead of the reverse. Historically, whenever the Church encountered new modes of thinking this encounter did not necessitate changes in her doctrine, but allowed for the *development* of doctrine, properly understood. With this in mind let us turn to the historical setting in which Paul VI issued *Humanae Vitae,* where he referenced the signs of the times of the 1960s:

> The fulfillment of this duty [of transmitting human life] has always posed problems to the conscience of married people, but the recent course of human society and the concomitant changes have provoked new questions. The Church cannot ignore these questions, for they concern matters intimately connected with the life and happiness of human beings. The changes that have taken place are of considerable importance and varied in nature. In the first place there is the rapid increase in population which has made many fear that world population is going to grow faster than available resources, with the consequence that many families and developing countries would be faced with greater hardships. This can easily induce public authorities to be tempted to take even harsher measures to avert this danger. There is also the fact that not only working and housing conditions but the greater demands made both in the economic and educational field pose a living situation in which it is frequently difficult these days to provide properly for a large family. Also noteworthy is a new understanding of the dignity of woman and her place in society, of the value of conjugal love in marriage and the relationship of conjugal acts to this love. But the most remarkable development of all is to be seen in man's stupendous progress in the domination and rational organization of the forces of nature to the point

that he is endeavoring to extend this control over every aspect of his own life—over his body, over his mind and emotions, over his social life, and even over the laws that regulate the transmission of life.[77]

The Holy Father asked whether or not these conditions warranted the Church's looking anew at her moral teaching—specifically, " . . . could it not be admitted that the intention of a less abundant but more rationalized fecundity might transform a materially sterilizing intervention into a licit and wise control of birth," whether or not " . . . the moment has not come for [man] to entrust to his reason and his will, rather than to the biological rhythms of his organism, the task of regulating birth?"[78] Paul VI was of a mind that these questions mandated a fuller reflection upon Catholic teaching on marriage and the family, founded on natural law and illuminated by divine revelation. But most importantly, before further study the Pope, citing Sacred Scripture and Catholic tradition reminded Catholics of the competency of the Magisterium to give this teaching:

> No member of the faithful could possibly deny that the Church is competent in her magisterium to interpret the natural moral law. It is in fact indisputable, as Our predecessors have many times declared, that Jesus Christ, when He communicated His divine power to Peter and the other Apostles and sent them to teach all nations His commandments, constituted them as the authentic

guardians and interpreters of the whole moral law, not only, that is, of the law of the Gospel but also of the natural law. For the natural law, too, declares the will of God, and its faithful observance is necessary for men's eternal salvation.[79]

Thus it is crucial for us to remember that *Humanae Vitae* was a *reaffirmation* of the infallible teaching of the ordinary magisterium forbidding contraception, taught from the very beginning of the Church, and prior to the close of the Second Vatican Council generally well-received by Catholics. What Our Lord teaches through His Church is the law of God, the will of Christ as taught by the Holy Spirit guiding the Church.

Not only Catholic teaching but the larger American culture was opposed to birth control until 1930, when the Anglican Church broke a centuries-old uniformity on the question by permitting contraception in marriage. So why the need to reaffirm an infallible moral teaching? In 1963, during the pontificate of John XXIII, theological speculation emerged that "the pill," since it did not appear to interfere with the physical integrity of sexual intercourse, was perhaps morally different from spermicides, IUDs and the diaphragm, and perhaps was similar to natural family planning and therefore morally licit. Indeed, the Holy Father formed a small commission to examine this view.

Following Pope John XXIII's death, Paul VI thought it prudent to delay judgment on this opinion until further study could be undertaken, being determined not to require of the faithful anything God did not ask of them. His goal was to give all who wished to weigh in on this question every chance to make their case, and so he enlarged John XXIII's commission to include married couples as well as bishops and their theological advisors, among them Archbishop Karol Wojtyla of Krakow. The majority opinion, comprised of nine of the sixteen bishops, Cardinals and their theologians, was not only that birth control pills were not morally different from other modes of contraception, but that contraception itself was morally acceptable.

As to the finding of the commission, we witness the hand of the Holy Spirit guiding the successor of St. Peter. After four months of study, in October, 1966, Pope Paul noted serious flaws in the commission's report, and under prayerful intense study he came to realize there was no other course than to reaffirm the teaching of the Church on contraception, the genesis of *Humanae Vitae*. During a delay in promulgation of the encyclical, those theologians and bishops who dissented from *Humanae Vitae*, having obtained an advanced copy, launched their propaganda campaign in the American media to maximize the impact of this dissent under the leadership of Fr. Charles Curran of Catholic University, among others.[80] Since his initial dissent on *Humanae Vitae*, Fr. Curran has repeatedly opposed centuries-old Catholic teaching on faith and morals, specifically Catholic doctrine on premarital sex, masturbation, contraception, abortion, homosexuality, divorce, and *in vitro* fertilization. Thus it was that dissent from Catholic teaching in the Church in the United States began over the issue of the moral use of man's God-given sexual power, and continued in opposition to Catholic moral teaching on other key issues.

In psychoanalytic thought, *libido* (from the Latin: *desire, lust*) is the psychic and emotional energy associated with man's instinctual biological drives (sexual desire). Though theoretically held in check by the ego and super-ego, in Freudian thought *libido* understands man as a sexual animal whose happiness derives from the unrestrained *libido*. The virtue of chastity in Freudian logic could only end in illness and unhappiness. Such thinking became normative in the United States in the 1960s, and it was not long before what the Church has always regarded as the greatest of natural mysteries, the marriage act, was reduced to an openly discussable "fun activity."[81]

In contrast, Paul VI offered *libido* as one way Satan, the "malign, clever seducer" undermines man's sexual morality with his "sophistry." The Devil's strategy here, as the Pope cautioned, is "eminently logical." He approaches man with what amounts to a false reason in one's mind, which, if dwelled on, can influence the will by rousing him to do something evil which seems to be good. Deceit is basic to his strategy. By way of one example, if one is gifted with a superior intellect, Satan will tempt to pride and sins of the mind. That some have not succeeded in resisting such temptation is evident in the contention on the part of some Catholic intellectuals that Catholic sexual teaching is out of touch with reality.

If one is worldly and hedonistic, Satan enters with temptations of the flesh. One hears often that the "liberation" of the human libido began in earnest in the United States in the "sexual revolution" of the 1960s. Americans, troubled over repressive attitudes toward human sexuality, hoped for a revolution that would free them from outdated moral and social constraints. The ensuing revolution resulted not in liberation but in license and a host of societal sexual crises. One has only to think of the tremendous increase in the number of post-1960s illegitimate births and abortions, sexually transmitted diseases, opposition to censorship of pornography (especially on the Internet), and the resulting sexual addiction (in some extreme instances resulting in murder). Consider too the tremendous blows to marriage and the family done by adultery, the battle over the homosexual lifestyle in the United States, Canada, and Europe (now to the point of the redefinition of marriage under the law); the increasing incidences of sexual harassment, child pornography on the Internet, Internet predators, date rape, and of course, the divorce rate.

Of late, on several Catholic College campuses it has been possible to attend a performance of Eve Ensler's *Vagina Monologues,* a play which, among celebrations of the female experience of the vagina, contains a "romantic" scene, where a 24-year-old woman seduces a 13-year-old girl. The woman invites the girl into her car, takes her to her house, supplies her with vodka, and seduces her, calling the experience "a kind of heaven." (One wonders what outcry would occur if priests with same-sex attractions were to come to the defense of the play).

It is surely reasonable to argue that these phenomena are the result of a turning away from traditional Catholic sexual moral teaching, revealed by God for our health and well-being. This rebellion has as its fruit not liberation but widespread suffering: the spiraling number of STDs, the millions of abortions, unintended sterility, global pornography, the sex trade, the vast increase in rape and child abuse, promiscuity's threats to marriage and family, and the hundreds of thousands of victims of AIDS. A sagacious observation on the infamous 1960s sums it up nicely: "I think it would be difficult to find a single decade in the history of Western culture when so much barbarism—so much calculated onslaught against culture and convention in any form, and so much sheer degradation of both culture and the individual—passed into print, into music, into art and onto the American stage as the decade of the Nineteen Sixties."[82]

In the United States, the 1960s thus marked the beginning of a breakdown in sexual mores and a rise in family disruption, coupled with rationalizations for departure from traditional morality. The United States underwent a massive social experiment linked to genuine progress for which the Church was not prepared—discrimination against African-Americans and women was coming to an end, and Catholics were ever-increasingly undergoing assimilation into contemporary culture. As a result, Catholics began placing their spiritual lives in one compartment and their daily activities in the secular arena in another, viewing their faith as an entirely private matter, and open to a "pick-and-choose" approach to doctrine. Many theologians, religious educators, and clergy provided intellectual cover for this practice. In such an atmosphere it was hard for the doctrinal teaching of Vatican II to be heard; what did get through was often not the true council, but a "spirit" of Vatican II.

The Devil's goal is to seduce, to lead people away from faithful obedience to God. All that he does with regard to human beings is willfully evil, in order that he might bring them spiritual, supernatural, eternal death. I remind the reader of Paul VI's insight quoted in the first chapter: "This matter of the Devil and of the influence he can exert on individuals as well as on communities, entire societies or events, *is a very important chapter of Catholic doctrine which should be studied again, although it is given little attention today. . . ."* It was the intellectual dishonesty of neomodernists theologians along with bishops sympathetic to their rebellion against the Magisterium which most impacted Catholics' opinions and practices regarding marriage and family in the face of the "sexual revolution" of the 1960s. In examining several of the more notable examples of this sophistry, let us remember that in Catholic teaching the Tempter is a "consummate deceiver" whose real designs are concealed behind what may seem to be divinely inspired, but are in reality instigated by him.

Following the CDF's letter informing Fr. Curran of his lack of suitability as a theologian in the Church, the result of his dissent from *Humanae Vitae,* a supporter wrote in his defense that the infallible status of the birth control encyclical had never been proclaimed, citing "Vatican officials" quoted in the New York Times.[83] In his discussion of the infallibility of the encyclical, he wrote:

> Msgr. Ferdinando Lambruschini, who introduced the encyclical to the press, was a personal friend of the Pope and a member of the birth control commission. We can be reasonably sure that he reviewed his statement with the Pope before he formally presented the birth control encyclical to the press. Lambruschini said that while most theologians think that moral issues can be taught

infallibly, no moral teaching has as yet been infallibly defined. He then explicitly stated that the birth control encyclical was not being taught infallibly.[84]

The author went on to question whether the head of the CDF could apply infallibility to moral issues not defined by Pope or an ecumenical council or the agreement of the college of bishops, especially in view of Canon 749, which says that "No doctrine is understood to be infallibly defined unless it is clearly established as such." Indeed, this was the offered line of argument in parish circles. As a young man in 1972, I was well aware of what I thought was authentic Church teaching—that one may disagree with Catholic teaching on contraception and still be considered a Catholic in good standing, an opinion that, judging by their behavior, millions of Catholics still hold today. This notion of the permissibility of contraception in good conscience is seductive in its argument that contraception is permissible because its prohibition was not taught infallibly. Back in the day, I trusted that priests and teachers would never intend to misrepresent Church teaching on so important a subject. What about this question of the legitimacy of dissent from "noninfallible teaching"? It is paramount to understand the full teaching of the Church in this matter, for it has been my experience in thirty years in Catholic education that the sophistry of those dissenting from

Humanae Vitae, employing neomodernist ideas, has deceived many of the faithful.

Prior to the promulgation of *Humanae Vitae,* moral theologians in the United States who predicted a change in Church teaching on contraception in light of the papal commission had gone on record as favoring a change in the Church's traditional ban on artificial contraception. In parishes, Catholics were counseled not to be concerned with obedience to a teaching that in their opinion was soon to change. Imagine the confusion on the part of the faithful and the reaction of the dissident theologians when *Humanae Vitae* appeared! The reputations of those who had predicted a change in Church teaching appeared tarnished. As we have seen, many priests and laymen in the United States wasted no time in denouncing the encyclical; the immediacy of their reaction surely prevented them from giving it careful study.

The bishops, the successors to the Apostles, shepherds of the flock both in Europe and the United States by and large supported the encyclical in their letter *Human Life in Our Day* of November, 1968. Tragically, very few spoke out publicly in defense of the Holy Father's reaffirmation of the centuries-old ban on artificial contraception. Furthermore, *Human Life in Our Day* contained one very questionable statement under the heading "Norms of Licit Theological Dissent" which read as follows: "The expression of theological dissent from the magisterium is in order only if the reasons are serious and well-founded, if the manner of the dissent does not question or impugn the teaching authority of the Church and is such as not to give scandal."[85]

By 1968, it was eminently clear that the neomodernists' dissenting position had indeed impugned Church teaching, openly challenging the authority of the Magisterium and giving grave scandal. Thus the bishops had opportune chance to quash the oft-given spiritual counsel that spouses could follow their consciences and decide the question of contraception for themselves. Instead they remained silent, abdicating their responsibility to remind Catholics of their duty to properly *form* their consciences by Scripture, Tradition, and magisterial teaching, lending credence to the false notion of licit dissent, creating abundant confusion for faithful Catholics.

All of this is reminiscent of Paul VI's words quoted earlier that, while we shouldn't see the Devil under every rock, ". . . . it is true that those who do not keep watch over themselves with a certain moral rigor are exposed to the influence of the 'mystery of iniquity' cited by St. Paul which raises serious questions about our salvation. *Our doctrine becomes uncertain,* darkness obscured as it is by the darkness surrounding the Devil. . . ." – this as Msgr. Lambruschini was reminding Catholics that *Humanae Vitae,* not having been taught infallibly, was thus reformable. The clear uncertainty sown here is how the divinely-inspired teaching that artificial contraception violates God's law, being contrary to the nature of marriage and married love, is reformable. In the decade of the sexual revolution most Catholics were not predisposed to read, study, and interiorize Church teaching on the matter. Most dutifully listened to clerical advice to decide "according to their conscience" and joined in the prevailing cultural practice of the use of the pill.

In response to the papal encyclical, over two hundred dissenting theologians, led by Fr. Curran, published their aforementioned statement in the *New York Times,* the text of which illuminates the sophistry in their response:

> As Roman Catholic theologians we respectfully acknowledge a distinct role of hierarchical magisterium (teaching authority) in the church of Christ. At the same time Christian tradition assigns theologians the special responsibility of evaluating and interpreting pronouncements of the magisterium in the light of the total theological data operative in each question of statement. We offer these initial comments on Pope Paul VI's encyclical on the regulation of birth.
>
> The encyclical is not an infallible teaching. History shows that a number of statements of similar or even greater authoritative weight have subsequently been proven inadequate or even erroneous. Past authoritative statements on religious liberty, interest-

taking, the right to silence, and the ends of marriage have all been corrected at a later date.

Many positive values concerning marriage are expressed in Paul VI's encyclical. However, we take exception to the ecclesiology implied and the methodology used by Paul VI in the writing and promulgation of the document: They are incompatible with the church's authentic self-awareness as expressed in and suggested by the acts of the Second Vatican Council itself.

The encyclical consistently assumes that the Church is identical with the hierarchical office. No real importance is afforded the witness of the life of the church in its totality; the special witness of many Catholic couples is neglected; it fails to acknowledge the witness of the separated Christian churches and ecclesial communities; it is insensitive to the witness of many men of good will; it pays insufficient attention to the ethical import of modern science.

Furthermore, the encyclical betrays a narrow and positivistic notion of papal authority, as illustrated by the rejection of the majority view presented by the commission established to consider the question as well as by the rejection of the conclusions of a large part of the international Catholic theological community.

Likewise, we take exception to some of the specific ethical conclusions contained in the encyclical. They are based on an inadequate concept of natural law: The multiple forms of natural law theory are ignored and the fact that competent philosophers come to different conclusions on this very question is disregarded. Even the minority report of the papal commission noted grave difficulty in

---

attempting to present conclusive proof of the immorality of artificial contraception based on natural law.

Other defects include: Over-emphasis on the biological aspects of conjugal relations as ethically normative; undue stress on sexual acts and on the faculty of sex viewed in itself apart from the person and the couple; a static world view which downplays the historical and evolutionary character of humanity in its finite existence as described in Vatican II's Pastoral Constitution of the Church in the Modern World; unfounded assumptions about the evil consequences of methods of artificial birth control; indifference to Vatican II's assertion that prolonged sexual abstinence may cause faithfulness to be imperiled and its quality of fruitfulness to be ruined; an almost total disregard for the dignity of millions of human beings brought into the world without the slightest possibility of being fed and educated decently.

In actual fact, the encyclical demonstrates no development over the teaching of Pius XI's *Casti Connubii* whose conclusions have been called into question for grave serious reasons. There reasons, given a muffled voice at Vatican II, have not been adequately handled by the mere repetition of past teaching.

It is common teaching in the church that Catholics may dissent from authoritative, non-infallible teachings of the magisterium when sufficient reasons for so doing exist.

Therefore, as Roman Catholic theologians, conscious of our duty and our limitations we conclude that spouses may responsible decide according to their conscience that artificial contraception

is some circumstances is permissible and indeed necessary to preserve and foster the values and sacredness of marriage.

It is our conviction also that true commitment to the mystery of
Christ and the Church requires a candid statement of mind at this
time by all Catholic theologians.[86]

Upon reflection we must ask ourselves, what did publication of this statement really mean? A select group of theologians had assigned to themselves the role of an alternative
magisterium without basis in Sacred Scripture and Tradition,
and proceeded to challenge official Church teaching on
ecclesiology,[87] on how Catholics should understand papal
authority, and on the Church's teaching on the natural law,
accusing her of physicalism.[88] With the *New York Times* statement, we have arrived at the core of the crisis of authority in
the Church which has in turn produced a profound crisis of
faith. Where were the shepherds of the flock amidst this rebellion? Most, but not all bishops, successors of the Apostles,
whose task it is to teach, sanctify, and govern in Christ's
name, demonstrated a good deal of uncertainty in their reaction to "faithful dissent" from *Humanae Vitae*. Many opted not
to reinforce its teaching, ignoring those Catholics who had
gone on record in defense of the encyclical.[89] Sadly, the lost
sheep had become the shepherds. Since the reasoning of these
theologians was persuasive to many Catholics in the United

States in the 1960s, a short critique of their position follows in light of Catholic teaching that the Devil has the capacity to use humans as instruments of his will, creating in us the desire for human recognition, inducing pride, the root of all other sins. Without knowing it, man can become the tool of the powers of darkness.

Let us begin with the assertion that the encyclical is not an infallible teaching. Writing in 1969 in reference to the 1917 Code of Canon Law, Fr. Curran persisted in his efforts to justify dissent from *Humanae Vitae*, maintaining that

> . . . those who defend the possibility of infallibility in teaching morality do not produce specific historical instances in which such teaching has been promulgated. According to the guidance of Canon 1223, No.3, of the Code of Canon Law nothing is to be considered defined *'nisi id manifesto [sic] constiterit'* (unless it is manifestly clear). There is no specific moral issue where this condition can be shown to obtain."[90]

Fr. Curran's point here is that any infallible *moral* teaching would have to meet the conditions proper to infallibly defined teachings, disregarding the possibility that, though not defined, the moral norms which they rejected might have been infallibly proposed by the ordinary magisterium. The applicable canon is 1323, not Fr. Curran's 1223. More importantly, the first section of the same canon necessitates that teaching proposed as divinely revealed by the universal and ordinary magisterium, as well as teaching solemnly defined, must be believed. This requirement is drawn, almost word for word, from Vatican I's solemn teaching on the same matter.[91] The Second Vatican Council Fathers gave the conditions for an infallible exercise of the Church's ordinary magisterium:

> In matters of faith and morals, the bishops speak in the name of Christ and the faithful are to accept their teaching and adhere to it with a religious assent. This religious submission of mind and will must be shown in a special way to the authentic magisterium of the Roman Pontiff, even when he is not speaking *ex cathedra;* that is, it must be shown in such a way that his supreme magisterium is acknowledged with reverence, the judgments made by him are sincerely adhered to, according to his manifest mind and will. His mind and will in the matter may be known either from the character of the documents, from his frequent repetition of the same doctrine, or from his manner of speaking.[92]

While it is true that Paul VI's teaching in the encyclical was not proposed *ex cathedra,* the red herring in the dissenting theologians' argument is their assertion that because this is so, infallibility is a nonissue as regards magisterial teaching on artificial contraception. I have mentioned that *Humanae Vitae* was a reaffirmation of a teaching already taught infallibly by the ordinary magisterium of the Church, accepted as such from her origins until at least 1962. The well-known footnote #40 to the excerpt from *Lumen Gentium* just quoted cites four previous Church Documents in corroborating that *Humanae Vitae* met the criteria for an infallible exercise of the Church's ordinary magisterium stated in Vatican II's Dogmatic Constitution on the Church.[93]

Some dissident theologians have also added that Church teaching prohibiting contraception from the time of the Church Fathers was not a reaffirmation of Biblical Christian teaching, but rather a development of early Christian moral teaching well-established in Sacred Scripture. This argument, that the dissenting position on *Humanae Vitae* represents a similar development of doctrine begun in the Church after 1962, is illustrative of the modernist idea that Christ did not found a Church with a divine constitution and unchangeable dogmas and moral standards. In their thinking, such standards were the result of so-called doctrinal evolution and must continue to develop and give place to others as times change. This cannot be reconciled with Vatican II's instruction that Church teaching on artificial contraception has been proposed infallibly by the ordinary magisterium. This "faithful dissent" still contradicts what the Church had always taught as infallible, and does not represent *authentic* doctrinal development as the Church understands and teaches it.

A second deception is found where the authors posit a novel understanding of the magisterium in endorsing the *sensus fidei,* the "mind of the faithful." Evident here is a coarse reduction of the fullness of conciliar teaching on the magisterium of the Church:

> The entire body of the faithful, anointed as they are by the Holy One, cannot err in matters of belief. They manifest this special property by means of the whole peoples' supernatural discernment in matters of faith when "from the Bishops down to the last of the lay faithful" they show universal agreement in matters of faith and morals.[94]

Here is one among numerous contemporary expressions of this argument:

> A very important event in the Church today is the re-emergence of an understanding of the Sensus Fidelium, what the Christian people believe, accept, and reject. It is here, the Sensus Fidelium, wherein resides the promise of Christ to protect us from error with the guidance of the Spirit. Church hierarchy (the rulers) have taught what to believe, accept, and reject, but always with acceptance or a corrective response by theologian (experts) and the faithful even from the very beginning. (Acts 15)
>
> This corrective response especially among the Church faithful, wherein the Spirit of truth resides, is a re-emerging tradition. Except in the early Church, never have so many faithful Christians been so educated in our faith and Church history and so aware of its meaning in our lives. We mark self awareness as a corner stone

in the development of the human species. It just might well be that our collective reawakening of a spiritual self awareness regarding truths of faith marks a corner stone in the concept of "Ecclesia semper Reformanda" (The church must always be reformed).

Herein lies present day conflict; the resistance of the hierarchy of the Church to recognize and honor the fact that the Spirit of truth speaks through the faithful who accept or reject their teachings. Theologians are suppressed and persecuted when attempting to express a better understanding of faith and morals that perhaps better reflects the sense of the faithful. This is not surprising since bishops are chosen because they echo mandates from Rome, and not because they reflect or listen to their people.

It has not always been thus in the Church and a re-awakening of the faithful people to their role in Ecclesia semper Reformanda is happening. It is long overdue.[95]

As a corrective we read in the same section of *Lumen Gentium:*

That discernment [*sensus fidei*] in matters of faith is aroused and sustained by the Spirit of truth. It *is exercised under the guidance of the sacred teaching authority, in faithful and respectful obedience to which the people of God accepts that which is not just the word of men but truly the word of God* [italics mine]. Through it, the people of God adheres unwaveringly to the faith given once and for all to the saints, penetrates it more deeply with right thinking, and applies it more fully in its life.

In the first chapter, I discussed the point that certain modernists prior to Vatican I saw human beings as emanations from the divine, leaning toward a pantheistic cosmology where God is equated with the world or a part of it. Believing that all revelation is through subjective experience, it follows that the people of God be the final authors of what should be believed. It would appear that the Vatican Council II Fathers had a more authentic view of the magisterium of the Church than these dissidents:

> But the college or body of bishops has no authority unless it is understood together with the Roman Pontiff, the successor of Peter as its head. The pope's power of primacy over all, both pastors and faithful, remains whole and intact. *In virtue of his office, that is as Vicar of Christ and pastor of the whole Church, the Roman Pontiff has full, supreme and universal power over the Church. And he is always free to exercise this power* [italics mine]. The order of bishops, which succeeds to the college of apostles and gives this apostolic body continued existence, is also the subject of supreme and full power over the universal Church, provided we understand this body together with its head the Roman Pontiff and never without this head. This power can be exercised only with the consent of the Roman Pontiff. For our Lord placed Simon alone as the rock and the bearer of the keys of the Church, and made him shepherd of the whole flock; it is evident, however, that the power of binding and loosing, which was given to Peter was granted also to the college of apostles, joined with their head.[96]

The third deception is the reference in the statement that historically the Church has issued authoritative statements on matters such as religious liberty, interest-taking, and the purpose of marriage and has corrected them at a later date, implying that such can be the case with the core teaching of *Humanae Vitae.* To this, one need only ask: was the Church's prohibition of usury, for example, *infallibly* proposed by the ordinary magisterium of the Church? Alas not. Further study of the alleged cases in the dissenters' statement (implying that a teaching proposed infallibly had been changed at a later date) shows that the teaching in these cases was not infallibly proposed in such manner as to meet the criteria set down in *Lumen Gentium.*

Fourthly, the authors maintained that ". . . Christian tradition assigns theologians the special responsibility of evaluating and interpreting pronouncements of the magisterium." Their intent here was to argue for an ongoing process of doctrinal development in which theological speculation would prove indispensible. At root here was their opposition to the teaching that there are moral absolutes in the area of sexual morality, a basic tenet of neomodernism of which Pope Benedict XVI has warned.[97] It should be clear here that these dissenters were interposing their erroneous speculation between the flock and the guidance of the principal shepherd of the Catholic Church. Most of the doubt about the

Church's ban on artificial contraception was sown by theologians who argued that Vatican II assigned them a prominent place within the magisterial authority of the Church. We are left wondering, where is this assignment mandated in Sacred Scripture by Our Lord? Where is this mandated in Sacred Tradition and the writings of the Fathers of the Church? In papal and conciliar documents, including Vatican II? Alas, the word "theologians" appears only *once* in the sixteen texts promulgated by Vatican II, a reality hardly commensurate with their self-assigned place as a core element in the full magisterial role of the Church.

One final argument against *Humanae Vitae* by the dissenting authors deserves careful study. It took issue with the following passage from the encyclical:

> The Church, nevertheless, in urging men to the observance of the precepts of the natural law, which it interprets by its constant doctrine, teaches that each and every marital act must of necessity retain its intrinsic relationship to the procreation of human life.[98]

In an article commemorating the twenty-fifth anniversary of *Humanae Vitae*, Fr. McCormick recounted Archbishop John Quinn's intervention during the bishops' synod on the family in the fall of 1984. The Archbishop opined that many Catholics still did not accept the encyclical's reiteration of the doctrine of the "intrinsic evil of each and every use of contraception,"[99] and as a result, "no longer look to the Church for enlightenment in the area of sexual morality."[100] Before discussing this rejection of the truth of the encyclical, an extended reading of the pertinent passages is in order. From *Humanae Vitae:*

> The sexual activity, in which husband and wife are intimately and chastely united with one another, through which human life is transmitted, is, as the recent Council recalled, "noble and worthy." It does not, moreover, cease to be legitimate even when, for reasons independent of their will, it is foreseen to be infertile. For its natural adaptation to the expression and strengthening of the union of husband and wife is not thereby suppressed. The fact is, as experience shows, that new life is not the result of each and every act of sexual intercourse. God has wisely ordered laws of nature and the incidence of fertility in such a way that successive births are already naturally spaced through the inherent operation of these laws. The Church, nevertheless, in urging men to the observance of the precepts of the natural law, which it interprets by its constant doctrine, teaches that each and every marital act must of necessity retain its intrinsic relationship to the procreation of human life.
>
> This particular doctrine, often expounded by the magisterium of the Church, is based on the inseparable connection, established by God, which man on his own initiative may not break, between the unitive significance and the procreative significance which are both inherent to the marriage act. The reason is that the fundamental nature of the marriage act, while uniting husband and wife in the closest intimacy, also renders them capable of generating

new life—and this as a result of laws written into the actual nature of man and of woman. And if each of these essential qualities, the unitive and the procreative, is preserved, the use of marriage fully retains its sense of true mutual love and its ordination to the supreme responsibility of parenthood to which man is called. We believe that our contemporaries are particularly capable of seeing that this teaching is in harmony with human reason.[101]

In a supportive effort to develop this timeless truth, Pope John Paul II wrote in *Familiaris Consortio:*

When couples, by means of recourse to contraception, separate these two meanings [procreative and unitive] that God the Creator has inscribed in the being of man and woman and in the dynamism of their sexual communion, they act as "arbiters" of the divine plan and they "manipulate" and degrade human sexuality-and with it themselves and their married partner-by altering its value of "total" self-giving. Thus the innate language that expresses the total reciprocal self-giving of husband and wife is overlaid, through contraception, by an objectively contradictory language, namely, that of not giving oneself totally to the other. This leads not only to a positive refusal to be open to life but also to a falsification of the inner truth of conjugal love, which is called upon to give itself in personal totality. . . .

When, instead, by means of recourse to periods of infertility, the couple respect the inseparable connection between the unitive and procreative meanings of human sexuality, they are acting as "ministers" of God's plan and they "benefit from" their sexuality according to the original dynamism of "total" selfgiving, without manipulation or alteration.[102]

In spite of this, sadly it is difficult not to agree with Fr. McCormick's reminder that Catholics have not accepted this truth in light of human reason, as Paul VI had hoped. Specifically, they would no doubt

> . . . . be incredulous at the proposition that the use of artificial birth control necessarily makes their sexual intimacy selfish, dishonest and unfaithful. Nor is their valuing of parenthood based on their experience of isolated sex acts as having a certain 'procreative' structure.[103]

Before turning to a discussion of all this, we note one final effort of dissenting theologians in their self-designated role of alternative magisterium to distort the divine law:

> The hidden supposition of this analysis [*Familiaris Consortio*] is that self-giving is determined by the *physical* openness of the individual act. The burden of the discussion since *Humanae Vitae* has been precisely the question of whether the *giving of self* can be tied so closely with the physical structure of the act.[104]

Catholic theologians such as Frs. Curran and McCormick and those influenced by their writings cannot comprehend why the Church teaches that contraception is morally wrong because in their thinking contraceptives seem only to interfere with the *physical* structure of the marital act (*e.g.*, condoms), or with the natural biological processes of the human body (*e.g.*, oral contraceptives). They accuse the Church of *physicalism,* that is, the idea that the Church places too much value on respecting the natural physical method or structure of sexual intercourse, and of being indifferent to sentiments similar to the one expressed by the Papal Birth Control Commission, that

> The morality of sexual acts between married people takes its meaning first of all and specifically from the ordering of their actions in a fruitful married life, that is, one which is practiced with responsible, generous and prudent parenthood. It does not then depend on the direct fecundity of each and every particular act.[105]

Moral theologians faithful to magisterial teaching refer to this thinking as *separatist,* that is, that which has "severed the existential and psychological bond between the life-giving or procreative meaning of human sexuality and its person-uniting, love-giving, unitive meaning,"[106] and which sees the procreative meaning as a biological task of sexuality. Because most Catholics are ignorant of these fundamentals of the faith, this separatist interpretation has proven most seductive.[107] As a corrective, we can look to Vatican II's *Gaudium et Spes:*

. . . . when there is question of harmonizing conjugal love with the responsible transmission of life, the moral aspects of any procedure *does not depend solely on sincere intentions or on an evaluation of motives,* [italics mine] but must be determined by objective standards. These, based on the nature of the human person and his acts, preserve the full sense of mutual self-giving and human procreation in the context of true love. Such a goal cannot be achieved unless the virtue of conjugal chastity is sincerely practiced. Relying on these principles, sons of the Church may not undertake methods of birth control which are found blameworthy by the teaching authority of the Church in its unfolding of the divine law.[108]

Thus, as the Catechism remind us, "Sexuality affects all aspects of the human person in the unity of his body and soul."[109] It is not simply biological, as the separatist position says, for we are a unity of body and soul. John Paul II has always written of marriage as a total self-donation of our bodies and wills, wherein husband and wife can give their very selves to the other. Sexual intercourse between the whole person of the spouses brings about this self-donation in the most intimate way humanly possible.[110] I am mystified as to why Catholics do not see this teaching as much more exciting than the separatist view of sex, except to say that for the reasons which appear in these pages, Catholics have hardened their hearts to the teachings of Jesus Christ in and through His Church, which sees the fertility of the husband and wife as a gift from God and the end (*telos*) of marriage where children are the fruit of the conjugal love, the total giving of self of husband and wife.[111] In this, husband and wife procreate; it is God who creates a new and immortal soul at each conception, a reality of which Vatican II sought to remind the faithful:

> All should be persuaded that human life and the task of transmitting it are not realities bound up with this world alone. Hence they cannot be measured or perceived only in terms of it, but always have a bearing on the eternal destiny of men.[112]

The alternative magisterium is strangely silent on this conciliar teaching, indicative of the apostasy of many of its members. Contraception is evil because of what it prevents; conception is an act of God. St. Paul warned that the Christian should not hope for the Church's wisdom to see eye to eye with "the wisdom of the world,"[113] for her moral teaching comes not from man but from God; *Humanae Vitae* teaches that artificial contraception obstructs the will of God, "based on the inseparable connection, established by God, which man on his own initiative may not break, between the unitive significance and the procreative significance which are both inherent to the marriage act."[114] The language of contraceptive intercourse says, so to speak, "I will give you all of myself, my person except my God-given ability to make a new life."

The other and, I think, principal reason Catholics persist in ignoring what Our Lord wished to teach us about the proper use of our sexuality is that contraception is a sin, and in speaking of it as an intrinsic evil the Church reminds us that it, *as does all sin,* separates us from God:

> Sin is an offense against reason, truth, and right conscience; it is failure in genuine love for God and neighbor caused by a perverse attachment to certain goods. It wounds the nature of man and injures human solidarity. It has been defined as "an utterance, a deed, or a desire contrary to the eternal law."

> Sin is an offense against God: "Against you, you alone, have I sinned, and done that which is evil in your sight." Sin sets itself against God's love for us and turns our hearts away from it. *Like the first sin, it is disobedience, a revolt against God through the will to become "like gods," knowing and determining good and evil.* [emphasis added] Sin is thus "love of oneself even to contempt of God." In this proud self-exaltation, sin is diametrically opposed to the obedience of Jesus, which achieves our salvation.[115]

In spite of his optimism in thinking that people would readily see the reasonableness of the Church's integralist understanding of the gift of our sexuality, Paul VI's later reflection in our first chapter on why this was so remains insightful analysis, and so I would like briefly to take up his challenge in order to give it greater attention in the world in which we live.

II.

I am not the slightest bit hesitant to say that I believe with the Church that we humans live in a world characterized by a spiritual war, and thus as baptized Catholics we are called to "put on the armor of God." In an Augustinian sense we must decide where our allegiance lies: are we citizens of God's kingdom, who happen temporarily to reside in a civil society, or are we full-fledged citizens of the city of men, making room for God when we are able? Catholic teaching on original sin continues to shed light on man's position in the world. As a result of the Fall, Satan has acquired "a certain domination over man" in spite of our free will. Widespread ignorance of this teaching is the root cause of the crisis of faith facing the Church today. The Catechism teaches the reality of this spiritual combat:

> The whole of man's history has been the story of dour combat with the powers of evil, stretching, so our Lord tells us, from the very dawn of history until the last day. Finding himself in the midst of the battlefield man has to struggle to do what is right, and it is at great cost to himself, and aided by God's grace, that he succeeds in achieving his own inner integrity.[116]

Contraception, like the original sin, like all sin, amounts to a revolt against God and his rights as Creator of all that is. Prideful man wills to become like God,[117] deciding subjectively what is moral and immoral for himself. As Cardinal Wojtyla explained at the time, we must probe into the reality of the Devil to explain this rebellion against God.[118] Cardinal Wojtyla's exegesis was telling in its reflection that Satan's temptation of Eve is rooted in his own rebellion against God, subsequently taught by the Catechism as well:

> Behind the disobedient choice of our first parents lurks a seductive voice, opposed to God, which makes them fall into death out of envy. Scripture and the Church's Tradition see in this being a fallen angel, called "Satan" or the "devil." The Church teaches that Satan was at first a good angel, made by God: "The devil and the other demons were indeed created naturally good by God, but they became evil by their own doing." Scripture speaks of a sin of these angels. This "fall" consists in the free choice of these created spirits, who radically and irrevocably rejected God and his reign. We find a reflection of that rebellion in the tempter's words to our first parents: "You will be like God." The devil "has sinned from the beginning"; he is "a liar and the father of lies."[119]

Wojtyla wished to remind his audience that our freedom as humans is limited: God told Eve that she might eat the fruit of all the trees in Eden except the one in the center (the "tree of the knowledge of good and evil"), "lest you die." Our existence as God's creatures requires us to acknowledge that only God knows what is truly good and what is evil. In seductive fashion the "father of lies" attempted to conceal this truth from Eve, to pass on to man his own *non serviam* or rebellion, which put him beyond the law of ultimate dependence on the Creator. Instead of dismissing the temptation, Eve permitted herself to ponder the falsehood, saw that it looked delightful, and a sinful disobedience was conceived in her heart. The spiritual war had begun: truth versus lies, good versus evil, life versus death.

In this immortal combat, St. Paul cautions us that we have spiritual enemies: "principalities," "powers," and "spiritual hosts of wickedness in the heavenly places."[120] Jesus too spoke of this, for when Peter rebuked Our Lord for talking of Calvary and the Cross, "he turned and said to Peter, Get behind me, Satan! You are a hindrance to me; for you are not on the side of God, but of men."[121] Jesus could see that his closest disciple had allowed himself to become the Enemy's mouthpiece. So, in teaching us that the gates of hell shall not prevail against His Church, Jesus warns that the Devil and his minions will continue to make war on His disciples, the offspring of "the woman," who is the bride of Christ.[122] That neomodernist theologians have failed to "take every thought captive to obey Christ"[123] does not change the reality!

The good news is that, as Cardinal Wojtyla reminded us, Satan did not succeed in sowing total rebellion on man's part; just in inducing us to "turn towards the world," in moving along a path "opposed to the destiny to which he has been called." Since the sin of our first parents the pattern, while remaining similar, has become more sophisticated: man asserts his independence of God, proving to himself that he, like God, may decide what is good for himself. In this, man, as a result of human pride, rebels against God instead of cooperating with Him, seeking what he and not God regards as truly good, truly human. Vatican II's *Gaudiam et Spes* refers to this worldly thinking as secularism, the view that created things in the end do not depend on the Creator, and may be dealt with by man as he wills. In reflecting on "the signs of the times," Wojtyla insightfully recalled St. Paul's words:

> for that day [the Second Coming] will not come, unless the rebellion comes first, and the man of lawlessness is revealed, the son of perdition, who opposes and exalts himself against every so-called god or object of worship, so that he takes his seat in the temple of God, proclaiming himself to be God. [124]

Cardinal Wojtyla's basic point was that modern man's anthropocentrism prevented him from acknowledging the rights of God as Creator of all that is, in turn rooting his life not in relation to his Maker but in himself. The soon-to-be Pope John Paul II warned his listeners of "rebellion"—the Greek term for this is *apostasia*, better translated as "apostasy"—a massive turning away from the Christian faith in the fullness of its revelation. The controversy surrounding *Humanae Vitae* is best understood in this light, as the occasion for mass apostasy. And, as we quoted Wojtyla earlier, "without the Creator, the Creature vanishes."

Before a brief look at what *Humanae Vitae* predicted would happen should man disregard God's design for our sexuality, I shall let St. Paul conclude my reflection on contraception as a "crack" through which the Devil has sown the seeds of rebellion, of apostasy:

> Now the Spirit expressly says that in later times some will depart from the faith by giving heed to deceitful spirits and doctrines of demons. . . . For the time is coming when people will not endure sound teaching, but having itching ears they will accumulate for themselves teachers to suit their own likings, and will turn away from listening to the truth and wander into myths.[125]

III.

In *Humanae Vitae* Pope Paul VI wrote of four evils that would result from a disobedience to Church teaching set down in his encyclical:

- That widespread contraceptive practice would lead to "conjugal infidelity and the general lowering of morality."
- Men . . . would "lose respect" for women and no longer care for their physical and psychological enjoyment.

- The contraceptive mentality would "place a dangerous weapon . . . in the hands of those public authorities who take no heed of moral exigencies."
- Contraception would lead humans into thinking they have unrestricted authority over their bodies.

It is easy to show from the historical record that the Holy Spirit guided the heart and mind of Paul VI to see clearly the consequences of the intrinsic evil of contraception. Jesus, the Way, the Truth, and the Life, teaches that *the truth* sets us free. Pope Paul VI was the Lord's herald in *Humanae Vitae,* and so understanding and assimilating its teaching is the key to human freedom in our sexually befuddled world.

The fulfillment of Pope Paul's predictions has been recounted in numerous studies. All show convincingly contraception's negative fruits in the areas of abortion, divorce, family disintegration, wife and child abuse, STDs, and illegitimate births.[126] These studies also show the dehumanization of women as men were released from accountability for their sexual aggression. And, as pro-life Catholics know all too well, population control is part and parcel of current United Nations policy debates *vis-à-vis* developing nations. Finally, the studies also reveal *in vitro* fertilization, cloning, genetic engineering and embryonic stem cell research for what they are: the fruits of the contraceptive mentality. I avidly recommend these studies to the reader, for I have found no shortage of Catholics intellectually dishonest in spouting off on this topic not having read these studies in light of *Humanae Vitae* and the tradition of the Church. At the very least, the Church which Jesus established, in teaching that contraception is shameful and intrinsically vicious, stands with Him as, to recall John Paul II's words, a "sign of contradiction" in our present culture's moral climate.

What I find both exciting and encouraging at present, however is that the discipline of social science, usually understood to be the preserve of progressive secular scholars, in following the available data has corroborated the evils Pope Paul had predicted. Recent research findings by scholars in the social sciences confirm contraception as the culprit behind the considerable rise in divorce and illegitimacy in the United States, both of which in turn have spawned other societal ills such as increased rates of criminal behavior and high school dropout rates. No surprise, it turns out that the poor are especially susceptible to the harms caused by the American contraceptive culture. These findings are the studied work of secular scholars, most of whom are regarded as slightly left of center on the sociopolitical spectrum.

To give but a few examples: Robert Michael of the University of Chicago has written that sudden widespread use of artificial contraception and the availability of abortion proved responsible for "about half of the increase in divorce from 1965 to 1976."[127] Nobel prize-winning economist George Akerlof of the University of California at Berkeley has given us an economic explanation for why the pervasive use of artificial contraception resulted in a rise rather than a decrease in illegitimate births, as had been predicted. He argues that traditional women, desiring either to remain chaste or at minimum obtain a promise of marriage from their boyfriend in the case of pregnancy, proved unable to compete with "modern" women who practiced contraception, creating an atmosphere in which fornication became the rule and women felt free or in some cases pressured to engage in premarital intercourse. Thus many traditional women ended up fornicating and having children out of wedlock, while many of the "free" women engaged in contraceptive intercourse or aborted so as to shun childbearing. This finding goes a long way in explaining why contraceptive practice was coupled with an increase in both abortion and illegitimacy.

On Paul VI's concern that men would objectify women, lose respect for them, and cease caring for their physical and psychological enjoyment, Mary Eberstadt writes that even noted Third Wave feminist author Naomi Wolf has come to realize that those feminists who had opposed pornography were right:

The whole world, post-Internet, did become pornographized. Young men and women are indeed being taught what sex is, how it looks, what its etiquette and expectations are, by pornographic training—and this is having a huge effect on how they interact.

But the effect is not making men into raving beasts. On the contrary: The onslaught of porn is responsible for deadening male libido in relation to real women, and leading men to see fewer and fewer women as "porn-worthy." Far from having to fend off porn-crazed young men, young women are worrying that as mere flesh and blood, they can scarcely get, let alone hold, their attention. . . . Today, real naked women are just bad porn.

As one more sign of the times in which we live, I find it noteworthy that after a recent talk of hers on pornography's effect on relations between male and female, Ms. Wolf inquired of a young man in the audience why he thought it necessary to move to sexual activity early in his acquaintances with girls:

Why have sex right away? Things are always a little tense and uncomfortable when you just start seeing someone. I prefer to have sex right away just to get it over with. You know it's going to happen anyway, and it gets rid of the tension.

"Isn't the tension kind of fun?" Wolf asked. "Doesn't that also get rid of the mystery?"

Mystery? I don't know what you're talking about. Sex has no mystery."[128]

In her vindication of *Humanae Vitae* Eberstadt wrote of "the Pill's bastard child, ubiquitous pornography."[129] It is my observation that she is on the mark. So Paul VI too was on the mark: "He is the malign, clever seducer who knows how to make his way into us through the senses, the imagination and the libido. . . ."

These recent secular findings on the effects of the contraceptive mentality in our culture show too that artificial contraception removes one of the key reasons for getting married — the moral incentive. They also reveal that while many middle and upper class men and women marry because it further serves their economic interest to do so, the poor are more likely to marry only for moral reasons. The result? In our contraceptive culture the poor have even less of an incentive to marry than do the other strata, and so have been hit harder by the negative consequences that resulted from the widespread use of contraceptives. In sum, the end results of the contraceptive revolution were promiscuity, the disintegration of the family, crime, and bitter relations between men and women, the poor among us paying the more steeply.[130]

I believe Paul VI would have been greatly vindicated had he lived to see all that developed in the final decades of the third millennium, and not just by the fulfillment of the warnings in his infamous encyclical. The crisis of authority which grew out of the response to *Humanae Vitae* in the United States entered other areas of "the Temple of God," namely its most sublime prayer, to which we turn presently. But all the news is not bad news. Consider a recent article which reports: ". . . . a different problem has crept up: More adult women are forgoing birth control, a trend that has experts puzzled—and alarmed about a potential rise in unintended pregnancies."[131]

CHAPTER FOUR

The Sacred Liturgy: The Holy Sacrifice of the Mass

In the past Canon Law and the rubrics dominated everything: priests conformed to their prescriptions with an obedience which was sometimes puerile, for want of being enlightened. Today, the reverse is the case: *it is the liturgy which must obey us and be adapted to our concerns,* [emphasis mine] to the extent of becoming more like a political meeting or a "happening." "We are going to celebrate our own life experience!"

Godfreid Cardinal Danneels

However, in these studies concerning ancient rites the due preparation of knowledge must not be overlooked, which should have as its companion piety and docile and humble obedience. And if these be lacking, any investigation whatever about ancient liturgies of the Mass will turn out to be irreverent and fruitless: for when the supreme authority of the Apostolic See in liturgical matters, *which deservedly rejects puffed-up learning* and, with the

Apostle, "speaks wisdom among the perfect" (1 Cor 8:1; 2:6), has been spurned, whether through ignorance *or a proud and conceited spirit,* [emphasis mine] the danger immediately threatens that the error known as modernism will be introduced into liturgical matters.

Pope Pius XI

A regular observance throughout my years as a Catholic educator has been that when Mass is celebrated on major Liturgical Feasts and Holy Days, the reaction of the student body at large is never generally one of excitement at the possibility of their sanctification and a chance to draw yet even closer to Our Lord. Furthermore, many students do not attend Mass regularly on Sundays, and many who do attend do so at the insistence of their parents. The Son of God Himself is present at Mass in the person of the priest, but especially in the Eucharist, body, blood, soul, and divinity. Think on it for a while — if Catholics *really* had faith that Jesus Himself was present at Mass, wouldn't attendance be more competitive than securing Super Bowl tickets?

Dr. Peter Kreeft of Boston College has written that since the time of the European Enlightenment and the genesis of modernism, and particularly following Vatican II, there has been a gradual departure from the orthodox Catholic faith now bordering on outright apostasy. Much as did Paul VI, Dr. Kreeft examines this reality in the context of a spiritual battle between the forces of light and the forces of darkness.[132] I contend that this development resulted in no small part from the failure of those bishops who, perhaps because they felt intimidated by the liturgical experts, allowed them to propagate teachings at odds with *Sacrosanctum Concilium,* the Council's document on the Sacred Liturgy. In effect, the bishops allowed the imposition of newfangled liturgical reforms on their flocks, resulting in a liturgy which has proven spiritually destabilizing in many cases.[133] The question which continues to puzzle is, why such poor shepherding? If Pope Celestine I's maxim *lex orandi, lex credendi* is true, and it is, then the lack of resemblance between what the Church teaches concerning the Holy Sacrifice of the Mass and the reality of what is taking place in its celebration in parishes in the United States today warrants that we come to understand those developments in the Liturgical Movement as it came under the influence of modernist thinking.

I have been offering a narration of Pope Paul VI's realization of the "invasion of the Church by worldly thinking," interpreted by him as Satanic penetration of the Roman Catholic Church. Paul VI reminded us that the Devil is a living spiritual force who perverts, who distorts a religious understanding of Creation; he is the Father of Lies. The Holy Father also spoke of the Devil's power to bring about deviations in man, "harmful because they seem to conform to our physical or mental makeup, or to our profound, instinctive aspirations." Rather than acknowledge the power of Satan, the Pope saw many among the faithful lapsing into *positivism* and other neomodernist ideological speculations in compensating for Church teaching on the Devil.

As discussed in our second chapter, positivism was a philosophy developed by Auguste Comte in the beginning of the 19th century which understood the scientific method to have eliminated the need for metaphysics as a branch of philosophy. It denied the existence of a transcendent God in favor of an anthropocentric approach to institutional religion. Thus Paul VI correctly saw positivism as another opening through which the Devil might "easily penetrate and change the human mind," as this philosophy denied a religious understanding of the created universe. Rooted in human pride, as is all sin, positivism can be understood as a consequence of man's ignorance of the effects of original sin, namely a wounded human nature prone to serious doctrinal errors.

In this chapter, we take up the story of how modernist thought influenced the preconciliar Liturgical Movement, a driving force behind Vatican II's *Sacrosanctum Concilium.* In so doing, let us keep in mind Fr. De LuBac's description of neomodernism's attempt to bring about "a different Church from that of Jesus Christ," that is, a man-centered, humanistic society in which individual experience is the norm, wherein the greatest good was to be sought in the here and now. This immanentist impulse viewed religion as an expression of human emotion, and strove to reduce or eliminate the importance of tradition.

How did such thinking impact the Mass, the re-representation of the Sacrifice of the Cross? Given the importance of subjective human experience in neomodernism, in the field of the Liturgy we can detect a de-emphasis on the Liturgy as the worship of Almighty God in favor of a community celebration of one's own life experience. After a high of seventy-four percent of Catholics who attended Mass in the United States in the post-WWII era, by 1965, sixty-five percent attended, compared with twenty-five percent in 2000.[134] What is more, the data reveal that only twenty percent of the generation of Catholics born after 1960 attends Mass once per week. One major reason for this decline was the collapse of the Liturgy after the misimplementation of *Sacrosanctum Concilium*, with the resulting harm to the faithful's understanding of dogma and morals over time. *Lex orandi, lex credendi.*[135]

I

Following Luther's 1517 revolt, Protestants rejected both what they perceived to be abuses in Church practice as well as the liturgy of the Church, choosing to break away from sacramental worship in favor of the reading of Scripture and preaching and the adoption of the vernacular in worship. This amounted to a breaking away from the historical evolution of the liturgy in conjunction with the reformer's heterodox beliefs.[136] The Church responded to the Protestant Reformation at the Council of Trent from 1543–1563, adopting liturgical reforms which remained substantially unchanged for the next four hundred years. In studying the history of the reform of the liturgy, it is important to note that the Council of Trent manifested reforms true to the traditional principles of organic development of the liturgy, as noted by a well-known liturgical authority:

> The Tridentine liturgical reform, initiated in order to correct abuse and ensure doctrinal orthodoxy, was thoroughly traditional. It produced nothing radically new. . . . And there *is no evidence of disparity between the mandate of the Council and the work of its liturgical commission.* It was another growth of the living organism that is the Roman rite, involving little substantial change[137] (emphasis mine).

One also observes instances in the history of the liturgy when organic development was not honored, an outstanding example of which is the sixteenth century reform of the Roman breviary. This reform attempt was significant because rather than adhering to traditional principles of organic liturgical development, its guiding principles were antiquarianism,[138] a disregard for liturgical development since antiquity, and "pastoral expediency."[139] In 1536, Pope Paul III promulgated this reform, seemingly rendering it beyond criticism; yet in August of 1558, Pope St. Pius V forbade this reformed breviary, which marked a "preeminent demonstration in liturgical history of the priority the organic development of the liturgy enjoys over approbation by competent authority."[140] Concerning this example of a Pope favoring a liturgical reform abhorrent to liturgical tradition, given the authority of organic development in that Tradition, papal approval as the sole principle of liturgical reform without subservience to objective liturgical tradition was to be rejected.

In the nineteenth century, as we have seen, the Church was confronted by the forces of modernism — positivism, rationalism, liberalism, socialism, and communism among others, all condemned by Pius IX's *Syllabus of Errors*. In response, Pius issued the summons for Vatican Council I to settle the questions of papal primacy and some revisiting of canon law to better meet the challenges posed by modernism. Regarding the liturgy, the Council confined itself to a confirmation of the Tridentine reforms, that the Church might maintain the dignity of liturgical worship. Thus it was not until the twentieth century liturgical movement that we observe the reformist impulse which gave rise to Vatican II's *Sacrosanctum Concilium*.

The movement's purpose was to draw the faithful nearer to God through a more profound attachment to the Liturgy. Dom Alcuin Reid sees as its foundation stone the wish of Pope St. Pius X:

> Filled as We are with a most ardent desire to see the true Christian spirit flourish in every respect and be preserved by all the faithful, We deem it necessary to provide before anything else for the sanctity and dignity of the temple, in which the faithful assemble for no other object than that of acquiring this spirit from its foremost and indispensable font, which is the active participation in the most holy mysteries and in the public and solemn prayer of the Church.[141]

The liturgical movement originated in an attempt to restore the liturgy to its ancient principles. Though it is difficult to discern principles of liturgical reform at the time of the formation of the Liturgy in the Early Church, Dom Reid has shown that the Liturgy was a living, developing entity, an "organism . . . capable of further growth,"[142] which is a traditional principle of true liturgical reform. We are further indebted to Dom Reid's exhaustive research for the elements of organic development in the complete history of the Roman Rite, which are:

1. a necessity for the development;
2. a profound respect for liturgical Tradition;

3. little pure innovation;

4. the tentative positing of newer liturgical forms along-side the old; and

5. the integration of the newer forms following their acceptance over time.[143]

Before examining the nineteenth century Liturgical Movement, it is important to keep in mind the aforementioned papal approval of liturgical reform without subservience to the authority of organic development. The record shows that the vicars of Christ began to understand their authority in the realm of *liturgical reform* as absolute.[144] As an example, in 1945 Pope Pius XII acceded to the request for a new Psalter prepared by the Jesuit scholars on the staff of the Pontifical Biblical Institute. In so doing, the Holy Father appeared sympathetic to their request for a translation reflecting developments in the historical critical method of biblical scholarship, what amounted to a major reform, as the style of the Latin texts were "improved" over those of St. Jerome's Vulgate. In promulgating this Psalter, Pope Pius made its use optional, revealing his regard for the Traditional Vulgate.

What proved to be harmful was the possibility of uncritical acceptance of liturgical reform at the hands of Papal authority whether or not the reform in question was consistent with Catholic liturgical tradition. Certainly in Pius XII's

1947 Encyclical *Mediator Dei* one detects a lack of regard for the priority of Liturgical tradition in organic development, and its emphasis on the role played by authority could be interpreted such that *any* duly authorized reform is permitted if it had Papal approval.[145] Here it is enlightening to read from Cardinal Ratzinger's famous Preface to Dom Alcuin's analysis, which we have been following:

> The author then agrees with the Catechism of the Catholic Church in emphasizing that 'even the supreme authority of the Church may not change the liturgy arbitrarily, but only in the obedience of faith and with religious respect for the mystery of the liturgy. . . .[146] [recalling] to mind what is the essence of the primacy as outlined by the First and Second Vatican Councils: the pope is not an absolute monarch whose will is law; rather, he is guardian of the authentic Tradition and, thereby, the premier guarantor of obedience. He cannot do as he likes, and he is thereby able to oppose those people who, for their part, want to do whatever comes onto their head. His rule is not arbitrary power, but that of obedience of faith.[147]

In his homily at St. John Lateran of May 07, 2005, Pope Benedict XVI reiterated the same teaching:

> The Pope is not an absolute monarch whose thoughts and desires are law. On the contrary: the Pope's ministry is a guarantee of obedience to Christ and to his Word. He must not proclaim his own ideas, but rather constantly bind himself and the Church to

obedience to God's Word, in the face of every attempt to adapt it or water it down, and every form of opportunism.[148]

Once underway, the liturgical movement found support in Pius X's *Motu proprio, Tra le Sollecitudini* and in *Mediator Dei* (1947), which rightly warned of false innovations and protestantizing influences in the movement. All things considered, the movement was positive until the promulgation of *Mediator Dei*, that is, it returned liturgical piety and active participation to their rightful place, that the wish of Pope St. Pius X be realized. However, in the period from 1947 until the dawn of Vatican II, the overall balance in the liturgical movement began to break down due to the efforts of a small number of influential liturgists active at liturgical conferences which "would do unprecedented violence to the objective traditional liturgy in the name of pastoral expediency."[149] We see in these few liturgists a wish to go beyond guidelines set down by the Holy See. Two ideas already mentioned—antiquarianism and the felt need for a more "pastoral" liturgy—were repeatedly emphasized by prominent scholars at the movement's various conferences. In this climate, the teaching of *Mediator Dei* (which Vatican II cites repeatedly) was in danger of becoming a dead letter. Notable among these liturgists was Vincentian Father Annibale Bugnini, director of the publication *Ephemerides liturgicae* in Rome. Father Bugnini was appointed to Pius XII's 1948 Commission for Liturgical

Reform, a forum which he ably used to push for the flawed theory of "reconstruction and innovation according to the perceived needs of modern man."[150] In other words, what Fr. Bugnini desired was a more "pastoral" liturgy, understood as separate from objective liturgical development.[151] The two ideas coalesced in the writings of the most influential of the liturgical reformers, Father Joseph Jungmann, S.J., whose

> . . . . principle of reform thus combines antiquarianism with pastoral expediency. It is a historical and pastoral principle that, precisely on historical grounds, fails to accord sufficient respect to organic development of the Liturgy beyond antiquity and, indeed, rejects organic development as the fundamental principle of liturgical reform, in favour of a "jerking" of the Liturgy into suitable shape for modern man. . . . [152]

If this principle were to prevail, it would permit the refashioning of the Liturgy not in accordance with objective tradition, but according to nonmajoritarian scholarly opinion and "the perceived needs of the day," echoing the words of Cardinal Danneels in the chapter's epigraph. While there were scholars within the Liturgical movement who remained faithful to authentic tradition — Fr. Romano Guardini and Fr. Louis Boyer, among them — by and large, as a result of what Pius XI referred to in the chapter's epigraph as the "puffed up learning" of a number of liturgical reformers, as Vatican

II drew near, the principle of the organic development of the objective liturgical tradition had been compromised.

II

As we have seen, as she prepared for the convening of Vatican II, the Church was faced with the prevailing modernist winds: the advance of Marxism in certain intellectual circles, rationalist thinking, positivism, the historical-critical method in biblical studies, and the appearance of the social sciences. There was also the confidence on the part of a few liturgists prior to the Council that what the Church needed was a new perspective on worship that she might be more viable in presenting her message to the modern world. In this they anticipated the call in *Gaudium et Spes* for the Church

> . . . . to adapt the Gospel to the grasp of all as well as to the needs of the learned, insofar as such was appropriate. Indeed this accommodated preaching of the revealed word ought to remain the law of all evangelization. For thus the ability to express Christ's message in its own way is developed in each nation, and at the same time there is fostered a living exchange between the Church and the diverse cultures of people. To promote such exchange, especially in our days, the Church requires the special help of those who live in the world, are versed in different institutions and specialties, and grasp their innermost significance in the eyes of both believers and unbelievers. With the help of the Holy Spirit, it is the

task of the entire People of God, *especially pastors and theologians, to hear, distinguish and interpret the many voices of our age,* [emphasis added] and to judge them in the light of the divine word, so that revealed truth can always be more deeply penetrated, better understood and set forth to greater advantage.[153]

It remains for us to observe how in their response to this call those liturgists assigned responsibility for the implementation of *Sacrosanctum Concilium* were led astray by the ideas and dispositions of modernity. Their proposed liturgical reform, "instead of providing an alternative vision of life to that of modernity, now cooperates with and disseminates principles that are destructive of Catholicism."[154] As Paul VI had warned, the Faith is endangered when modern secular thinking begins to determine the Church's understanding and transmission of the gospel message. Space allows us time for only one example of this—today it is possible for a Catholic to encounter in a popular Catholic magazine a theological de-emphasis on Our Lord's sacrifice on the Cross for our salvation:

.... the concept of atonement—that God and humanity have been reconciled through Jesus—hasn't always focused so exclusively on Jesus' death as a sacrifice and payment for sin. Like most teachings, *it has evolved over the past 20 centuries* of Christian thought, and today *is being critiqued by some as problematic,* not only for what is says about God, but also for what it may mean for victims of violence [emphasis added].[155]

It would seem that the author is unaware that doctrine does not evolve (change meaning) but develops in stages over time, resulting in a clearer presentation of the doctrine by the Church, toward a more profound understanding of truth. It does not present new doctrine or revelation. Again, Paul VI warned that those who do not think with the mind of the Church may be exposed to the influence of the "mystery of iniquity," in evidence when "the spirit of the Gospel is watered down or rejected. . . ." The reason for this neglect of the authority of the documents of divine revelation was the reformers' assimilation of the principles of modernity. Fr. Jonathan Robinson has painstakingly shown "how various Enlightenment themes have played a role in the formation of the modern consciousness as it has impinged most directly on the Church."[156] To cite one example of this, Fr. Hans Urs von Balthasar criticized the Enlightenment's understanding of religion in his analysis of its influence on Fr. Rahner's anthropocentric theology:

The Enlightenment was the change from a theocentric to an anthropocentric viewpoint; for religion . . . this means the change from a positive historical religion to a religion valid for man in general, who is essentially religious. . . . Everywhere in the world and in history, God's self-communication takes place in the Holy

Spirit offered to every human being, a self-communication which itself already possesses as such the character of a revelation of truth and which finds in Jesus Christ, crucified and risen, only its full historical tangibility. Positive dogmas, based on history, are transcendentally outlined in human nature. . . . The better the Enlightenment understands its own program, the less it will seek this absolute in contingent historical facts rather than in the inner enforcement of truth in the subject. This also applies to the Church, which wants to make the transposition of Christian faith into today's modes of understanding her business. As a necessary consequence, there must ensue a shift of accent from the objective dignity of truth in itself to recognition of and respect for the dignity of the subjective awareness of truth.[157]

At the time, Cardinal Ratzinger had written that the best measure of theological speculation is its spiritual consequences; given his position as the most influential speculative theologian after Vatican II, Rahner's capitulation to Enlightenment religious thinking has proven poisonous to the both Christian gospel and the Liturgy, to which we now turn.

As we have seen, the drawing up of the *schemata* for the Constitution on the Sacred Liturgy was turned over to the liturgists on the specialized commissions, many of whom had become enchanted with the forces of modernism. Fr. Robinson has dubbed them "wingless chickens":

Wingless chickens are cripples who have had the religion bred out of them. This means it is increasingly difficult [for them] to say anything about Catholicism that registers with our contemporaries, and not only with nonbelievers, but with Catholics as well. The message and mysteries of Christianity, whether loved or hated, are no longer part and parcel of most people's awareness.[158]

How Enlightenment ideas have played a role in shaping modern secular consciousness is a rewarding study. The Enlightenment refers to a historical intellectual movement which advocated reason as a means to establish an authoritative system of aesthetics, ethics, and logic. The leaders of this movement saw themselves as an elite group whose purpose was to lead the world toward progress and out of a long period of doubtful tradition, irrationality, superstition, and tyranny, which they argued began during a historical period they called the Dark Ages. As is well-known, the movement presented an intellectual framework for the American and French Revolutions, and also led to the rise of liberalism and the birth of socialism and communism. For some it is the source of all that is good in the modern world; for others it is just the reverse:

The eighteenth century has been variously characterized as the century of Enlightenment and Revolution or alternatively as the Age of Reason. Whatever the merit of these designations, they embody a denial of cognitive value to spiritual experiences, attest *to the atrophy of Christian transcendental experiences* and seek to enthrone the Newtonian method of science as the only valid method of arriving at truth. The *apostatic* revolt, for such it was, released a movement of ideas which would shape decisively the political structure of the West. With the formal abolition of Christianity as the authoritatively unifying spiritual substance of mankind, *the particular community substances* could move into the vacuum. The mystical bodies of the nations which had been growing ever since the high Middle Ages had achieved by the eighteenth century a considerable coherence and articulation and now they could begin to substitute with increasing effectiveness for the mystical body of Christ.[159]

Present in this analysis of the Enlightenment are the three themes which played an integral part in the disintegration of the liturgy: the denial of the transcendent, the resulting apostasy, and the exaltation of the community. That the movement was hostile to revealed Christianity is beyond debate. At bottom, the Enlightenment was hostile to Christian revelation's teaching that salvation comes through Jesus Christ alone. In its stead, the *philosophes* substituted a rational religion which emphasized the universal moral law shared by all men by virtue of their reason, not what they regarded as the untrustworthy historicity of the life message of Jesus. They saw this rational religion as a refining of, not a repudiation of, Christian moral teaching.

For example, the Mass, which celebrates the revelation that Christ's sacrificial death reconciles us to the Father and to each other, and makes present to the believer the one sacrifice of the Cross, was reduced to a mere celebration of a good man's death. In like manner, Enlightenment thinkers eliminated doctrines fundamental to Scripture and tradition in favor of an equating of revelation with the dictates of the individual conscience. Because these subjective principles were common to all religions, the *philosophes* believed all men had it in their power to make themselves acceptable to God. We may detect the fruits of this thinking in the way in which our present liturgy as a celebration of the core mysteries of our Catholic faith—especially the sacrificial nature of the Eucharist—means less and less to the people in the pews.

Fr. Robinson has given us an eye-opening critique of "what happens to Christianity when we begin to discount the Bible and the Creeds,"[160] in an enlightening look at the influence of Immanuel Kant on Catholic theologians.[161] Kant is largely responsible for the modernists' subjective approach to things religious in his contention that the source of what is moral lies not in anything outside the human subject (the metaphysical), either in nature or given by God, but rather only the good will itself—that is, the acceptance of the moral law. Kant's "good will" is one that acts from duty in accordance with the universal moral law that the autonomous individual freely gives himself. This law obliges one to treat humanity — understood as rational agency, and represented through oneself as well as others — as an end in itself rather than (merely) as the means.[162]

With this in mind, Robinson turns to Kant's thinking on religion. In his *Religion within the Limits of Reason Alone*, Kant puts forth his version of a classic philosophical argument for God's existence, the argument from morality. Briefly summarized, because human beings are typically aware of actions as being right and wrong, this awareness seems to bind us toward certain obligations, regardless of our subjective goals and ends. In this sense, moral qualities have the appearance of universality and objectivity. The best explanation for this moral normativity is a moral law-giver, God — therefore God exists. Kant adds that apart from human effort to live moral lives, man knows nothing of God in any metaphysical or religious way.[163] Clearly Kantian thought precludes the necessity for any Church or religion founded on Christian revelation; Christianity contained truth only to the extent that it corresponded to his definition of religious truth as consisting in morality. Sacred traditional Christian dogmas should thus be given a moral construct that we might build the Kingdom here on earth. Kant viewed the Jesus of the gospels as an example of the greatest possible moral excellence.

It should not be difficult to see just how far Kant's rational religion is from the Catholic faith. The ideas discussed above

were in no small part responsible for the post-conciliar subjective approach to religion which says, in effect: "the way I
feel about things is the way they are."[164] Fr. Robinson's analysis of Kantian thought makes a persuasive case as to how
"accommodation with that history [of philosophy], in the
interests of comprehensiveness or *learning from the world,* has
helped to destroy the liturgical dimensions of Catholicism."[165]
I found it interesting that in his seminary days at Freising,
Joseph Ratzinger in his philosophical studies was delighted
to "detect a return to metaphysics, which had become inac-
cessible since Kant."[166]

We complete our summary of Fr. Robinson's analysis of
the negative influence of modern thought on liturgical reform
with his study of the influence of Georg Wilhelm Freidrich
Hegel on Western civilization's understanding of God, man,
society, and community. Whereas both Kant and the empiricists argued that metaphysics was impossible, as man could
not know things as they were in themselves, Hegel thought
the nature of reality was knowable to us. Briefly stated, Hegel
saw the totality of ideas used in the complete body of knowledge of his day — the arts and sciences, religion, political philosophy, history — as unified in what he termed the Absolute
Mind or Absolute Spirit, a God who is total reality and truth
who reveals himself to finite human intellects in every area
of knowledge. In his metaphysical system, reality was the

vast totality of rational concepts, also referred to as Absolute Idealism and exemplified in the maxim, "the Real is the Rational, and the Rational is the Real." Human beings for Hegel were aspects of this Absolute Mind or Spirit, in need of a fuller understanding of themselves.[167]

In his masterpiece, *The Phenomenology of Spirit,* Hegel recounts how throughout history opposing philosophical schools competed with one another to establish themselves as the sole repository of truth, each competing for adherents — Plato versus Aristotle, for example. Aristotle's followers, convinced they had the final truth, denied truth to all competing schools and attempted to destroy their standing, firm in the belief that one philosophy can reach ultimate truth. Hegel posits that when seen properly, these historical competing schools of thought demonstrate not conflict but necessary stages in the expansion of whole truth, building blocks of an organic unity. In this, Hegel espoused the philosophical doctrine of organicism, which emphasized an analogy with living organisms whose parts only are what they are because of, and can only be understood in terms of, their contributions to the whole. This is Hegel's model for understanding the personality, societies and societal institutions, history, philosophy, and especially ethics. For him, the moral life is life lived in an organized society, a community; indeed, all ethics is social ethics.[168] His first argument on why community is important was that the need for other human beings was integral to what it means to be truly human.[169] Hegel next concerned himself with how communities fit into larger entities in his discussion of civil society:

> The dialectics of civil society create a universal dependence of man on man. No man is an island anymore, and each finds himself irretrievably interwoven into the texture of production, exchange, and consumption.[170]

By civil society Hegel meant the economic aspect of modern capitalistic society wherein men related to each other in terms of satisfying their individual economic needs and interests under a division of labor, with the inevitable division of society into bourgeoisie and proletariat. Civil Society was for him a new modern form of community distinct from the state and necessary for one's self-development. It was this notion of civil society that was later appropriated by his prize student, Karl Marx. Fr. Robinson shows us that the origins of contemporary rhetoric on community are found in these two post-Enlightenment thinkers.[171] In Hegel especially we detect a reactionary Romantic emphasis on the subjective self and one's feelings, which as we have said requires others to become fully human. Thus for Hegel man's living in rational civil society begins "to build communities and develop the human person."[172]

If contemporary Christian rhetoric on community is reminiscent of Hegel's civil society, Robinson rightly reminds us that the Christian community belongs to God and not to Caesar—in other words, in the Catholic view community cannot be said to be just one more group of people pursuing satisfactory economic relationships, though as we know there are Catholics who think this Hegelian community the appropriate model for the Church in the world:

> In worship there is an emphasis upon people together, a family, a community of equals who deeply care for one another. The community of God's people overwhelms our great diversity, whereas in society those differences often are magnified. Though individuality is respected, each person honored, excessive individualism is addressed and steadfastly challenged by our sense of belonging to a community. Sometimes a gift from another part of the church can be illuminating. Consider the Xhosa proverb from the church in southern Africa: *Umntu ngumntu ngabantu*. It translates, *"A person is a person because of other people."* An African Christian would see his/her identity grounded in the community, among the people. A similar sense of corporate identity is to be found within the church in northern Canada, among the Dene. The Dene people speak of a sense of community that transcends time and space. For example, they speak of their land as being held in trust by their generation from their ancestors for their descendants. *The land is not theirs individually, but belongs to the people.* Such a community dimension infuses the church of Christ: we are a people— the people of God[173] [emphasis added].

148

In Hegel the Deistic theology, the unemotional rational religion of the Enlightenment with its belief that God created but does not intervene in the world, was replaced by a view that increasingly rejected the idea of a transcendent God altogether in favor of Hegel's notion of God as Absolute Mind/ Spirit. Sadly, a main body of nineteenth century philosophical thought was influenced by this idea of a "God who had been recast in the light of the needs of the community," and who is found in society.[174] In his exalting of the community at the expense of a transcendent God, it is easy to see the disastrous influence of Hegel's thought for the liturgical life of the Church.

The German philosopher rejected as groundless the teaching that Christianity was a historical (and therefore authoritative) religion. His religious writings are significant for our study because he thought a spirit of reconciliation among men could be achieved without Our Lord's salvific death, in effect a heartfelt "Christian" community devoid of a transcendent, Trinitarian God. For Hegel, the Gospels were first and foremost a body of moral philosophy, and Jesus a great moral preacher who taught in parables and by personal moral example. Thus Hegel's theory of the community as God launched a political and social schema into the practice of the faith:

It is the constant theme of critics of the present liturgical arrangements that these arrangements leave little room for adoration and
contemplation and that they are almost exclusively concerned
with the needs and aspirations of the community. . . . with the
new emphasis on community, the sense of the Church as the sacramental presence of God among us is in danger of being lost. . . .
the center of interest of the liturgy, which ought to be the mystery
of Christ and the adoration of the living God, has been shifted into
a forum for ideological or social reflection.[175]

Fr. Robinson concludes by showing the negative impact
of the distortion of community by Hegelian thought and its
influence on the European reformers who were the driving
force in drawing the *schema* for *Sacrosanctum Concilium:*

The focus of the Liturgy as God-directed has been displaced, and
any sense of mystery and awe at being in the presence of God has
disappeared. Behind this, whether it is recognized or not, is the
philosophical belief that the community is necessary for God to be
totally real. The dynamic of this new emphasis on the community
has led to a total exclusion of any reference to God as transcendent. . . . In fact the community from having first of all displaced
the focus of divine worship is in danger of becoming itself the
object of worship.[176]

Hegel's influence is easily discerned in the idea that at
Mass we gather to speak our faith in community, and, by
speaking it, to renew and deepen it. Modern liturgists rarely
if ever reference God's saving grace, implying that we can

develop supernatural virtue in ourselves without the need to receive it as the gift of Our Lord's saving grace.

In my thirty years as a Catholic educator, I have observed innumerable such communal concerns displacing the reenactment of the saving passion, death, resurrection, and ascension of Our Lord. It will be recalled that Paul VI referred to this excessive concern with communal aspirations as the result of positivism, discussed at the beginning of this chapter, wherein God has become society, the ultimate reality. I would add that this particular crack through which Satan entered God's Temple is an accurate explanation of the disregard for organic development in the liturgical reform of Vatican II. Thus as the Church began her *aggiornamento*, she presided over a disintegration of her most relevant instrument for presenting the truth of Jesus Christ to the modern world, the Holy Sacrifice of the Mass, now at the mercy of liturgical commissions wishing to make the liturgy more pastoral. Let us also remember Paul VI's teaching that Satan is always seen as active where the spirit of the Gospel is watered down, as in the reformers' efforts to accommodate Gospel revelation to the forces of modernity.

III

In 1959, Pope John XXIII saw a true need for liturgical renewal within the Roman Rite in accordance with the principle of organic development, the aim of the Liturgical Movement endorsed by Pope St. Pius X.[177] In authentic organic development, the Church listens to what liturgical scholars deem necessary for the gradual improvement of liturgical tradition, and evaluate the need for such development, always with a careful eye on the preservation of the received liturgical tradition handed down from century to century. In this way, continuity of belief and liturgical practice is ensured. As Cardinal Ratzinger wrote at the time, the principle of organic development ensures that in the Mass, "only respect for the Liturgy's fundamental unspontaneity and pre-existing identity can give us what we hope for: the feast in which the great reality comes to us that *we ourselves do not manufacture,* but receive as a gift"[178] [emphasis mine]. Organic development was the symbol employed by the key figures in both the Liturgical Movement and hence in *Sancrosanctum Concilium:*

> That sound tradition may be retained, and yet the way remain open to legitimate progress, careful investigation is always to be made into each part of the liturgy which is to be revised. This investigation should be theological, historical, and pastoral. Also the general laws governing the structure and meaning of the lit-

urgy must be studied in conjunction with the experience derived from recent liturgical reforms and from the indults conceded to various places. Finally, there must be no innovations unless the good of the Church genuinely and certainly requires them; and care must be taken that any new forms adopted should in some way grow organically from forms already existing.[179]

Thus as the Council convened in the fall of 1962, John XXIII had it in mind not to reform the Roman Missal but to restore it, and articulate general norms for making the liturgy "better suited to signifying the mystery it celebrates."[180] The Holy Father was aware of the intimate connection between the liturgy and dogma, and so intimate that reform of the liturgy could be salutary only to the extent that such reform would effect a deepening of dogma and a greater sanctification of the faithful. As *peritus* Fr. Ratzinger observed, the question of liturgical reform was pressing only for the Council Fathers from France and Germany, the two countries that in 1962 enjoyed theological leadership in the modern liturgical movement. Along with Belgium and the Netherlands, these countries pushed through the *schema* in spite of the less-than pressing need for liturgical reform at the Council.[181]

Ominously, in 1960 Fr. Anibale Bugnini, professor of liturgy at the Lateran University, was given the position of Secretary to the Preparatory Commission on the Liturgy. In this position, he proved to be the prime mover behind the drafting of the *schema* to be considered by the Council Fathers, the very first of the *schemata* to be discussed. The document proposed a more active participation by the faithful in the liturgical actions, and in this, exposed its bias in favor of the pastoral concerns of the liturgical movement at the expense of contemplative participation consistent with genuine organic development. In its final form *Sancrosanctum Concilium's* "*participatio actuosa*," is more accurately translated *actual* (and not active) participation. To be clear — it is most certainly not the case, as is often said, that Vatican II introduced active participation into the liturgy.[182] The best source for what the Fathers meant by *participatio actuosa* is Pope John Paul II:

> Since the Liturgy is the exercise of the priesthood of Christ, it is necessary to keep ever alive the affirmation of the disciple faced with the mysterious presence of the Lord: "It is the Lord!" (Jn 21:7). Nothing of what we do in the Liturgy can appear more important than what in an unseen but real manner Christ accomplishes by the power of his Spirit. A faith alive in charity, adoration, praise of the Father and silent contemplation will always be the prime objective of liturgical and pastoral care.[183]

In the Constitution on the Sacred Liturgy, there was no question of new constructions or modifications of the Mass — only guidelines toward making the Mass more effective in signifying the mystery it celebrates. The text of *Sacrosantum*

Concilium was approved by the Council in December, 1962, and gave special emphasis to the pastoral aspect of the liturgy, reassuring the more traditional among the Fathers:

> Lastly, in faithful obedience to tradition, the sacred Council declares that holy Mother Church holds all lawfully acknowledged rites to be of equal right and dignity; that she wishes to preserve them in the future and to foster them in every way. The Council also desires that, *where necessary, the rites be revised carefully in the light of sound tradition, and that they be given new vigor to meet the circumstances and needs of modern times* [emphasis added].[184]

Here is reflected the Fathers' belief that in the face of the modern world, new liturgical guidelines were necessary to more effectively proclaim the truth of the Christian message. The Fathers were no doubt also reassured by Article Twenty-three's assertion that prior to any proposed revision of the rites, a sound "theological, historical, and pastoral" investigation should be made, with "no innovations unless the good of the Church genuinely and certainly requires them, and care must be taken that any new forms adopted should in some way grow organically from forms already existing."[185] Thus one would expect that after approval of the Constitution on the Sacred Liturgy, no major changes in the Mass would be forthcoming, but this was not to be. In retrospect, it seems difficult to comprehend just how the Church could remain true to sound tradition, to organic, authentic liturgical development while simultaneously revising the rites to meet the circumstances and needs of modern times.

As we have seen, the liturgists on the *Consilium ad Exsequendam Constitutionem de Sacra Liturgia*, charged with implementing *Sacrosacntum Concilium*, did not in fact produce what John XXIII and the Council Fathers desired.[186] I have already discussed the negative side to the Liturgical Movement after 1947, when modernist liturgists in ascendancy at the dawn of Vatican II pushed for innovation according to the needs of modern man, disregarding organic development in favor of antiquarianism and pastoral expediency. In this, as I have argued, they were able to do violence to traditional liturgy.

Hindsight reveals that the source of the problem of the *Consilium's* fabrication of the liturgy in disregard for the organic, living process of growth and development over centuries was certain ambiguous passages in *Sacrosanctum Concilium* (as in the passage just cited from No. 4). These passages were included at the instigation of the *periti* in order that they might later be given a neomodernist interpretation by the *Consilium* when implementing the general principles of the document.[187] In this, the Council Fathers were deceived by Fr. Robinson's wingless chickens. And so it was that the Constitution on the Sacred Liturgy was rendered dead on arrival following its passage, and was paid little attention as a foundation for the authentic liturgical reform John XXIII intended.

In 1964, the first instruction on the carrying out of *Sacrosanctum Concilium, Inter Oecumenici*, was issued by the Sacred Congregation of Rites, taking effect in January 1965. Though the form of the rite was substantially preserved, there were major changes to the 1962 Missal, including the following: use of the vernacular was permitted, not mandated; the priest was permitted to face towards the congregation if he wished; there were some textual changes; and Mass vestments were simplified. By October 1967, the *Consilium* had produced *a complete draft revision of the liturgy*, and this revision was presented to the Synod of Bishops that met in Rome. In response to several bishops' concerns, some changes were made to the text; Paul VI then promulgated this revised rite of the Mass with his Apostolic Constitution *Missale Romanum* on April 3, 1969. The following changes were made from the 1962 Roman Missal:

- To the Roman Canon of the previous edition were added three alternative Eucharistic Prayers, and the number of prefaces was increased.
- The rites of the Ordinary of the Mass were "simplified, due care being taken to preserve their substance." "Elements that, with the passage of time, came to be duplicated or were added with but

little advantage" were eliminated, especially in the rites for the presentation of the bread and wine, the breaking of the bread, and communion.

- "Other elements that have suffered injury through accidents of history" were restored "to the tradition of the Fathers," that is, the homily and the general intercessions or prayer of the faithful.

- The proportion of Sacred Scripture read at Mass was greatly increased through an increase in the number of readings and the introduction of a three-year cycle of readings on Sundays and a two-year cycle on weekdays.[188]

With the promulgation of the *Missale Romanum*, the traditional principle of organic development of the liturgy was violated. The promulgation marked another example of a Pope favoring a liturgical reform abhorrent to liturgical tradition, as discussed above. Given the authority of organic development in Church Tradition, papal approval as the *sole* principle of liturgical reform without subservience to objective liturgical tradition is to be rejected.

Cardinal Ratzinger, in his memoirs, recalled both joy at the promulgation of this now binding missal after a time of liturgical experimentation (1965–70) which had denigrated the Mass, and dismay at the complete prohibition of the 1962 Missal, an unprecedented event in the history of the liturgy. [189] Recall that the Roman Missal had been reworked by Pius V in 1570 in response to the Reformation; subsequent papal reworkings (as in 1962) had been carried out without opposing the reworking to its predecessor in a "continual process of growth and purification in which continuity was never destroyed."[190] In her history, there had never been a prohibition of a previous edition of a missal that had been approved by the apostolic authority as valid — until Paul VI's promulgation of "The Missal of 1970" as it came to be known. Now the forbidding of the organically grown 1962 missal began a discontiniuty in the history of the liturgy that has proven tragic. Cardinal Ratzinger's assessment is impressive:

> . . . . the old building was demolished, and another was built, to be sure largely using materials from the previous one and even using the old building plans. There is no doubt that this new missal in many respects brought with it a real improvement and enrichment; but setting it as a new construction over against what had grown historically, forbidding the results of this historical growth, thereby makes the liturgy appear to be *no longer a living development but the product of erudite work and juridical authority; this has caused us enormous harm.* For then the impression had to emerge *that liturgy is something "made,"* not something given in advance but *something lying within our own power of decision.* From this it also follows that *we are not to recognize the scholars and the central authority alone as decision makers, but that in the end each and every "community" must provide itself with its own liturgy. When liturgy is self-made, however, then it can no longer give us what its proper gift should be: the encounter with the mystery that is not our own product but rather our origin and the source of our life.* A renewal of liturgical awareness, a liturgical

reconciliation that again recognizes the unity of the history of the liturgy and that understands Vatican II, not as a breach, but as a stage of development: these things are urgently needed for the life of the Church. *I am convinced that the crisis in the Church that we are experiencing today is to a large extent due to the disintegration of the liturgy, which at times has even come to be conceived of etsi Deus non daretur:*[191] *in that it is a matter of indifference whether or not God exists and whether or not he speaks to us and hears us.* But when the community of faith, the worldwide unity of the Church and her history, and the mystery of the living Christ are no longer visible in the liturgy, where else, then, is the Church to become visible in her spiritual essence? Then *the community is celebrating only itself, an activity that is utterly fruitless.* And, because the ecclesial community cannot have its origin from itself but emerges as a unity only from the Lord, through faith, *such circumstances will inexorably result in a disintegration into sectarian parties of all kinds – partisan opposition within a Church tearing herself apart.* This is why we need a new Liturgical Movement, which will call to life the real heritage of the Second Vatican Council[192] [emphasis added].

The Constitution on the Sacred Liturgy teaches that "the Liturgy is the summit toward which the activity of the Church is directed; it is also the font from which all her power flows,"[193] and necessary for catechizing the faithful that Christ Jesus may fully work in them in transforming them. If this is so, and it is, then Cardinal Joseph Ratzinger got it right when he noted that the disintegration of the liturgy is behind the crisis of faith that confronts the Church at present, for when man falls from worshipping God in the way that He wants to be worshipped "in favor of the powers and values of this world," he loses his freedom, and returns to captivity through loss of the moral law which governs true humanity.[194]

The Cardinal wrote that worship, that is, the right kind of relationship with God, is the indispensable ingredient for truly human existence in the world, as it "allows light to fall from that divine world into ours."[195] He spoke too of a danger in worship concerned only with the interests of the community — a horizontal phenomenon — and not the primacy of celebrating the paschal mystery of Christ properly understood. Authentic liturgy is about God responding to man and revealing how man can worship him, a *vertical* phenomenon. The speculation of the liturgists in "the Spirit of Vatican II" notwithstanding, this in turn means true liturgy does not depend solely on human participation, imagination or creativity, but requires, in Cardinal Ratzinger's words, "a real relationship with Another, who reveals himself to us" and transforms our lives. *Sacrosanctum Concilium* makes this point best:

> Rightly, then, the liturgy is considered as an exercise of the priestly office of Jesus Christ. In the liturgy the sanctification of the man is signified by signs perceptible to the senses, and is effected in a way which corresponds with each of these signs; in the liturgy the whole public worship is performed by the Mystical Body of Jesus Christ, that is, by the Head and His members.[196]

In contrast, Cardinal Ratzinger perceptively likened the positivist approach to the behavior of the Israelites after Moses' extended absence atop Mount Sinai:

> Worship becomes a feast that the community gives itself, a festival of self-affirmation. Instead of being worship of God, it becomes a circle closed in on itself: eating, drinking, and making merry. The dance around the golden calf is an image of this self-seeking worship. . . . a warning about any kind of self-initiated and self-seeking worship. . . . an apostasy in sacral disguise. All that is left in the end is frustration, a feeling of emptiness.[197]

In this chapter, we have seen the fruit of the disintegration of traditional liturgy as the introduction of ideas and sentiments having no place in Catholic worship, having been shaped by the forces of modernity warned against by Pope Paul VI. In the words of one prominent scholar, "the Liturgy, instead of providing an alternative vision of life to that provided by secular modernity, now cooperates with and disseminates principles that are destructive of Catholicism."[198] It is at Mass where most Catholics encounter Christ and his message in His Church — *lex orandi, lex credendi*. With the disintegration of the liturgy at the hands of these experts, small wonder that pastors and theologians have floundered in judging, distinguishing, and interpreting the many voices of modernity in the light of the divine word, so that revelation might be more deeply penetrated, understood, and set forth for our earthly happiness and ultimately eternal life.

In this divergence from the original intent of the Liturgical Movement, one is reminded of Paul VI's words in an earlier chapter: "He [the Devil] is the malign, clever seducer who knows how to . . . bring about in us deviations that are all the more harmful because they seem to conform to our physical or mental makeup, or to our profound, instinctive aspirations." Earlier I noted how those *periti* who believed the Church had to speak more effectively to the modern world underwent a division in their ranks, as many lapsed into the arrogance born of false pride, styling themselves an alternative magisterium which claimed authority for reforms "the spirit of Vatican II." As such, these men viewed the documents of Vatican II as an inadequate reference for subsequent theology. Specifically, I have tried to show that it was the neomodernist ideology operative within the ranks of this group, at whose mercy were the Shepherds, the Bishops of the Church, whose misimplementation of *Sacrosanctum Concilium* over time has contributed much to the crisis of faith bordering on apostasy in the Church at present. These liturgists and theologians are not the enemy; as Dr. Kreeft has written, they are our patients, the deceived, the victims the Church is trying to save.[199]

In the end, I think it wise for us to heed Paul VI's caution in our first chapter concerning the supreme underlying agent in the present crisis, "the hidden enemy that sows errors and misfortune in human history." The history of the Liturgical Movement and the subsequent misimplementation of *Sacrosanctum Concilium* offer examples of how ideas destructive of Catholicism entered the Temple of God. Let us remember Jesus' words to Peter, "Simon, Simon, behold, Satan demanded to have you, that he might sift you like wheat, but I have prayed for you that your faith may not fail; and when you have turned again, strengthen your brethren." (Lk: 22:31) St. Peter took these words to heart, for in his first letter he advised us:

> Be sober, be watchful. Your adversary the devil prowls around like a roaring lion, seeking someone to devour. Resist him, firm in your faith, knowing that the same experience of suffering is required of your brotherhood throughout the world. And after you have suffered a little while, the God of all grace, who has called you to his eternal glory in Christ, will himself restore, establish, and strengthen you (1 Peter 5: 8–10).

Pope Leo XIII too was aware of this spiritual war. As the nineteenth century drew to a close, a journal from Rome published in 1947 gives an account of a priest who worked at the Vatican during the time of Leo XIII, Fr. Domenico Pechenino. Fr. Pechenino related that while the Pope was attending Mass, he began to look upwards and displayed an unusual expression on his face. He left Mass and went to his private office, and a short time later called for the Secretary of the Congregation of Rites, handing him a document. This document contained a well-known prayer, which the Pope made part of a set of prayers to be recited on behalf of the Church at the end of Low Mass. This prayer was taught to every member of the faithful, as Dr. Kreeft has written, until:

.... the 1960s. And that was exactly when the Catholic Church was struck with the incomparably swift disaster that has taken away half its priests, two-thirds of its nuns and nine-tenths of its children's theological and moral knowledge by turning the faith of our fathers into the doubts of our dissenters. It's been a diabolical reversal of Christ's first miracle at Cana, converting the wine of the gospel into the water of psychobabble, an antimiracle by the Antichrist.[200]

Pope Leo wrote:

Saint Michael the Archangel,
defend us in battle.
Be our protection against the wickedness and snares of the devil.
May God rebuke him, we humbly pray;
and do Thou, O Prince of the Heavenly Host–
by the Divine Power of God–
cast into hell Satan and all the evil spirits
who roam throughout the world seeking the ruin of souls. Amen.

CHAPTER FIVE

Religious Life

.... for I betrothed you to Christ to present you as a pure bride to her one husband. But I am afraid that as the serpent deceived Eve by his cunning, your thoughts will be led astray from a sincere and pure devotion to Christ. For if some one comes and preaches another Jesus than the one we preached, or if you receive a different spirit from the one you received, or if you accept a different gospel from the one you accepted, you submit to it readily enough.

2 Corinthians 11:2–5

Christian charity exceeds our natural capacity for love: It is a theological virtue. It therefore challenges the giver to situate humanitarian assistance in the context of a personal witness of faith, which then becomes a part of the gift offered to the poor. Only when charitable activity takes the form of Christ-like self-giving does it become a gesture truly worthy of the human person created in God's image and likeness God's love is offered to everyone, hence the Church's charity is also universal in scope, and so it has to include a commitment to social justice. . . . changing unjust structures is not of itself sufficient to guarantee the happiness of the human person. . . . Rather, her mission is to promote the integral development of the human person. For this reason, the great challenges facing the world at the present time, such as globalization, human rights abuses, unjust social structures, cannot be confronted and overcome unless attention is focused on the deepest needs of the human person: the promotion of human dignity, well-being and, in the final analysis, *eternal salvation* [emphasis added].

Pope Benedict XVI

The words of the Consecration make me sick.

Joan Keller-Maresh

I

*I*n many ways the story of religious life after Vatican II is the saddest to tell, one that still causes grief when I revisit childhood memories and think on the turbulent history of religious life since the Council. In general, in the explosion of movements whose alleged purpose was to bring forth the spirit of the Council, the evangelical foundation of conciliar teaching became diluted. Many religious seemed unable or unwilling to assert Catholic doctrine over culture. A prominent author and scholar describes this best:

If anyone over the past 35 years paid attention to Paul's assertion of the primacy of contemplation in the council's work, I have not noticed it. And it's a shame, because it is clear that Paul, in line with the best in the tradition, did not emphasize contemplation *instead of* engagement with the world. Rather, he sees it as the central point and final culmination of a whole Christian life, which gives order and direction to the many other quite necessary worldly obligations that we all must fulfill. (The Council's declaration on religious life also counseled commitment to contemplation.) But there is no confusion in Paul VI that somehow the mission to the world could replace or be put on an equal footing with our living relationship with God. The first commandment seemed to have set that point straight long ago. . . .

If we've learned anything from the past 35 years, it is that the world does not need more social workers and activists who also happen to say prayers. It desperately needs contemplatives who understand that their love for God — and the graces they get in prayer — are the source and guide to their love of neighbor. That was the revolution Vatican II introduced into the modern world.[201]

How it was that religious orders came to exchange charisms for "psychological nostrums and social work"[202] has always mystified me. I have found no more convincing analysis than Pope Paul VI's warning that the loss of a sense of personal sin following Vatican II "becomes the occasion and the effect of interference in us and our work by a dark, hostile agent, the Devil . . . a living, spiritual being that is perverted and that perverts others . . . who sows errors and misfortune in human history."[203]

Surely it is not inconsistent with Catholic doctrine to see in the unraveling of religious institutes after Vatican II the influence Satan can exert on "whole communities," to borrow Paul VI's phrase. As to errors sown by the Evil One, one need only browse the post-conciliar works of many prominent religious sisters, many of whom bear the title of theologian, to see evidence of positivistic neomodernist ideas and lack of contemplation of God's self-revelation in Sacred Scripture, Tradition, and magisterial teaching in favor of "engagement with the world."[204] Pope Paul opined that such sentiments could only result from an invasion of worldly thinking into the Church, and that the Devil's hand could be seen in the consequent doctrinal uncertainty, so evident in the experimentation in religious communities after council, and in the abandonment of a living relationship with God in favor of the mission to the world.

Paul VI wisely asked us to revisit the Parable of the Sower and the Seed: "When anyone hears the word of the kingdom and does not understand it, the evil one comes and snatches away what is sown in his heart; this is what was sown along the path."[205] Our Lord reminds us here that His teaching on the Kingdom of God in its fullness remains fruitless for those who see the Kingdom as merely an earthly kingdom, having rejected its supernatural dimension. This seed bears no fruit, and its fate is the spiritual fate of the hearer. What the Sisters of Notre Dame DeNamur taught me in my formative years was that there was more to my existence than things temporal, challenging me to work toward holiness and the salvation of my soul *Ad Majorem Dei Gloriam* that I might enjoy happiness with Him forever.

In this chapter's look at religious life since the Second Vatican Council it is not my intention to chronicle "the tragic unraveling" of religious orders, especially religious sisters, for this has been incomparably done.[206] My hope rather is to highlight neomodernist ideas, which influenced those responsible for the unraveling. The picture that emerges is one of many religious communities judging all things according to human perceptions, values, and experiences, producing Fr. De Lu Bac's "immanentist apostasy" under cover of "renewal" geared toward building God's Kingdom here and now.[207] Paul VI was of the mind that Satan is skilled at making his way into us through such a methodology.

By way of background, prior to Vatican II, sisters were often taken for granted by the faithful and the hierarchy in the United States, and were rarely consulted as to their own needs and thinking as religious.[208] Due to the tremendous demands of their community life, teaching, and continuing education, community self-analysis remained low on their list of priorities. Coupled with the formalism and authoritarian nature of conventual life, the result was overburdened sisters, some of whom were perhaps not adequately prepared for their assignments, and who often were treated as children by superiors. A Dominican sister insightfully summarizes the state of religious life before Vatican II:

> The period before Vatican II was not particularly notable for its emphasis on a reasoned faith, which is probably why religious communities fell apart on a massive scale after the Council.
>
> Up to that point they had held together, not only through the sheer rigidity of their life-structures and mores, but also, it should be noted, by the sheer heroism of most of the members who were strong in their belief, self-sacrificing in their fidelity to religious duty and often passionate in their devotion to Christ, His Mother, the saints and all things divine.
>
> Faith itself was eminently visible in many religious before the Council, and we should assume that they have now attained a shining reward for that faith. But they were often deprived of the capacity to live the spiritual life and vows to the fullest extent because the whole dimension of human reason and understanding was held up to suspicion as a threat to good order and personal asceticism.
>
> Few religious would have studied philosophy, and doctrine was often understood in a skeletal and piecemeal way that was not

proof against certain theological predators who came into their own from the early days of the Council.

Yet another less than rational element of religious life before the Council was its sheer formalism which turned not only on a multiplicity of small legalities, retained because they had always been "done," but on foundational things like the vows.

If there was and has been a revolution in religious life during the last 40 years, it is because there were in the Church distinct elements of suppression and deprivation of the kind that tend to spark off any revolution in any place and in any era.[209]

Under the Holy Spirit's prompting, Holy Mother Church realized she had no choice but to call for renewal. Indeed, Pope Pius XII had already beckoned women religious globally to examine routine prayer exercises which might preclude the development of spiritual insights; in the United States, due to their workloads, religious superiors were slow to begin such self-examination. It was in this setting that John XXIII convened the Second Vatican Council, mandating that religious update and renew their orders.

Earlier I remarked that it was a real eye-opener for me when I immersed myself in the Vatican II documents, rather than rely on what new theologians said was the teaching within them. Perhaps nowhere is the contrast more vivid than between conciliar teaching on the reform and renewal of religious life, and what the principal women's religious leadership groups and leaders themselves were claiming was the teaching of the council.

On August 6, 1966, Paul VI issued *motu proprio*[210] his Apostolic Letter *Ecclesiae Sanctae* in order to begin implementation of Vatican II's *Perfectae Caritatis*. The letter mandated that all religious institutes prudently promote a "renewal of spirit" adapted to each institutes' life and particular discipline through both a study of *Lumen Gentium,* Chapters 5 and 6, and *Perfectae Caritati*s itself. It is significant that the Holy Father felt this a *sine qua non* for the careful maturation of the Council's fruits.

I would recommend that all Catholics read *Lumen Gentium,* Chapter 5, as the Church here teaches a truth that had become obscured over the preceding decades: *all* Catholics are called to holiness. Only God is holy, but Jesus tells us, "You, therefore, must be perfect, as your heavenly Father is perfect."[211] Therefore, to become holy we must be open to the Holy Spirit working in us to keep the greatest commandment, to *love the Lord our God with all our heart, soul, mind, and strength,* [emphasis mine] and "to love your neighbor as yourself."[212] We can keep the greatest commandment and achieve holiness if, with God's grace, we are open to His will for us. *Perfectae Caritatis* teaches us also that holiness is fostered by the evangelical counsels of poverty, chastity, and obedience, in which the laity are called to participate.

Lumen Gentium instructed that religious were to live out the counsels in community to a greater degree in service to the Church (living for God alone), and in doing so model for the laity what grace can accomplish.[213] Reflecting upon why God made us, which is to share in His life forever, religious were to be a road sign for the rest of humanity pointing the best way to love of neighbor. Paul VI, expanding on *Lumen Gentium*, alluded to this in *Evangelica Testificatio*, his Apostolic Exhortation of June, 1971:

> It is precisely for the sake of the kingdom of heaven that you have vowed to Christ, generously and without reservation, that capacity to love, that need to possess and that freedom to regulate one's own life, which are so precious to man. Such is your consecration, made within the Church and through her ministry — both that of her representatives who receive your profession and that of the Christian community itself, whose love recognizes, welcomes, sustains and embraces those who within it make an offering of themselves as a living sign "which can and ought to attract all the members of the Church to an effective and prompt fulfillment of the duties of their Christian vocation . . . more adequately manifesting to all believers the presence of heavenly goods already possessed in this world.[214]

The religious life, then, according to Vatican II, is to reveal the transcendence of God's Kingdom, which *takes precedence* over all earthly considerations.[215] The hierarchical Church for its part is empowered "to make wise laws for the regulation of the practice of the counsels," and ensure that religious institutes, whose members were to respect and obey bishops in accordance with canon law, develop and flourish in harmony with the spirit of their founders.[216]

Perfectae Caritatis set forth general principles for renewal and intended for religious institutes to return to the very sources of the Christian lifestyle and the primitive inspiration of their institute, adapting all to the conditions of the times. Specific renewal principles for religious institutes included:

- Setting the following of Christ as the highest rule.
- Letting the spirit and aims of each founder as well as their sound traditions be faithfully held in honor.
- Adapting as their own and implementing in accordance with their own characteristics the Church's undertakings and aims in biblical, liturgical, dogmatic, pastoral, ecumenical, missionary, and social matters.
- Promoting among their members a proper understanding of men, the social conditions of the times, and the needs of the Church to be able to more effectively assist men.
- Keeping in mind that that even the best adjustments made in accordance with the needs of our age will be ineffectual unless animated

by *a renewal of spirit. This must take precedence over even the active ministry*[217] [emphasis mine].

So it was that *Perfectae Caritatis* challenged religious to imitate the virginal and poor Christ, who sanctified man by His obedience unto death. Under the impulse of this model of God's love religious were to live ever more like Christ and His Body—the better done, the more fruitful the apostolate. Their type of community life, prayer, work, and government all were to be examined anew in light of the aims of the apostolate, the needs of their members, the nature of the religious institute, and the prevailing economic, social, and cultural environment. Toward this end, religious institutes were to hold community-wide conferences to amend their rules and constitutions to reflect conciliar teaching on religious life. The chapters were to set up norms for appropriate renewal and legislate it, providing for experimentation; superiors were to find effective means to consult their sisters and listen to them. Most importantly, institutes were directed to seek the Holy See's and the local bishops' approval "when the law requires this."[218]

Obedience was emphasized as both the member's cooperation in humility and the superior's charge to foster a spirit of voluntary obedience in consecrated life. *Perfectae Caritatis* also affirmed the importance of common life in prayer and in the sharing of the same spirit. The religious habit was explained

as a sign of consecration that should be "simple and modest
. . . poor and becoming," and also consistent with the neces-
sities of health and adapted to various times and places and
apostolic needs.[219] It is noteworthy that entire portions of the
document would be included in the revised Code of Canon
Law of 1983 to underscore its importance.

Paul VI's *Ecclesiae Sanctae* directed that all religious institutes were to hold a special general chapter on renewal to
approve constitutional reforms that would permit experimentation, thus responding to the Vatican II directives. Obsolete
rules were to be discarded, and experimentation was to be
short-term and to maintain the purpose, nature, and character
of the institute. Upon completion, the experiments were to
be assessed and those proving beneficial might be incorporated in the constitutions. Further experimentation would be
sanctioned if deemed necessary, subject to the same assessment process just described. *Ecclesiae Sanctae* also expressed
the Pope's wish that conferences of religious superiors would
cooperate with episcopal bodies and the Sacred Congregation
for Religious "with confidence and reverence."[220]

Unhappily, both *Perfectae Caritatis* and *Ecclesiae Sanctae*
were either deliberately disregarded or interpreted wrongly
by many Superiors. There were institutes which made reforms
in conformity with Vatican II, but these were the exception, as
most institutes thoroughly disregarded their essentials of reli-

gious life as taught by the council during the experimentation years:

> Some communities gave their members total freedom in deciding when and how they would pray, where they would live, what work they would do, what hours they would keep, and what they would wear — a freedom that led to excesses, such as mini-skirted nuns smoking, drinking, and dating. And some sisters simply took it upon themselves to change religious life. Sister Elizabeth Kolmer of the Adorers of the Blood of Christ wrote that: "Frequently enough individual sisters did not wait for those in authority to make the first move or, faced with reluctance on the part of the superior, made their own decision." Many sisters left religious life because of this rapid transformation in their lifestyle, since their communities no longer resembled in any way the communities they had entered.[221]

By 1967, a tremendous amount of unauthorized experimentation had begun, all proceeding from erroneous interpretations of the mind of the Church. For example, some sisters abandoned their orders to form noncanonical experimental communities: an effort to establish what they called new forms of religious life for the third millennium, that is, doing away with the bureaucratic, authoritarian structures they erroneously blamed for massive defections after Vatican II. Religious superiors were eliminated, and sisters abandoned the communal life for apartment living, sought employment in non-teaching professions, and ceased wearing their habits.

The most celebrated of these radicals was the cabal which separated from the Sisters of the Immaculate Heart of Mary in Los Angeles, which numbered 637 sisters prior to Vatican II. When these sisters began experimentation in 1967 by abandoning the religious habit and the practice of communal prayer, the bishop, James Cardinal McIntyre, barred them from teaching in schools in his diocese. In violation of Vatican II, the radicals then said that they could not uncritically accept the decision of ecclesiastical superiors, and demanded apostolates that the Council had deemed proper to the laity. Prayer and communal life were to be left to the discretion of individual sisters if the new manner of service infringed upon traditional practice. The leadership also claimed that the reanimation of their community according the charism of their founder was unnecessary if communal discernment indicated otherwise.

A Vatican commission sent to inquire into the affair proposed a compromise: the 315 radicals, led by Sr. Anita Caspary (formerly Mother Humiliata) were granted more time to experiment, after which their decision as to the type of religious life they would pursue would be sent to Rome for Vatican approval. The remnant 50 sisters might continue their teaching in diocesan schools. In fact, the radicals were moving toward the view that a more genuine community life could be experienced outside existing structures and canon law. So it was that the majority of Sisters joined Sr. Caspary, their self-styled President in requesting dispensation of their vows that they might begin the Immaculate Heart Community, an independent secular organization devoted to service in the spirit of the Gospel. The community was to be open to lay Catholic married couples and singles, claiming Vatican II now saw the Church as "ourselves."[222]

As one might expect, the Holy See mandated that the sisters abandon their departures from Catholic tradition, to which Sr. Caspary replied:

> If you bought the whole package of self-determination, and you were being stopped every little while, then it seemed logical to break away. While I saw the break as inevitable, I didn't really want it. But I wondered how much energy you could spend fighting authority when you could spend that same energy doing what you should be doing.[223]

What the sisters ended up doing was recounted over two years hence:

> Today 260 of the original 300 "defectors," as they are called in canon law, remain active. In a bold redefinition of a religious order, they have added to their ranks three married couples and one Protestant woman, who are considered full members of the

community and, like the sisters, contribute part of their earnings to a common fund. Says Sister Anita Caspary, the community's moving spirit and the former head of the mother group: "Our own strength and liberation as women came from our past experiences in the Immaculate Heart order, when we were forced to take top administrative roles and do work usually assigned to men in the outside world.²²⁴

What secular news coverage of the Los Angeles affair never revealed were some of the fruits of this break with magisterial teaching on religious life. By no means were the sisters in California the only women's order to rebel against the Church.²²⁵ Sisters in many traditional orders who were once a bastion of Catholic life in the United States began leaving their institutions in ever-increasing numbers to pursue secular ministries that had little to do with the evangelical counsels as understood by the Church. The names of many who remained are recognizable as being in the forefront of challenging Church teaching on abortion rights, women's ordination, and a more democratic church organization.

We must remember that *ressourcement,* a return to original charisms, an emphasis on biblical, spiritual, and pastoral theology in religious formation and a fuller ecclesiology emanated from the Church's awareness of the effects of their absence prior to the Council. Thus far, I have briefly described the process by which implementation of *Perfectae Caritatis* in many instances went beyond what the council's reform of religious life positively required.

When conciliar teaching precluded such deviant reforms, an appeal to "the spirit of Vatican II" was made by the defectors. Religious themselves were sent to seminars, conferences, and think-tanks which pressured them to abandon hierarchical structures in favor of the democratic, to question traditional doctrinal certainties, and to demand reasons for those things formerly regarded as sacred, the most important of which was the basis for their vocation to the religious life. They became exposed to new anthropologies under the influence of psychology, sociology, and other social sciences, acceptance of which many sisters were naturally compliant under obedience—all this in spite of the obviousness that such changes were not approved by Rome and threatened the existence of their communities.[226] In other words, the desired *ressourcement* of the council Fathers, rather than providing the guiding atmosphere in which *aggiornamento* was to occur, was ignored in favor of "updating." We now turn to a look at the fruits of this betrayal of *Perfectae Caritatis* and subsequent magisterial teaching done "in the spirit of Vatican II."

II.

The decade of the 1960s was hardly the most favorable time for the Church to inaugurate a reform of religious life, given the simultaneous cultural turmoil of the sexual revolution and women's liberation movements of this decade into which the Church was drawn. Simultaneous with their attempt to understand what Vatican II meant for religious life, priests, seminarians, and religious observed secular young Americans protesting the corruption of "the system," becoming activists for change, and demanding a better future for everybody through a dismantling of capitalism. Young people in religious life came to think that they were confronting the same reactionary element in the Church that secular youth were encountering during the Johnson and Nixon years, and adopted a radical spirit and vision to oppose the hierarchy. They desired greater freedom in matters of conscience and a more open dialogue with the secular world.

In opening Vatican II, Pope John XXIII wished to see a more fruitful presentation of the truths of the Catholic Faith to individuals, families, and society in the modern world. To effect this, he remarked that:

> . . . . it is necessary first of all that the Church should never depart from the sacred patrimony of truth received from the Fathers. But at the same time she must ever look to the present, *to the*

new conditions and new forms of life introduced into the modern world [emphasis mine], which have opened new avenues to the Catholic apostolate.[227]

Thus the Pope envisioned a new enthusiasm in the Church from a more effective proposal of her doctrine to the world through reform of her discipline and catechesis on the documents of Vatican II. Instead, what resulted was a situation wherein the Church was confronted with a process of decadence unfolding under a false *aggiornamento,* the offspring of an inordinate "love affair with the times." Interviewed almost two decades after John XXIII's summons, Cardinal Joseph Ratzinger saw this clearly:

> I am convinced that the damage we have incurred in these twenty years is due, not to the 'true' council, but to the unleashing *within* the Church of latent polemical and centrifugal forces; and *outside* the Church it is due to the confrontation with a cultural revolution in the West . . . with its . . . liberal-radical ideology of individualistic, rationalistic and hedonistic stamp.[228]

Renewal was made more difficult by the failure of the American bishops to call for a diocesan-wide comprehensive study of the documents of Vatican II during the period 1966–1971, and by the ongoing revision of the Code of Canon Law during the experimentation period. How were the institutes to know whether their experimentation would be in keeping with the unpromulgated code, and how to reverse experiments which contradicted it?

A proper respect and reverence for *Perfectae Caritatis* and subsequent instruction would have greatly mitigated experiences such as the one endured by the Immaculate Heart Sisters. So too would have competent shepherding by the bishops in the United States; alas, many bishops present at the council, my own Archbishop John Dearden among them, returned from The Eternal City amenable to naïve advocacy of changes beyond what the council had intended or approved.[229] The depressing fact is that most American bishops at the time failed to systematically catechize their sheep under their care on the council's authoritative teaching, something done wonderfully by Archbishop Karol Wojtyla in his diocese of Krakow upon his return from Rome. Indeed, many American bishops appeared not to have understood the full meaning of the council, and so deferred to pseudo-experts in renewal, whose number seemed legion. As we have seen, these neo-modernist-inspired experts appealed to conciliar texts where favorable, but, more commonly, ignored the texts when they precluded the desired changes.

That the aforesaid California experience occurred at all is not surprising when one traces the events following national coordination of preparation for the call to renewal from the Vatican, which began in November, 1956. Two hundred thirty-five superiors gathered in Chicago that year to attempt this task requested by the Holy See. By a unanimous vote, they launched the Conference of Major Superiors of Women (CMSW) whose goals were to promote the spiritual welfare of the women religious in the United States, ensure growing efficacy in their apostolate and encourage closer fraternal cooperation with all religious of the United States, the hierarchy, the clergy, and Catholic associations. Following the sought-after Vatican approval for CMSW, in its initial phase the conference professed the confidence and reverence requested of them by the Congregation for Religious in Rome:

> The conference professes and declares to the Apostolic Delegate and to the hierarchy of the United States the profound respect which is due to those whom the Holy Spirit has appointed to govern the Church, and a perfect allegiance in full conformity with canonical legislation.[230]

As Vatican II was sitting in 1964, the first CMSW National Conference took place, assembling the members at a single site for the first time. Their program included a formal business meeting, at which Sr. Consolatrice Wright, BVM, challenged communities to listen to the "eternal now" of the Spirit. Sr. Mary Luke Tobin, a Sister of Loretto, was elected national chair and sent to Rome by the National Executive Committee to see what she could learn at the Third session of the council. On the way to Rome, the Vatican extended Sister Luke an invitation to be one of a handful of women observers. In 1965, CMSW held a national conference centered on the theme "Sisters and the Council," initiating a Canon Law Committee so that American women religious might have a voice in the revision of canon law. Since its inception in 1956, CMSW had proven a wonderfully positive force in the education of women religious, the quality of community life, and relationships with the Church hierarchy. Ominously, speakers at the 1965 conference included *peritus* Fr. Bernard Haring, theologian Fr. Bernard Cooke, S.J. and psychologist Fr. Eugene Kennedy, none of whom had given evidence of faithfulness to true conciliar teaching.[231]

Following the close of Vatican II and the Sisters and the Council conference, CMSW conducted a survey in 1966 of active women religious in the United States under the direction of Sr. Marie Augusta Neale, S.N.D. This massive socio-psychological survey of some 139,000 religious would prove nothing less than a tool for the reeducation of sisters. Modern polling techniques have shown that accurate data can be gathered with random sampling with a slight margin for error, precluding the need to survey the entire field. Why then, were nearly all sisters surveyed? It was to introduce into American convents a concept of renewal that had been conceived of by an elite group of sisters—an understanding of renewal differing greatly from those in *Perfectae Caritatis*.[232] A cursory look at the Survey sheds further light on neomodernist penetration of reform efforts in the 1960s, resulting in the near-demise of religious life in the United States.

The Sister's Survey consisted of 778 questions in the areas of belief, the religious life, obedience, preferred reading, and related items. The questions were derived from a work entitled *The Changing Sister*, a collection of essays written by consultants for the survey, which clearly prioritized the sociological and temporal aspects of religious life over the purely spiritual. Sr. Marie Augusta Neale deceptively claimed that the survey was based on the documents of Vatican II, but promulgation of *Perfectae Caritatis* and *Ecclesiae Sanctae* in the Unites States had not yet taken place.[233] Instead, the questions mirrored the subjective humanistic philosophies of the survey's authors. From the survey:

> 44. Since *Christ speaks to us through the events of our times,* sisters cannot be apostolically effective in the modern world unless they understand and respond to social and political conditions.

> 69. The traditional way of presenting chastity in religious life has allowed for the development of isolation and false mysticism among sisters.

> 79. One of the main characteristics of the new poverty will be openness and liberality of mind, heart, and goods.

90. The vow of obedience is a promise to listen to the community as it speaks through many voices.

91. Every religious community in the Spirit of the council must adjust to the changed conditions of the times. This means *that no community can continue in traditional form and be working with the mind of the church* [emphasis mine].

643. The only purpose of the vows of poverty, chastity and obedience is *to create a community wherein people can effectively channel their human energy* [emphasis mine] to the most immediate realization of the Gospel.[234]

In her interpretation of the data gathered from the survey, sociologist Sr. Neale described as "pre-Vatican II" sisters who preferred reading traditional theologians and agreed with survey items such as:

5. The mystery of the Trinity is so profound and so central I feel I should humbly accept it as given and not seek to plumb its depths.

12. I sometimes wish I had been alive at the time of Christ rather than now so that I could have really known Him.

33. I like to attend as many Masses as possible each day.

95. I feel that the parochial school is still the most effective means for educating Catholics.

97. Personal sanctification comes first, then duties of apostolate.

312. Christians should look first to the salvation of souls; then they should be concerned with helping others.

319. The best contribution sisters can make to world problems is to pray about them.

322. I think of heaven as the state in which my soul will rest in blissful possession of the Beatific Vision.

324. What my daily work consists of matters little, since I see it as a way to gain merit for heaven.[235]

Sisters who read dissenting theologians Frs. Hans Kung, Charles Curran, Gregory Baum, Gabriel Moran, and Edward Schillebeeckx thus responded favorably to the following and scored high in the category of "post-Vatican thinking:"

6. I regard the word of God as speaking always and in diverse ways through events, other persons, and my own conscience, as well as through the Bible and the Church's magisterium.

14. I prefer to think of Jesus as our Mediator with the Father, rather than as the Second Person of the Blessed Trinity.

64. If a sister shuns involvement with persons I think she betrays the purpose of her vow of chastity.

76. The drama of renewal will consist largely in laying aside power, ownership, and esteem.

94. Holiness consists in utter self-sacrificing involvement in human needs.

100. It seems to me that sisters should be especially interested in establishing centers where people could come together to experience Christian community through worship, discussion, and the joy of shared activity.[236]

As one can readily detect, attitudes labeled "pre-Vatican II" by Sr. Neale were in fact quite consistent with the conciliar document on religious life; "post-Vatican thinking" reflected the influence of the neomodernist writings we have examined. What was even more cunning was Sr. Neale's statement that problems in achieving renewal were the fault of these "pre-Vatican II" sisters, whose attitudes witnessed to "the irrelevancy of religious life" in the post-conciliar era.[237] Apparently their desire for prayer and faithfulness to the evangelical counsels inhibited involvement in worldly pursuits and secular relationships, and was thus offered as the main reason for the defections from religious life after Vatican II!

In reality, the abandonment of religious life by many was due much more to the neomodernist re-indoctrination of religious in opposition to the true council. The Sisters Survey was utilized in many renewal chapters, where it, coupled with the thought of rebellious theologians was incorporated into many reformed chapter decrees, fostering a feminist, antihierarchical, democratic view of the Church in opposition to the teaching of Vatican II and canon law.

As the survey results were made known to the CMSW, a restructuring of religious life in the United States was begun, following the principles of de-emphasis of the transcendent aspects of religious life, altered concepts of authority (*i.e.*, collegiality, subsidiarity), independence from ecclesiastical authority (especially the Magisterium), and creation of a national secretariat to be managed by a core executive group. Thus, by the fall of 1970, the CMSW, contemptuous of the Vatican's manner of treating American women religious, was prepared to resist the anticipated Vatican regulations, renaming itself the Leadership Conference of Women Religious in 1971, its new name implying that the women would determine their own future rather than take directions from Rome.[238]

A study done in 2003 showed that religious institutes which embraced the vision of religious life entertained in the Sister's Survey, one of democracy and liberation, have all experienced declining vocations and a precarious future.[239] It should not surprise one that young women of today are not attracted to the rebel sisters' self-styled way of life, largely due to the political maneuvering and constitutional management of activist sisters pursuing their neomodernist and feminist-influenced vision, and, under the LCWR, a new leadership entity for women religious independent of the Church which challenges her teaching as a matter of principle. Unhappily, for many dissenting sisters neomodernism's subjective "lived experience" became the theological reference point which took precedence over the Holy Spirit's guidance of renewal after Vatican II.

There remains the real tragedy of faithful, mostly elderly, sisters, who suffer in communities that are dying because of ill-considered reforms. I have visited with some in retirement at their motherhouses, a few of whom still wear habits. These are fortunate; in other communities leaders sold off mother-houses and convents to show solidarity with the poor. Older nuns in such congregations must either attempt apartment living or go to nursing homes, in some cases having to take outside jobs to make ends meet. These sisters have endured a real martyrdom of exclusion and hostility as they tried to remain faithful to the evangelical counsels. An essay written by one such sister makes for subdued reading:

> The present turbulent time in the Church is a challenge to everyone, but what is it like to go through it as an older religious? I can tell you, from experience, that it is both a time of martyrdom and a time of Faith. Most religious my age—50 years in religious life—came from homes in which our Faith was nurtured from the cradle on. We were led to love and respect our Church and its leaders. We had a deep and abiding devotion to the Mass. When

we became old enough to go to school, the sisters and the pastors of our parishes took up where the family left off, and our faith continued to grow and deepen in Catholic schools.

When we entered the novitiate, the Faith was again the very reason for our choice. Customs and training—at times a little ridiculous—took place in an atmosphere which always had the transcendent as backdrop. After novitiate, we went out to serve the Church. That's how we understood our role then: to SERVE in the Church. In our order that meant going into Catholic classrooms all over the United States to teach about God and the things of God. Don't laugh, but for a while there, we even put God into the math and grammar books. Who of my age group does not recall teaching *Progress in Arithmetic*'s lesson on how many cupcakes were needed for the Little Jesus party? And *Voyages in English,* with all its religious and moral sentences and paragraphs? Maybe we did overdo it a little, but when I look at our world today and our world then, I have to conclude that it was better to err on the side of Faith.

One of history's "turmoil periods" hit us in the 1960s. Turmoil entered the novitiates, too, and strange formation programs (so-called) began to emerge. In many cases, persons as yet unformed themselves, began to be appointed as formation directors, replacing older, experienced, seasoned religious. The rationale was that older religious were unable to give the "young"—if you can call women in their 30s and 40s young the training needed to "adapt to the times." The results of that mistake are evident in religious congregations today: A generation of religious who haven't the slightest notion of what religious life is about, and who are so "adapted to the times" that they cannot grasp the concept that religious life is supposed to be countercultural rather than adapted to every un-Christian ideology.

In the 30 years that followed 1960, all hell broke loose in some congregations. Questionable elections were held, and carefully controlled processes were used to give the stamp of legality to decisions which were totally unacceptable to the majority of Sisters, most of them older and irrevocably loyal to the magisterium of the Church and the original charism of their congregations.

The reactions to this state of affairs have been varied. Most sisters, accustomed to obedience by long practice of their vow, and untrained in how to deal with the bulldozing methods of controlled (and at times dishonest) processes, suffer martyrdom in silence and in indescribable pain at seeing their congregations being turned into entities to which they can in no way relate, and at witnessing the destruction of the original values, charisms and traditions of their founders and foundresses.

Other sisters, unable to endure being cut off, threatened, and persecuted, are giving lip-service to a leadership whose actions they despise, because they don't know what else to do. A third group of sisters, outraged by the injustice and oppression being inflicted upon the majority of sisters by their misguided leaderships are reacting courageously and fearlessly, in spite of threats and persecutions.

One thing is certain; no matter what the reaction, all of these sisters share in the martyrdom being inflicted upon older religious at this time. They are shamed and saddened by the public behavior of their leadership, who brazenly and openly dishonor and ridicule the Holy Father, the magisterium, the Catholic priesthood, and the sacred traditions of the Church concerning Faith and morals. The radical feminist leadership of besieged congregations devalue the Eucharist, the Creed, Scripture, and all things sacred, putting in their place the worship of goddesses, sacrilegious liturgies, and support of immorality and deviant sexual behavior.

When I said this turmoil period (1960s to 1990s) is a time of martyrdom for older religious, I was not using a metaphor. Physical martyrdom is merciful compared to the assault being made upon the Faith, the values and the sacred traditions of older sisters in congregations whose leadership has been seized by radical feminists. But, besides being a time of martyrdom, this period is also a time of faith for older religious. These sisters who are reacting to this tragedy with silence are not helpless bystanders. As never before, they have intensified their prayer life, spending long hours before the Blessed Sacrament and/or slipping their rosary beads through their fingers, interceding for their congregations, hour after hour, day after day. Those older sisters who, confused, give lip-service to radical feminist leaders do so because they don't know what else to do, and this seems the safest course of action to them. They, too, have deepened their faith life; amid their attempt to deal with opposing ideologies and matters of conscience is no small contribution to the welfare of their congregations. Then, there are those older sisters, who, armed with fortitude and prayer, with the strength which comes from the Eucharist and with an overwhelming sense of outrage in the face of injustice, have resolved that their congregations will NOT be secularized and/or destroyed without a struggle on their part.

Realizing that the era of peace before the 1960s did not prepare them for this crisis, they have begun to study the documents of the Church concerning religious. They have unearthed the documents and histories of their congregations in order to be able to get a clearer idea of specific charisms, of the real meaning of their consecration and their role in the Church. They are taking a second look at the vows, community life, personal and communal prayer for the purpose of updating them. They are becoming acquainted with canon law for religious and communicating with persons and organizations in the church whose responsibility it is to give assistance to religious congregations. They are beginning to network among themselves, not only in their own congregations, but with other congregations who may be experiencing the same problems. In this way, sisters who refuse to accept the secularization of their congregations can give one another support and encouragement and share research and insights so that we can act as responsible Christians.[240]

My response is to pray for the sustenance of this sister's discipleship, and to note that the intercessory prayer being done by these martyrs for the faith is already producing much fruit, as we shall see.

In addition to rebel sisters, priests, and theologians, the laity as well played a part in the unraveling of religious communities. Let us now take up another radical ideology in evidence during these years, also warned against by Paul VI — humanistic psychology. Dr. William Coulson is a licensed psychologist and founder and director of the Research Council on Ethnopsychology.[241] In the decade of the 1960s, Dr. Coulson was a research associate to Carl Rogers and Abraham Maslow at Western Behavioral Sciences Institute in La Jolla, California. Coulson co-edited a seventeen-volume series on humanistic education with Rogers and helped organize the country's first program of facilitator training. There he was assigned to assemble a core group of facilitators to infiltrate the aforementioned California community of nuns and later many other orders, including the Sisters of Mercy, the Sisters of Providence, and the Society of Jesus.

In 1971, Dr. Coulson began to experience doubts about his belief in psychotherapy after its vicious effects on the religious orders and on the Church and society in general became obvious to him. Having abandoned his once-lucrative practice, as of this writing he devotes his life to lecturing to Catholic and Protestant groups on the dangers of psychotherapy.[242] What follows is an interview he gave in 1995. I have edited it to include topics relevant to this chapter's thesis concerning the impact of neomodernist thought on postconciliar religious life; though extensive, it is remarkably illuminating in this regard. The interviewer is Dr. William Marra (now deceased), then professor of Philosophy at the Jesuit Fordham University.

"We" being you and Rogers?

We inundated that system with humanistic psychology. We called it Therapy for Normals, TFN. [They] had some 60 schools when we started; at the end, they had one. There were some 560 nuns when we began. Within a year after our first interventions, 300 of them were petitioning Rome to get out of their vows. They did not want to be under anyone's authority, except the authority of their imperial inner selves.

Who's that on page 180 of that book?

This is Sister Mary Benjamin... Sister Mary Benjamin got involved with us in the summer of '66, and became the victim of a lesbian seduction. An older nun in the group, "freeing herself to be more expressive of who she really was internally," decided that she wanted to make love with Sister Mary Benjamin. Well, Sister Mary Benjamin engaged in this; and then she was stricken with guilt, and wondered, to quote from her book, "Was I doing something wrong, was I doing something terrible? I talked to a priest—" Unfortunately, we had talked to him first. "I talked to a priest," she says, "who refused to pass judgment on my actions. He said it was up to me to decide if they were right or wrong. He opened a door, and I walked through the door, realizing I was on my own."

This is her liberation?

How excited they were, to be delivering someone into God's hands! Well, instead they delivered her into the hands of nondirective psychology.

But to mitigate your own guilt, Dr. Coulson, psychologists don't know what they are doing when it comes to the inner depth of the human person; and one would think the Catholic Church, with 2,000 years' experience, does know what it is doing. This priest was a co-culprit. Had he nipped this in the bud—but he sounds like Rogers: "Well, it seems to me that perhaps you might perhaps do this or that."

"What does it mean to you?" not "What does it mean to me?" Or to God. The priest got confused about his role as a confessor. He thought it was personal, and he consulted himself and said, "I can't pass judgment on you." But that's not what confession is. It is not about the priest as a person, making a decision for the client; rather it's what God says. In fact, God has already judged on this matter. You are quite right to feel guilty about it. "Go thou and sin no more." Instead he said she should decide.

Okay. Now, why did you choose the ...order in the first place? Or did they choose you?

Well, they hustled us pretty good. They were very progressive to begin with. A shoestring relative of one of Rogers' Wisconsin colleagues was a member of the community. By then we were at the Western Behavioral Sciences Institute (WBSI) in La Jolla, which is a suburb of San Diego; as a Catholic, I was assigned to exploit the connection. I spoke to the California Conference of Major

Superiors of Women's Religious Orders, and showed them a film of Carl Rogers doing psychotherapy.

And Rogers' reputation had already grown.
Oh yes. Rogers had a great reputation. He was former president of the American Psychological Association; he won its first Distinguished Scientific Contribution Award. And WBSI was also the occasional home of Abraham Maslow, the other great figure in humanistic psychology.

What do you mean by humanistic psychology?
Well, it's also called third-force psychology. Maslow referred to it as Psychology **Three**. By that he meant to oppose it to Freud, which is Psychology One, and Skinner and Watson, the behaviorism which is Psychology Two. We Catholics who got involved in it thought this **third force** would take account of Catholic things. It would take account of the fact that every person is precious, that we are not just corrupted as Freud would have it, or a tabula rasa, which is available to be conditioned in whatever way the behaviorist chooses: hut rather we have human potential, and it's glorious because we are the children of a loving Creator who has something marvelous in mind for every one of us.

That could be very seductive even for Catholics who could reject the other two with a simple wave of the hand. Okay, continue now with the story...
As I said, [they] were pretty progressive, but some of the leadership was a little bit nervous about the secular psychologist from La Jolla coming in; and so I met with nearly the whole commu-

nity; they were gathered in a gymnasium at Immaculate Heart High School in Hollywood, on an April day in 1967. We've already done the pilot study, we told them. Now we want to get every-body in the system involved in nondirective self-exploration. We call it encounter groups, but if that name doesn't please you, we'll call it something else. We'll call it the person group. So they went along with us, and they trusted us, and that is partly my respon-sibility, because they thought, "These people wouldn't hurt us: the project coordinator is a Catholic." Rogers, however, was the principal investigator. He was the brains behind the project, and he was probably anti-Catholic; at the time I didn't recognize it because I probably was, too. We both had a bias against hierarchy. I was flush with Vatican II, and I thought, "I am the Church; I am as Catholic as the Pope. Didn't Pope John XXIII want us to open the windows and let in the fresh air? Here we come!" And we did, and within a year those nuns wanted out of their vows.

How did you do this — just with lectures?
Yes, there were lectures; and we arranged workshops for their school faculty, those who would volunteer. We didn't want to force anybody to do this, which was a symbol of how good we were.

But at first you had a plenary session for the community.
That was *my* lecture. I told them what we wanted to do, and I showed them a film of an encounter group; and it looked pretty holy. The people in that film seemed to be better people at the end of the session than they were when they began. They were more open with one another, they were less deceitful, they didn't hide

their judgments from one another; if they didn't like one another they were inclined to say so; and if they were attracted to one another they were inclined to say that, too. Rogers and I did a tape for Bell and Howell summarizing that project; and I talked about some of the short-term effects and said that when people do what they deeply want to do, it isn't immoral. Well, we hadn't waited long enough. The lesbian nuns' book, for example, hadn't come out yet; and we hadn't gotten the reports of seductions in psychotherapy, which became virtually routine in California. We had trained people who didn't have Rogers' innate discipline from his own fundamentalist Protestant background, people who thought that being themselves meant unleashing libido. Maslow did warn us about this. Maslow believed in evil, and we didn't. He said our problem was our total confusion about evil. (This is quoting from Maslow's journals, which came out too late to stop us. His journals came out in '79, and we had done our damage by then.) Maslow said there was danger in our thinking and acting as if there were no paranoids or psychopaths or SOBs in the world to mess things up. We created a miniature utopian society, the encounter group. As long as Rogers and those who feared Rogers' judgment were present it was okay, because nobody fooled around in the presence of Carl Rogers. He kept people in line; he was a moral force. People did in fact consult their consciences, and it looked like good things were happening.

But once you had those 560 nuns broken down into their encounter groups, how long did it take for the damage to set in? Well, in the summer of '67 [they] were having their chapter. They had been called, as all religious orders were, to reevaluate their mode of living, and to bring it more in line with the charisms of their founder. So they were ready for us. They were ready for an intensive look at themselves with the help of humanistic psychologists. We overcame their traditions; we overcame their faith. . . .

Marvelous, indeed. How many years did it take to destroy this ...order?
It took about a year and a half.

Of the 560, how many are left?
There are the retired nuns, who are living in the motherhouse in Hollywood; there is a small group of radical feminists, who run a center for feminist theology in a storefront in Hollywood —

They're hardly survivors.
No, they're not a canonical group.

But the order as a whole, the Immaculate Heart of Mary, which ran all those schools?
There are a few of them in Wichita whom I visited recently, who are going to make a go of it as traditional teaching nuns;[243] and there are a few doing the same in Beverly Hills. There may be a couple of dozen left all together, apart from whom, kaput, they're gone.

And the college campus —
The college campus was sold. There is no more Immaculate Heart College. It doesn't exist. It's ceased to function, because of our good offices. One mother pulled her daughter out before it closed,

saying, "Listen, she can lose her faith for free at the state college." Our grant had been for three years, but we called off the study after two, because we were alarmed about the results. We thought we could make [them] better than they were; and we destroyed them.

Did you do this kind of program anywhere else?
We did similar programs for the Jesuits, for the Franciscans, for the Sisters of Providence of Charity, and for the Mercy Sisters. We did dozens of Catholic religious organizations, because as you recall, in the excitement following Vatican II, everybody wanted to update, everybody wanted to renew; and we offered a way for people to renew without having to bother to study. We said, we'll help you look within. After all, is not God in your heart'? Is it not sufficient to be yourself, and wouldn't that make you a good Catholic? And if it doesn't, then perhaps you shouldn't have been a Catholic in the first place. Well, after a while there weren't many Catholics left.

Now, you mentioned that the religious orders had received a mandate from Vatican II to renew themselves according to the original spirit of their founders, which would have been wonderful.
Yes.

For example, the original spirit of the Jesuits was Saint Ignatius Loyola . . .
That's right. Speaking of Saint Ignatius, I brought with me a letter that Carl Rogers got, after we did a workshop at a Jesuit univer-

sity in the summer of '65. One of the young Jesuits, just about to be ordained, wrote as follows about being with Rogers at an encounter group for five days:

"It seemed like a beautiful birth to a new existence. It was as if so many of the things that I valued in word, were now becoming true for me in fact. It is extremely difficult to describe the experience. I had not known how unaware I was of my deepest feelings, nor how valuable they might be to other people. Only when I began to express what was rising somewhere deep within the center of rile, and saw the tears in the eyes of the other group members because I was saying something so true for them, too—only then did I begin to really feel that I was deeply a part of the human race. Never in my life before that group experience, had I experienced me so intently; and then to have that me so confirmed and loved by the group, who by this time were sensitive and reacting to my phoniness, was like receiving a gift that I could never—"

"Reacting to my phoniness"?

"My phoniness." But what is his phoniness'? Well, his phoniness is among other things his Catholic doctrine. Because if you look within yourself, and you find the Creed, for example, you can imagine someone saying, "Oh, you're just being a mama's boy, aren't you'? You're just doing what you were taught to do; I want to hear from the real you." The proof of authenticity on the humanistic psychology model is to go against what you were trained to be, to call all of that phoniness, and to say what is deepest within you. What's deepest within you, however, are certain unrequited longings, including sexual longings. We provoked an epidemic of sexual misconduct among clergy and therapists —

And it seemed to be justified by psychology, which is supposed to be a science. . . .

That's right. I'll tell you what Rogers came to see, and he came to see it pretty quickly, because he really loved those women. I'm going to quote him in a tape that he and I made in '76: "I left there feeling, Well. I started this damned thing, and look where it's taking us: I don't even know where it's taking me. I don't have any idea what's going to happen next. And I woke up the next morning feeling so depressed, that I could hardly stand it. And then I realized what was wrong. Yes, I started this thing, and now look where it's carrying us. Where is it going to carry us'? And did I start something that is in some fundamental way mistaken, and will lead us off into paths that we will regret'?"

That's a credit to him, that he at least had pangs of conscience; whereas these other orders, like the Jesuits, even when they saw that [they] were almost extinct, nevertheless they invited the same team in.

Oh, yes. Well, actually we started with the Jesuits before we started with the nuns. We did our first Jesuit workshop in '65. Rogers got two honorary doctorates from Jesuit universities. . . . A good book to read on this whole question is Fr. Joseph Becker's *The Re-Formed Jesuits*. It reviews the collapse of Jesuit training between 1965 and 1975. Jesuit formation virtually fell apart; and Father Becker knows the influence of the Rogerians pretty well. He cites a number of Jesuit novice masters who claimed that the authority for what they did — and didn't do — was Carl Rogers. Later on when the Jesuits gave Rogers those honorary doctorates, I think that they wanted to credit him with his influence on the Jesuit way of life.

But do you think there were any short-term beneficial effects? Did it seem as if you were getting somewhere in the good sense? Well, priests and nuns became more available to the people that they worked with; they were less remote. . . . But we didn't have a doctrine of evil. As I've said, Maslow saw that we failed to understand the reality of evil in human life. When we implied to people that they could trust their impulses, they also understood us to mean that they could trust their evil impulses, that they weren't really evil. But they were really evil. This hit home again for Rogers in the 1970s, when rumors began to circulate about a group that had spun off from ours. By then we had become the Center for Studies of the Person in La Jolla, having spun off from WBSI; and at the same time there spun off another group called the Center for Feeling Therapy in Hollywood. Well, charges were brought against the guys at the Center for Feeling Therapy — one of three founders of that, by the way, being a Jesuit who had left the order — and among the things that the State of California was perceptive enough to charge them with was killing babies. Eleven times, women who became pregnant while they were in the compound, the Center for Feeling Therapy, were forced to abort their babies. The State of California charged them with this crime —

Was this before *Roe v. Wade*?

No, this happened after Roe, but the State Medical Board held that it was unethical for those men to force the women to have abortions, because those women wanted their babies.

And this is a result of psychological feeling therapy?

Yes. . . . Humanistic psychotherapy, the kind that has virtually taken over the Church in America, and dominates so many forms of aberrant education like sex education, and drug education, holds that the most important source of authority is within you, that you must listen to yourself. Well, if you have a baby you're carrying under your heart, get rid of it. Women who came into the Center for Feeling Therapy with I children were forced to put them up for adoption. . . .

Is there an assumption in humanistic psychology, a modernist, Teilhardish kind of assumption, that human nature has altered, and therefore old values, old models, don't apply?

I don't think that humanistic psychology assumes any alteration of human nature, but rather John Dewey's idea that because we live in times of rapid social change, what we've always done is precisely what we should no longer do.

Sure.

Now the odd thing is, we've been living in terms of Dewey's theory for almost a hundred years now. We're living in Dewey's past, and not in our own present. That's what makes a movement like Roger McCaffrey's and Bill Marra's so progressive: it doesn't pretend that the last fifty years have worked out very well.[244]

When I first read this account, I was immediately taken by Dr. Coulson's candid admission of the force of a loss of a sense of personal sin which lay behind the doctrinal errors and gross perversions of reform. Neomodernist thinking had done its work, as Coulson recounted in a later interview:

> We thought what we were doing was immanently human. It turned out to be all *too human,* because one of the things we could achieve was that we freed everybody from local doctrine. They were no longer constrained by rules because we persuaded them to make their own rules for themselves. *Each individual would follow now his own life. Each individual had direct access to God, and this was through self-consultation. . . . We freed them from the constraints of doctrine.* When we *freed them from Catholic doctrine,* Catholic religion, there were *no more certitudes* available to them, and it allowed their impulses to bubble to the surface. Jesuits of the Northwest province stopped their young men from coming to LaJolla because they saw that these young men had become just exactly what Rogers said they should become: quiet revolutionaries, subversives. It is not the case that we didn't believe in institutions. We believed only in our own. So, it was stupid for the Church to allow this to happen because *it was inviting the enemy in.* We were the Trojan horse[245] [emphasis mine].

Dr. Coulson's story points out the immanentist contention that religious truth is *thought* by the individual, not received from the Creator. Embedded as well is the misinterpretation of Vatican teaching on reform of religious life, styled as an uncritical turning toward the world and humanistic psychology. Further it contains the neomodernist idea that traditional Catholic teaching on Original Sin and its wounding of human nature was relative to the subjective conscience. The resultant lack of awareness of the reality of evil in human life facilitates Satan's goal of transmitting his rebellion to one who chooses to go uncritically toward the world, the territory of man's temptation, where human pride seeks not God's glory but one's own satisfaction—the world over which he is Prince. How effective He has been is seen in declining Mass attendance, induced mass defections from the Catholic faith, the rapidly decaying moral fabric, and the doctrinal illiteracy of generations.

John Paul II's *Fides et Ratio* proposes the solution in teaching that the human quest is for God who is Truth Itself but also that He Himself is the way to Truth. Neither subjectivism nor rationalism by themselves leads to The Way. We must seek for knowledge, understanding, and wisdom where they are to be found—in God's revelation, properly understood and then assimilated by human reason. In this way, we think with the mind of the Church under the Holy Spirit's guidance and not in our own subjective way, which only allows the Devil a crack through which he may enter time and time again.

III.

In 1973, when Paul VI first observed that *aggiornamento* had led to an infiltration of the Church by worldly thinking, and her subsequent need to be defended from the evil we call the Devil, he enumerated signs of this presence—sexual licentiousness, seductive ideological errors and doctrinal uncertainty, a radical denial of God, and wherever the Good News of Jesus Christ was diluted or rejected. Because of Original Sin, the Devil has acquired a certain domination over man, though he retains his free will. Ignorance of or denial of this "Original Wound"[246] in our nature, the Catechism says, gives rise to serious errors in the realm of catechetics, politics, social action, and morality. The present day evils of heresy and apostasy on the part of some baptized Catholics are a consequence of sin, pure and simple. The Catechism also teaches that:

> Sin sets itself against God's love for us and turns our hearts away from it. Like the first sin, it is disobedience, a revolt against God through the will to become "like gods," knowing and determining good and evil. Sin is thus "love of oneself even to contempt of God." In this proud self-exaltation, sin is diametrically opposed to the obedience of Jesus, which achieves our salvation.[247]

In my years in Catholic education, I have witnessed colleagues who maintain a nostalgic reverence for the sisters who educated them, many from elementary school through the college years. What displeases them is that their children have been denied the identical educational opportunity, largely the result of the feminism which has been devouring institutes of religious women in the United States since the 1960s. This ideology first appeared in the Church when, as part of their updating during the early sixties, the Sister Formation movement advised that sisters earn the same academic qualifications as their secular peers. Superiors were naturally suspicious of secular academic pursuit, fearing that novices would be exposed to error, but were met with the argument the truths of the Faith and of reason were not antithetical, that degrees in education, psychology, catechetics, and theology would instead produce a more valuable apostolate.[248] It was thus in the realm of American higher education that many younger sisters were first exposed to neomodernism. What resulted was for the most part a falling away from the Deposit of the Faith as sisters became favorably disposed to this ideology.

The question which had always mystified me was, how did we arrive at the present condition of religious life? A most neglected element, I believe, lies in Paul VI's warning of Chapter 1 that an adversary power lies behind the present "day of clouds and storms, of darkness, of searching and uncertainties." He reminded all who would give ear to listen that evil is not merely an absence of good but an active force, a living, spiritual being that is perverted and that perverts others. In the first chapter we saw that as a fallen angel, Satan, in Catholic teaching is the clever seducer who in Paul VI's words knows how to lead us from God "through the senses, the imagination, the libido, through utopian logic, or through disordered social contacts in the give and take of our activities, so that he can bring about in us deviations that are all the more harmful because they seem to conform to our physical or mental makeup, or to our profound, instinctive aspirations."

My reading of feminist theology gives cause to assert that by the 1980s this is precisely what had happened to many feminist religious. Having come under the sway of neomodernist errors, they rejected belief in the Incarnation and other core doctrines of the Deposit of the Faith—apostasy pure and simple. At present they offer social work, liberal political nostrums, a feminist interpretation of Sacred Scripture, and the contention that the lived experience of religious women transcends Vatican directives in defining religious life for our times. But this is not all they offer, as we shall see.

We have seen that the process by which *Perfectae Caritatis* was to be implemented frequently went beyond what the document mandated, and that when the Council's teaching disallowed these unexpected reforms, an appeal to "the spirit of Vatican II" was made by the defectors. Seeking higher education as a means to more effective apostolates, many young sisters became exposed to what I, too, upon entering the Jesuit University of Detroit encountered — neomodernist anthropologies influenced by psychology, sociology, and other social sciences, which reduced doctrine to mere symbols of human aspirations. Offered as well was a reinterpretation of Sacred Scripture proposed by Rudolph Bultmann's form criticism, which was widely assented to by many sisters under obedience to what they thought was conciliar teaching.

This pseudoscientific approach and its immanentist perspective has played an integral part in the ideology of Catholic feminism which, in forgoing its belief in the inerrancy of Sacred Scripture and in the immutability of revealed dogmas, cast out belief in the Real Presence of the Mystical Body of Christ. Following the council Sisters also attended seminars and conferences which urged the abandonment of a hierarchical Church structure in favor of the democratic, the questioning of traditional doctrine, and a demand that reasons be given for things formerly *believed* to be sacred, including the basis for their vocation to the religious life. *Ressourcement,* rather than guiding *aggiornamento,* was ignored in favor of the latter, the result in too many instances being the loss of faith on the part of baptized Catholic sisters. The community-wide disruption faced by many religious began what Ann Carey has named "the tragic unraveling of women's religious communities," followed by the emergence of secular feminist ideology to replace the void created by the loss of faith.

Such apostasy is best understood in light of Cardinal Wojtyla's preaching on Genesis, chapter 3, in 1976.[249] The future Pope in his preaching on Original Sin discussed in our first chapter had said that the Devil was identifiable "solely from the content of his words," concluding that history would be "subject to rule by the Word and the anti-Word." In the Fall, the "anti-Word," Satan speaks the temptation, the source of which is his own rebellion and denial: "Were you to eat it your eyes would open and you would become like God, acquiring knowledge of good and evil." The truth inherent in the story is that man's status as creature requires him to acknowledge that only God may author the moral law. Thus the nature of the temptation was and is Satan's attempt "to transmit to man his own rebellion," that is, "the attitude with which he—Satan—has identified himself and by which he has, in consequence, placed himself outside the truth; which means outside the law of dependence on the Creator."

Cardinal Wojtyla further noted that in the story Satan failed in his attempt at sowing in man the seeds of total rebellion, but was successful in "inducing man to turn towards the world, and to stray progressively in a direction opposed to the destiny to which he has been called." This rendered the world the "terrain of man's temptation," where human pride seeks not the glory of God but its own greater satisfaction. He reminded his listeners that the council warned against this secularism: "Without the Creator the creature vanishes," he said, quoting *Gaudium et Spes:* "When God is forgotten, however, the creature itself grows unintelligible." From the standpoint of doctrine, this is exemplified clearly in the writings of women in the Catholic feminist movement, which has contributed to the demise of American religious communities.

Donna Steichen has contributed by way of a history of feminist influence on American Catholic communities a comprehensive analysis of the unintelligibility of Catholic feminism, [250] a great deal of which is premised upon male-generated neomodernist philosophy. In short, sisters acquired from neomodernist professors and theologians an ability to give new and alien meanings to traditional religious vocabulary, employing process theology as a doctrinal base for their new religion, according to which God "needs creation" and "needs fulfillment and relationships in order to be real," because "everything is relative, even the deity."[251] As Steichen correctly notes, such a theology can make a virtue out of *any* action which may seem self-actualizing: "revolution . . . divorce, abortion, lesbianism, witchcraft, voodoo, demon marriages or any of the other desperate acts taking place in the tragic, perilous, self-inflicted feminist wilderness exile."[252]

Her opening chapter, "From Convent to Coven" is instructive in allowing the feminists, both secular and religious, to speak for themselves.[253] As of this writing, Mankato State University hosts an annual Women and Spirituality conference, and the 1985 conference was especially illustrative of Catholic feminist influence in "the spirit of Vatican II." Earlier in the chapter I mentioned that *Perfectae Caritatis* spoke of following Christ as the highest norm for religious life, charging religious with imitation of "the virginal and poor Christ," and His body. At Mankato State, Rosemary Radford-Reuther was the only presenter to even mention the name of Jesus, done in the context of a useful symbol.[254] The concept of sin was referenced only by way of ridicule, except for the "original sin," sexism.[255] Vatican II's *Dei Verbum* (Dogmatic Constitution on Divine Revelation) was ignored in favor of "imaging God" as both male and female, or—denying God's existence altogether—as either "the goddess within" or "the Divinity in each us."[256]

Mrs. Steichen also recounts instances of witchcraft—Wicca—within the Catholic feminist movement.[257] Wiccans accept as immanent in each of us "a life force energy that some of us call the goddess, a part of ourselves."[258] This of course eliminates the need for a Church to intercede between the deity and the individual. Presenter Jade River assured the Mankato conference attendees that Wiccans were not

Satanists, exclaiming: "I don't even believe there is a Satan. . . . And not necessarily a true good and evil."[259] This relativism downplays both the existence of evil itself and the idea of absolute good, and has proven a scourge on mankind, which Pope Benedict XVI has signaled out for pointed criticism.

Contrasted with Catholic teaching—that all of us have a good, but fallen, sinful nature as a result of Original Sin and are redeemed through faith in a crucified and risen Christ by God's grace manifest in our good works here on earth— there is no need for redemption in Catholic feminist anthropology.[260] It is as though good and evil are two sides of the same coin, both parts of a greater oneness and of each other. In the absence of absolute good and evil, we must ask ourselves, at what point does one go over to the "dark side" and who draws the line?[261] Wicca does not say. Blessed Mother Theresa does: "Words that do not give the light of Christ increase the darkness."[262] We would do well to take to heart the following example of demonic oppression undergone by one Wiccan:

> When I was a witch, I performed rituals. I evoked spirits. I called entities. I cast spells, burned candles, concocted brews. The only thing I didn't do was fly on a broom, but I probably would have figured it out if given time. But where did it lead to? Into darkness, depression and the creation of an aura of gloom around me. I was frequently under demon attack. The house where I lived was alive with poltergeist activity . . . due to residual "guests" from rituals.

My friends and family were afraid of me. I knew I had no future; all I had was a dark present. I was locked in by oaths and "destiny." But I had *power,* something I'd always wanted. It wasn't Satan's fault. He didn't exist — or so I thought. I gave it all up, and came to Jesus on my knees. . . . He freed me from the oppression and gave me back my soul — the one I had so foolishly given to evil in exchange for power. . . . Our salvation was bought at a great price and all we have to do is reach out for it. But we cannot serve two masters.[263]

In the fall of 1978, I took a job as a catechist in a suburban parish high school, where my department chair, Sr. Fran, incessantly made reference to her "creation-centered" approach to teaching the Faith, acquired through attending conferences centered around Dominican Fr. Matthew Fox's new spirituality. As a newly-certified catechist, I remember being grateful to her for not insisting that I adopt this approach to instruction; though at the time I assumed it must be licit, simply because Sr. Fran was one of the kindest people I have ever known, and being green behind the ears I trusted her judgment.

Fox's creation spirituality has had a significant influence upon Catholic feminism since its inception. By 1987, Creation-Centered Catholic Communities were calling for a creation spirituality that "begins with mystical union . . . with the Cosmos-Earth-planet."[264] Such spirituality posits knowledge of God through experience, usually mystical, over any revelation outside of man. Fr. Fox insists that God can only be truly known through these otherworldly experiences, because this "mystical dimension of our psyches is part of our true self."[265]

This is the age-old heresy of Gnosticism, the doctrine of salvation by knowledge, derived from the etymology of *gnosis,* "knowledge."[266] Whereas the Church teaches that the soul attains its salvation by obedience of mind and will to God, by grace through faith working in love, Gnosticism places the soul's salvation solely in one's possession of a quasi-intuitive knowledge of the mysteries of the universe, and of magic formulae indicative of that knowledge. Mrs. Steichen has done us an invaluable service indeed by exposing the influence of Gnosticism on Catholic feminist ideology.[267] Creation spirituality's influence on Catholic feminism thus appears to be one in which the subjective goddess within takes the place of "I AM who AM" and is worshipped as such.

My own vicarious encounter with a prominent figure in the Catholic feminist movement movement came, ironically, in the course of my research for this book. I had occasion to interview a longtime colleague about her recollection of the years of *aggiornamento.* When I asked her why she joined her order, she replied that she felt it was what the Lord called her to do. She had always taught in the lower grades of various Catholic elementary schools in a large urban area, largely because she loved teaching such children. Obedient to the Father's call and to the prompting of the Spirit, she daily shows that religious life is a way of following Christ, in order to devote oneself to Him with an undivided heart.[268]

During the course of the hour I spent with her, she told me of another sister of her order in the days after Vatican II, covetous of advanced learning, who had told her one day, "I could never do what you do." When I asked what became of this sister, my interviewee smiled, mischievously. She said the sister was now a well-known theologian. Further research on my part turned up that she now holds an STL in patristics from the *Institut Catholique,* Paris, and an STD in scripture and spirituality from the Gregorian University in Rome. The author of several feminist theological works, she is currently professor of New Testament and spirituality at a well-known graduate school. In October, 1986, she spoke at the first Women in the Church conference held in Washington, D.C., where she called on American women religious to be independent of Vatican control, noting that nuns are "laypersons" in possession of the right "to enjoy the same freedom as the rest of the world." Referring to an "invisible church" composed of *those directly illumined by the Holy Spirit* [emphasis mine], she stated that there has been a "gradual espousal of a pneumatological ecclesiology which is not really compatible with the reigning ecclesiology of the Vatican," resulting in "a self-understanding and praxis among religious which is in contrast, even opposition, to official teaching about religious life and Church law regarding it."[269] This sister also hailed the "costly but real victory" of the superiors who refused to intimidate or banish the religious signers of a Catholics for a Free Choice 1984 *New York Times* advertisement on abortion.

At the Women and Spirituality conference, Sr. Madonna Kolbenschlag, H.M. blasphemously referenced the Trinity as "a good ole boy, associating intimately only with two other divine males," together who had "legitimated religious bigotry, racism, classism, imperialism, clericalism and all the other isms you can think of."[270] But apparently not feminism, as Sr. Kolbenschlag continued:

> The myth of the Father God ensured a world of dominance and dependence. . . . Patriarchy, embedded in the creation story of Genesis, *is* the universal religion. What explains the persistence of the myth? What explains its selection? There were other myths available at the time. . But the Genesis myth marked the establishment of monotheism and the legitimation of patriarchy as the way of nature—as God's will.[271]

Sr. Kolbenschlag's subjective feminist interpretation corroborates Cardinal Woytyla's preaching on the effects of the original temptation on man:

> Eve, reaching for the Tree of Life, for the fruit of knowledge and power, full of desire for godlikeness . . . True daughters and sons of Eve will, in increasing numbers, reach for the Tree of Life and

the fruits of knowledge and power, seeking godlikeness. The question is, how long will other men and women go on reaching for the fruits of patriarchy?[272]

She went on to offer this interpretation of the Fall:

Adam and Eve's sin was, first, a sexual transgression: they knew they were naked. In the ancient world, images of the snake were always associated with the goddess of fertility, the goddess of life. Thus the snake is a symbol of pre-eminent female power and also of the threat of chaos: female power out of control. The banishing of the snake is the banishing of the goddess and, symbolically, of Eve's free and autonomous expression of her sexuality. [The second transgression,] *"You shall be as gods"* [emphasis mine] — is a transgression of power. Because of her autonomous act, her curiosity and her aggressive desire to *know,* she is to be punished by being excluded from knowledge and from the experience that is power. It's not just the triumph of the "One True God" over the fertility goddesses and the cults. It is a clear condemnation by Yahweh of female sexuality exercised freely and autonomously. It is above all a condemnation and prohibition of the exercise of female power and authority. . . . So now we see what a seamless web this is: the Vatican preoccupation with contraception, abortion, female altar servers, ordination, nun's habits and constitutions. It's all part of one piece! It's not about 'the mind of Christ.' And the abortion controversy is not about life. It's about control over women's sexuality and power![273]

The rebellion of those religious seduced by this particular "spirit of Vatican II" at present is an attack on Christ's Church.

Recall that in Cardinal Wojtyla's catechesis on the Fall, the nature of the first temptation was Satan's bid to transmit to man the attitude on which He had fixed his will and by which he has placed himself outside the Truth, the law of dependence on the Creator. Rebelling against the authority of God, He said, "You will be like gods." In this, the Devil was successful only in persuading man to turn towards the world, a direction opposed to the eternal destiny God intended for him, making the world the terrain of man's temptation, where pride seeks not the glory of God but its own greater satisfaction.

In this overview of religious life after Vatican II, we have seen also a rebellion against the vow of chastity, remembering the Serpent in Genesis had recommended that our first parents reclaim their own reality by giving free vent to their sexual desires. Among religious who succumbed, there is an obvious rage and anger against God and against their own womanhood, which only serves to make one more susceptible to the advice of a fallen angel who has no love of either sex. Those who rebel thus against this teaching on the Fall are condemned to repeat it.

In sum, the following are the fruits of feminist ideology since Vatican II: rejection of the Deposit of the Faith under the influence of theological neomodernism, dabbling in the occult, susceptibility to the Gnostic heresy, uninhibited libido, and exclusion of other apostolates in favor of social and political activism.[274] As an ideology it has proven fruitless because ideas such as the following do not appeal to young women of the new millennium: [Women] "must emancipate themselves from Jesus as Redeemer and seek a new redemptive disclosure of God and of human possibility in female form."[275] *Perfectae Caritatis* challenged religious to imitate the virginal and poor Christ, who sanctified man by His obedience unto death. It challenged religious to live ever more like Christ and His Body — the better done, the more fruitful the apostolate. We have seen how the reverse is also true.

I close with a look at how the prayers of the sister whose essay appears above are being answered daily.[276] Himself a leader of a reform movement of Capuchin Brothers, Sisters, and Priests, Fr. Benedict Groeschel, C.F.R. has recently observed that after forty years of a process of collapse of the large religious orders in the United States,

A surprising and welcome development at the present time is the emergence of a whole wave of young men and women interested in authentic religious life. They provide proof of the ongoing presence of God's grace. . . . These young people surprise us by their willingness to join even communities beset by obvious theological confusion and little observance of their traditional rule. If they manage to survive for twenty years, the appearance of the sinking communities may change. In some communities there is an absurd phenomenon similar to a theological sandwich: The youngest and the oldest, who are in agreement, are like slices of bread. The age group in the middle reminds us of mayonnaise.

Something in human nature has been calling people to religious life for thousands of years — and gospel teaching and church tradition have aimed this human hunger at a strong form of Christian dedication. We should have learned by the disastrous experience of the twentieth century that we cannot afford the luxury of frivolous attempts at silly spirituality and self-seeking. We cannot continue to be misled by untested and unscientific sociological and psychological theories.

There hardly seems a mistake that religious orders did not make. *Corruptio optimi pessimum*, the old Latin proverb runs: Corruption of the best becomes the worst. We have seen it for forty years. The generation formed since John Paul II became pope is clamoring for something better.[277]

This is not surprising, for the Pope whom this generation loved said of the religious life:

In every age there have been men and women who, obedient to the Father's call and to the prompting of the Spirit, have chosen this special way of following Christ, in order to devote themselves to him with an "undivided" heart. Like the Apostles, they too have left everything behind in order to be with Christ and to put themselves, as he did, at the service of God and their brothers and sisters. In this way, through the many charisms of spiritual

227

and apostolic life bestowed on them by the Holy Spirit, they have helped to make the mystery and mission of the Church shine forth, and in doing so have contributed to the renewal of society.[278]

We have surveyed the trials which consecrated life is undergoing in the Church in the modern world, the theme of which has been that "the mystery of evil also threatens those who dedicate their whole lives to God."[279] Any reform of religious life will wither unless, as the Council taught, it sets the following of Christ as the highest rule.

There is good news on the horizon, however. Cardinal Franc Rode's Prefect for the Congregation for Institutes of Consecrated Life and Societies of Apostolic Life, began in December, 2008, an Apostolic Visitation of the major Religious Institutes of Women in the United States. It will collect and assimilate data about religious life under the direction of Mother Mary Clare Millea, A.S.C.J., who will report to the Prefect upon completion of her mission, expected sometime in 2011.

A related news item gives indication of much of what Mother is likely to encounter, as the Congregation for the Doctrine of the Faith is also investigating the Leadership Conference of Women Religious, conducting a "doctrinal assessment" due to the suspect content of speeches delivered at the Conference's annual meetings. In addition to rejecting Church teaching on homosexuality and women's ordination, the LCWR refuses to accept the CDF's declaration *"Dominus Jesus"* on the unicity and salvific universality of Jesus Christ and the Church. Furthermore, at a recent assembly, Dominican Sister Laurie Brink spoke of the need to go "beyond Jesus," adding that He "is not the only son of God."[280] Indeed, as of this writing many leaders of women's religious orders in the U.S. are refusing to answer questions submitted to them as part of the apostolic investigation. To date only about one percent of the religious have responded by the expected deadline to the questions submitted by Mother Mary Clare, indicating "almost universal resistance" to the Vatican.[281]

I wholeheartedly implore Catholics to visit some of the social communication of Religious Orders faithful to Vatican II via the Internet.[282] Doing so makes one feel as though John Paul the Great still beckons to our youth: "Dear young people, Be not afraid!" And Jesus says to all of us called to holiness, "In the world you have tribulation; but be of good cheer, I have overcome the world."[283]

CHAPTER SIX

Catechesis

Why do you not understand what I say? It is because you cannot bear to hear my word. You are of your father the devil, and your will is to do your father's desires. He was a murderer from the beginning, and has nothing to do with the truth, because there is no truth in him. When he lies, he speaks according to his own nature, for he is a liar and the father of lies. But, because I tell the truth, you do not believe me.

John 8:43–45

I charge you in the presence of God and of Christ Jesus who is to judge the living and the dead, and by his appearing and his kingdom: preach the word, be urgent in season and out of season, convince, rebuke, and exhort, be unfailing in patience and in teaching. For the time is coming when people will not endure sound teaching, but having itching ears they will accumulate for themselves teachers to suit their own likings, and will turn away from listening to the truth and wander into myths. As for you, always be steady, endure suffering, do the work of an evangelist, fulfill your ministry.

2 Timothy 4:1-5

I.

I am grateful to Our Lord, my mother, and the Sisters of Notre Dame De Namur for instilling in me a clear sense of the transcendent, Triune God as I was growing up in the 1950s. In retrospect, my gratitude stems from the Father's gifts of the workings of baptismal grace, a mother who knew how to mother in a Catholic family, and devout religious sisters who taught and lived the fundamentals of the Deposit of the Faith. In the end all of this shielded me against the wiles of neomodernist-motivated religious education professionals who directed my catechist formation in the 1970s. We turn in this chapter to the deviations in catechesis in the United States following Vatican II, toward the corroboration of Pope Paul VI's assessment concerning the "smoke of Satan" working in the Church.

"Go therefore and make disciples of all nations, baptizing them in the name of the Father and of the Son and of the Holy Spirit, teaching them to observe all that I have commanded you; and lo, I am with you always, to the close of the age." It was thus that Jesus commanded his Apostles, giving them the

Holy Spirit that they might explain with authority all that He had taught them. From the beginning, catechesis has always meant the Church's effort to win disciples for Our Lord, to lead others to faith in Him as the Son of God that they might have the fullness of life in His name. Catechesis has also meant to instruct disciples of Christ to build up the Church through teaching the Deposit of the Faith in an organic, systematic manner. Until Vatican II, catechesis was primarily doctrinal, consisting in instruction in the *didache*, the "Doctrine of the Twelve Apostles" before baptism.[284] This doctrine was encapsulated in the Apostles Creed, the twelve fundamental doctrines which summarized Apostolic teaching in the form of a profession of faith. Over time, the fundamentals of the Faith came to be divided into Creed, Commandments, Sacraments, and Prayer, the structure of our present-day Catechism.

I am one of the generational Catholics schooled in the Faith by the teaching of the Baltimore Catechism prior to Vatican II, which the postconciliar religious education establishment had branded as defective pedagogy; my quarrel with them is not over their contention concerning the *style* of teaching, but rather their belief that the truths of the Catholic faith on the existence and nature of God, the creation and Fall, the Incarnation and Redemption, and the Church set down in the Baltimore Catechism were defective as well.

Vatican II's Decree Concerning the Pastoral Office of Bishops in the Church mandated for the future that a "directory should be composed concerning the catechetical instruction of the Christian people; this directory will consider the fundamental principles of such instruction, its disposition and the composition of books on the subject," taking care that particular attention should be given to the views expressed by the council Fathers.[285] The mandate was fulfilled in 1971 with the publication of the Sacred Congregation for the Clergy's papally-approved General Catechetical Directory, which marked an abandonment of the Church's usual practice of issuing a catechism, as she did for example after the Council of Trent. Nevertheless, the Directory was an orthodox document, approved by Paul VI, and stressed the importance of doctrinal propositions and cognitive learning after Vatican II. The intent of the Directory was to provide basic principles taken from the Magisterium and from the Second General Vatican Council — "by which pastoral action in the ministry of the word can be more fittingly directed and governed."[286] Most telling was the Congregation's explanation for the need for the Directory:

> Such a course of action was adopted especially for the following reason: *the errors which are not infrequently noted in catechetics today* can be avoided only if one starts with the correct way of understanding the nature and purposes of catechesis and also the truths

which are to be taught by it, with due account being taken of those
to whom catechesis is directed and of the conditions in which they
live.[287]

The errors originated in a turning away from the teaching
of Catholic doctrine in favor of experimental liturgical activity
and social protest. This prepared the way for the application
to catechesis of the malevolent concept of "ongoing revelation" under the leadership of Gabriel Moran.[288] For disciples
of Moran, God was to be sought in the modern world, from
which it follows that catechesis should be centered on finding
meaning in one's lived experience, the approach which was
said to be authoritative following Vatican II. The following
characteristics give indication of neomodernist inspiration in
catechesis after the Council:

- The prioritization of inquiry over the handing on of the Deposit of
  the Faith, wherein students under the catechists' direction explore
  the meaning of their own experience; the net result of this method
  was to downgrade the bishop from the role traditionally assigned
  him as chief catechist in his diocese in deference to the "professional" expert more versed in the "new catechesis."[289]
- The derision of Church Tradition and authority, which was viewed
  as "indoctrination" because it offered absolutes and authoritative
  answers. The truth of these answers was now styled as relative to
  the age in which they appeared and did not necessarily speak to
  the modern age. That Jesus came to set men free was interpreted
  to mean that one was then free to decide for himself the meaning

of Christ's teaching, and under no obligation to follow magisterial teaching. The immediate fruits of this approach were dramatic declines in attendance at Confession and at Mass.

- The priority given to subjectivity over objective reality in the "new catechesis;" one's religion now being understood as personal, it was argued that the believing Catholic could decide for himself the meaning of Jesus' teaching.[290]

In the face of parental objection to the new approach to catechetics, which made the interpretation of one's life experience the norm for catechesis, the religious education professionals disingenuously replied that what the parents were demanding was a return to the "pre-Vatican II" method of indoctrination, of memorizing the Baltimore Catechism. The diabolic element in the new approach was in the reception it received.

One of America's premier orthodox catechists, then Director of the NCEA, Fr. Alfred McBride, *O. Praem.*, delivered a talk at the Catholic University of America in the summer of 1969 on the transcendence of God. He noted that his students, budding nuns, priests, seminarians, brothers, and laymen, seemed content rich but pedagogically destitute. Fr. McBride correctly discerned that a more efficacious catechesis could be had by *both* an immanent dimension to *complement* the transcendent dimension, in faithfulness to Vatican II's *Gaudium et Spes* (and later recommended by John Paul II).[291] As he recalled, Fr. McBride assumed that his students had grasped and assimilated both dimensions when they had not, and sensed that worldly thinking had invaded their minds:

> After three years teaching my human dimensions course, I realized that secularity had intruded into the consciousness of many of these students. A number of them had succumbed to a modernity that rejected history and tradition. What's modern is good. What's pre-modern is outdated and useless. That virus was there, even though I did not recognize it initially. I found myself, tragically, nourishing it with all my talk about modern drama, poetry, fiction, philosophy, mid communications theory. These particular students failed to see the culture as instrumental, as a means to an end, an opening to revelation. Instead they swallowed it indiscriminately as an end in itself. The transcendent was collapsing before my eyes, but at first I did not recognize it. It was probably no coincidence that the famed 1966 Easter cover story of Time magazine, "Is God Dead?" coincided with the initiation of my course.[292]

Fr. McBride noted that for the remainder of the decade of the 1960s, catechetical materials had become doctrinal wastelands concerned with activities about friendliness and stories of secular saints. In short, pedagogy began to stress process rather than the message, the result being a doctrinal illiteracy that undermined the beliefs, attitudes, and practices of his students. In the first chapter we saw how Paul VI believed he had been indiscreet in the face of the invasion of modernist thinking into the Church, and sorrowfully I admit that as I began to write I would have agreed. But as I delved further and further into the Holy Father's response to the crisis of faith spawned by the invasion, my concerns quickly vanished.

What follows is a look at the events which gave rise to Pope Paul's *Creed of the People of God* of August 10, 1968, which mapped the battle plan against the crisis of faith brought about by the misinterpretation of Church teaching after the Second Vatican Council. We begin with an examination of the main neomodernist errors identified in the infamous Dutch Catechism by the commission of Cardinal theologians sent by Paul to the Dutch hierarchy late in 1967. I humbly ask the reader to examine his present beliefs concerning these points to see whether or not he has been misinformed of the Church's teaching on them (as I had in the 1970s). The actual teaching of the Church on the points outlined is reproduced in the brackets. I make no apology for the extensive quotation, as doctrinal literacy is served by it. They are as follows:

1. *Points concerning God the Creator*. It is necessary that the [Dutch] Catechism teach that God, besides this sensible world in which we live, has created also a realm of pure spirits whom we call Angels. [Here the Cardinals cited Vatican I's *Dei Filius*, and Vatican II's

Lumen Gentium nos. 49, 50]. Furthermore, it should state explicitly that individual human souls since they are spiritual [here citing *Gaudium et Spes*, No.14] are created immediately by God [again, citing Pius Xll's Encyclical *Humani Generis*].

2. *The Fall of Man in Adam.* [*Cf Lumen Gentium*, n. 2]. Although questions regarding the origin of the human race and its slow development present today new difficulties, to be faced in connection with the dogma of original sin, nevertheless in the New Catechism the doctrine of the Church is to be faithfully proposed, that man in the beginning of history rebelled against God [*Cf. Gaudium et Spes*, nos. 13, 22] and so lost for himself and his offspring that sanctity and justice in which he had been constituted, and handed on a true state of sin to all through propagation of human nature. Certainly those expressions must be avoided which could signify that original sin is only contracted by individual new members of the human family in this sense that from their very coming into the world, they are exposed within themselves to the influence of human society where sin reigns, and so are started initially on the way of sin.

3. *With regard to the conception of Jesus by the Virgin Mary.* The Commission of Cardinals has asked that the Catechism openly profess that the Blessed Mother of the Incarnate Word always enjoyed the honor of virginity, and that the fact itself of the virginal conception of Jesus which is in such great conformity with the mystery of the incarnation itself, he taught clearly. In consequence the Catechism should offer no excuse for abandoning this factual truth — in face of the ecclesiastical Tradition founded on Holy Scripture — retaining only a symbolic signification, such as the complete gratuity of the gift which God has given to us in His Son.

4. *The "Satisfaction" made by Christ Our Lord.* The essential elements of the doctrine of the satisfaction of Christ which pertains to our faith are to be proposed without ambiguity. God so loved sinful men as to send His Son into the world to reconcile men to Himself. [*cf.* 2 Cor 5:19]. As St. Augustine says: "We were reconciled to a God who loved us even when we were at enmity with Him because of sin" [*In Ioannes Evangelium* Tract. 110 n. 6]. Jesus therefore, as the first-born among many brethren [*cf. Rom.* 8:29] died for our sins [*Cf.* 1 *Cor.* 15:3]. Holy, innocent, immaculate [*cf Hebr.* 7:26], he underwent no punishment inflicted on him by God,

but freely and with filial love, obedient to His Father [*cf. Phil.* 2:8] he accepted, for his sinful brethren and as their Mediator [*cf.* 1 *Tim.* 2, 5], the death, which for them is the wages of sin [*cf. Rom.* 6:23; *Gaudium et Spes,* no. 18]. By this His most sacred death, which in the eyes of God more than abundantly compensated for the sins of the world, He brought it about that divine grace was restored to the human race as a good which it had merited in its divine Head [*cf Hebr.* 10:5–10; Council of Trent, sess. VI, Decr. *De justificatione,* cap. 3 and 7, can. 10].

5. *The Sacrifice of the Cross and the Sacrifice of the Mass.* It must be clearly stated that Jesus offered Himself to His Father to repair our wrong-doing as a holy victim in whom God was well pleased. For Christ . . ."loved us, giving himself up in our place as a fragrant offering and a sacrifice to God" [Eph, 5:2]. The sacrifice of the Cross is perpetuated in the Church of God as the eucharistic sacrifice [*cf.* Sacrosanctum Concilium, No, 47]. In the eucharistic sacrifice Jesus as the principal priest offers Himself to God through the consecratory oblation which priests perform and to which the faithful unite themselves. That celebration is both sacrifice and banquet. The sacrificial oblation is completed by commu-

nion, in which the victim offered to God is received as food, to unite the faithful to Himself and to join them with one another in charily [*cf.* 1 *Cor* 10:17].

6. *The Eucharistic Presence and the Eucharistic Change.* It is necessary that in the text of the Catechism it be brought out beyond doubt that after the consecration of the bread and wine the very body and blood of Christ is present on the altar and is received sacramentally in Holy Communion, so that those who worthily approach this divine table are spiritually renewed by Christ Our Lord, Furthermore, it must be explained that the bread and wine in their deepest reality (not in appearance or phenomenologically), once the words of consecration have been spoken, are changed into the body and blood of Christ; and so it comes to pass that where the appearance of bread and wine (the phenomenological reality) remain, there, in a way most mysterious, the humanity itself of Christ, lies hidden together with His Divine Person.

Once this marvelous change has taken place, a conversion which in the Church is termed *transubstantiation* [emphasis mine], the appearance of bread and wine, — since they actually contain and present Christ Himself, the fountain of grace and charity to be communicated through the sacred banquet, — take on as a consequence indeed a new signification and a new end. But they take on that new signification and that new end precisely because transubstantiation has taken place [here the cardinals cite Paul VI's *Mysterium Fidei*].

7. *The Infallibility of the Church and the Knowledge of Revealed Mysteries.* It should be more clearly stated that the infallibility of the Church does not give her only a safe course in a continual research, but the truth in maintaining doctrine of faith and in explaining it always in the same sense [*cf.* Vatican I's *Dei Filius,* cap. 4, and Vatican II, *Dei Verbum,* cap, 2]. "Faith is not only a seeking of the truth but is above all certain possession of truth" [Paul VI, *ad Episcoporum Synodurn,* 1967]. Nor is it to be allowed that readers of the Catechism think that the human intellect arrives only at verbal and conceptual expressions of the revealed mystery. Care must be taken rather that they understand that the human intellect is able by those concepts "through a mirror in an obscure way" and "in part," as St. Paul says [1 *Cor.* 13:12], but in a way that is altogether true, to express and grasp the revealed mysteries.

8. *The Ministerial or Hierarchical Priesthood and the Power of Teaching in the Church.* Care must be taken not to minimize the excellence of the ministerial priesthood, that in its participation or the priesthood of Christ, differs from the common priesthood of the faithful not only in degree, but in essence [cf. *Lumen Gentium,* no. 10].

Care should be taken that in describing the priestly ministry there is brought out more clearly the mediation between God and men which they exercise not only in preaching the word of God, in forming the Christian Community and in administering the Sacraments, but also and chiefly in offering the Eucharistic Sacrifice in the name of the whole Church [here citing Vatican Il's *Lumen Gentium,* no. 2 and *Presbyterorum ordinis,* nos. 12, 13].

Furthermore, the Cardinals asked that the new Catechism clearly recognize that the teaching authority and the power of ruling in the Church is given directly to the Holy Father and to the Bishops joined with him in hierarchical communion, and that it is not given first all to the People of God to be communicated to others. The office of Bishops, therefore, is not a mandate given them by the People of God but is a mandate received from God Himself for the good of the whole Christian community.

It is to be brought out more clearly that the Holy Father and the Bishops in their teaching office do not only assemble and approve what the whole community of the faithful believes. The people of God are so moved and sustained by the spirit of truth that they cling to the word of God with unswerving loyalty and freedom from error and the leadership of the Magisterium to whom it belongs authentically guard, explain and defend the deposit of faith. Thus it has come about that in understanding the faith that has been handed down, in professing that faith and in manifesting it in deed, there is a unique collaboration between bishops and the faithful [cf. *Lumen Gentium,* no. 11, and *Dei Verbum,* no. 10]. Sacred Tradition and the Sacred Scripture — which constitute the one and only holy deposit the Word of God — and the Magisterium of the Church are so joined that one cannot stand without the other [cf. *Dei Verbum,* no. 10].

Finally, that authority by which the Holy Father directs the Church is to be clearly presented as the full power of ruling, a supreme and universal power which the Pastor of the whole Church can always freely exercise [*cf. Lumen Gentium*, no. 2].

9. *Various points concerning Dogmatic Theology.* In the presentation of the mystery of the three Persons in God, the Catechism should not seem to deny that Christians do well to contemplate them with faith and love them with filial devotion not only in the economy of salvation where they manifest themselves but also in the eternal life of the Divinity, whose vision we hope for.

The efficacy of the Sacraments should be presented somewhat more exactly. Care must be taken that the Catechism does not seem to say that miracles can only be brought about by divine power insofar as they do not depart from that which the forces of the created world are able to produce.

Finally, let open reference be made to the souls of the just, which, having been thoroughly purified, already rejoice in the immediate vision of God, even while the pilgrim Church still awaits the glorious coming of the Lord and the final resurrection [*cf. Lumen Gentium*, no, 49, 51].

10. *Certain points of Moral Theology.* The text of the Catechism is not to make obscure the existence of moral laws which we are able to know and express in such wise that they bind our conscience always and in all circumstances. Solutions of cases of conscience should be avoided which do not sufficiently attend to the indissolubility of marriage. While it is right to attach great moment to the moral habits, still one must be on guard lest that habit be presented without sufficient dependence upon human acts. The presentation of a conjugal morality should be more faithful in presenting the full teaching of Vatican II and of the Holy See.

The above observations, though not few and not insignificant, still leave untouched by far the greater part of the New Catechism with its praiseworthy pastoral, liturgical, and biblical character. Neither are they opposed to the laudable purpose or the authors of the Catechism, namely, to present the eternal good tidings of Christ in a way adapted to the understanding and the thinking of the present day man. Indeed the very fine qualities which make this an outstanding work demand that it ever present the true teaching of the Church in no way obscured or overshadowed.[293]

Since the publication of the Dutch Catechism's English translation in 1967, the doctrinal errors cited by the Cardinal's commission circulated in the development of local catechisms, the catechetical texts which were studied by children and young people with the assistance of catechists, teachers and parents. As we shall see, no corrective was offered to these texts as late as the 1990s, a major reason for the present doctrinal illiteracy in the Church. In the United States, such basic religion textbooks based on the Dutch Catechism were published by William E. Sadlier, Inc., Benziger Brothers, Allyn and Bacon, and Paulist Press. In effect, a second magisterium of theologians and religious education experts had arisen, taking upon itself the authority to say what Catholic teaching was and was not after Vatican II. Paul VI noted this, alarmed at the apostasy of these neomodernists in not believing the fullness of Catholic teaching handed down from the Apostles and interpreted for the faithful by the Vicar of Christ in union with the successors of the Apostles. The Pope's alarm was evident in his call for the Church to observe a "year of faith" in honor of Saints Peter and Paul:

> We wish to address a special exhortation to those engaged in the study of Sacred Scripture and theology, to collaborate with the hierarchical teaching authority of the Church in defending the true faith from all error and in sounding its unfathomable depths, in correctly expounding its content and in drawing up reasoned

247

norms for its study and spread. This same appeal we make to preachers, to teachers of religion and to catechists.[294]

In announcing the year of faith, what concerned the Holy Father was a crisis of faith bordering on apostasy, the result of neomodernist ideas attacking the Church from inside:

And while man's religious sense today is in a decline, depriving the faith of its natural foundation, new opinions in exegesis and theology often borrowed from bold but blind secular philosophies have in places found a way into the realm of Catholic teaching. They question or distort the objective sense of truths taught with authority by the Church; under the pretext of adapting religious thought to the contemporary outlook they prescind from the guidance of the Church's teaching, give the foundations of theological speculation a direction of historicism, dare to rob Holy Scripture's testimony of its sacred and historical character and try to introduce a so-called "post-conciliar" mentality among lie People of God; this neglects the solidity and consistency of the Council's vast and magnificent developments of teaching and legislation, neglects with it the Church's accumulated riches of thought and practice in order to overturn the spirit of traditional fidelity and spread about the illusion of giving Christianity a new interpretation, which is arbitrary and barren. What would remain of the content of our faith, or of the theological virtue that professes it, if these attempts, freed from the support of the Church's teaching authority, were destined to prevail?[295]

Paul VI furthered his crusade against this threat from within the Church Jesus built upon Peter in his *Credo of the People of God*. The genius of the *Credo* was in its twofold purpose of confirming the brethren against the errors in the Dutch Catechism which had brought about widespread doubt and uncertainty, and doing so by a positive expanded restatement of the traditional creedal outline derived from the Nicene Creed. Thus we see answered all of the doubts raised by the Dutch Catechism and its sympathizers on the topics of original sin, the Mass as sacrifice, the real presence of Christ in the Eucharist, creation from nothing, the primacy of Peter, the virginity of Mary, the Immaculate Conception, and the Assumption; in short, a reaffirmation of Catholic belief in the face of the errors his theological commission had found in the Dutch Catechism.[296]

To fully comprehend how what Paul called "new opinions in exegesis and theology" remain evident in catechesis at present, recall Paul VI's 1972 warning that the Devil can be presumed to be at work where "the denial of God becomes radical, subtle and absurd," and where the spirit of the gospel is watered down and rejected." Though Paul had intended in the *Credo* to bind all Catholics in his exercise of ordinary magisterial teaching as prescribed by *Lumen Gentium,* Catholic scholars among the alternate magisterium paid little heed.

Nevertheless the Holy Father issued a final exhortation on the role of authentic catechesis in evangelization:

> A means of evangelization that must not be neglected is that of catechetical instruction. The intelligence, especially that of children and young people, needs to learn through systematic religious instruction the fundamental teachings, the living content of the truth which God has wished to convey to us and which the Church has sought to express in an ever richer fashion during the course of her long history. No one will deny that this instruction must be given to form patterns of Christian living and not to remain only notional. Truly the effort for evangelization will profit greatly — at the level of catechetical instruction given at church, in the schools, where this is possible, and in every case in Christian homes — if those giving catechetical instruction have suitable texts, updated with wisdom and competence *under the authority of the bishops*. The methods must be adapted to the age, culture and aptitude of the persons concerned, they must seek always to fix in the memory, intelligence and heart the essential truths that must impregnate all of life. It is necessary above all to prepare good instructors — parochial catechists, teachers, parents — who are desirous of perfecting themselves in this superior art, which is indispensable and requires religious instruction. Moreover, without neglecting in any way the training of children, one sees that present conditions render ever more urgent catechetical instruction under the form of the catechumenate, for innumerable young people and adults who, touched by grace, discover little by little the face of Christ and feel the need of giving themselves to him. . . .[297]

And so it was that as the twentieth century waned, the dogged persistence of the neomodernist view of the Church's magisterium and the bishops' failure to correct it caused many Catholics to lose faith in the Church and the guidance She provides under God the Holy Spirit.

II

The Dutch Catechism's influence in the United States is best studied in the careers of the principal religious education theorists at the university level. First among them was Fr. Gerard Sloyan, an instructor in Catholic University of America's Religious Education Department from 1950–1967. In 1956, Fr. Sloyan traveled to Antwerp, Belgium, where he had become acquainted with Fr. Piet Schoonenberg, S.J., who, with Fr. Edward Schillebeeckx were theologians involved with the Dutch Catechism.

Upon his return to the United States, Fr. Sloyan was appointed Chair of the Religious Education Department at the Catholic University of America in 1957. During his seventeen-year tenure he transmitted to a whole generation of under-graduate and graduate students the new catechetics in the "spirit of Vatican II." That Fr. Sloyan developed an attraction to European neomodernist ideas was evident in his *Speaking of Catholic Education* (1967), whose general thesis was that children cannot learn doctrine—they are only capable of experiencing religious emotions. He also erroneously implied that until Vatican II, memorization of Catholic doctrine was the sole catechetical pedagogy, completely ignoring sacramental practice, liturgical and popular prayer, and the study of biblical stories and saint's biographies. The author of *Speaking of Catholic Education* had high praise for the Dutch Catechism, later offering the following review in the catechism's English translation:

> A remarkable synthesis of Christian revelation and human life. Beautifully written and well translated, this volume is in every way a suitable guide to the meaning of Christian life in today's world. *It can very well stand as the catechism of the Second Vatican Council.* [298] [emphasis added].

One is left wondering why the General Catechetical Directory made reference to errors in catechesis in 1971 if the *Dutch Catechism* was the catechism of the Second Vatican Council, and how one might also square this with Paul VI's assertion that the council documents themselves were "the great catechism of modern times."[299]

Sloyan protégé and ex-Christian Brother Gabriel Moran was instrumental in applying to catechetics the concept of ongoing revelation.[300] For Moran, God was to be sought in the modem world, from which it followed that catechesis should center on finding meaning in one's lived experience, an approach which claimed to be authoritative following Vatican II. Students were taught to relate the Gospel to their subjective experiences, for it was here that one encountered God's revelation.

In 1970, as I prepared to enter the Jesuit University of Detroit, Moran wrote a piece for *Commonweal* entitled "Catechetics R.I.P.," in which he stated that "anyone who sets out to educate in the field of religion has to put Scripture, liturgy, and Christian theology in a broader context that does not afford Christianity a normative role." Moran challenged Catholics to stop being concerned over heresy when for him the bigger question was whether or not Christianity itself was true.[301]

Here we have a renowned Catholic religious education professional stirring up doubt by writing in a major Catholic publication that historical Christianity did not establish the field of Catholic religious education! Given what we have said about an alternate magisterium in the Church, it should not surprise the reader that as late as 1991, Moran remained a much sought after keynote speaker at summer catechetical institutes.

Simultaneous with publication of Moran's *Commonweal* piece, there appeared a popular textbook billed as a modern presentation of the Catholic faith for adults, Anthony

Wilhelm's *Christ Among Us,* which I observed being used extensively by pastors and religious educators at the outset of my career. Though the text eventually sold over two million copies, what I did not know at the time was that its *Imprimatur* had been revoked by the Congregation for the Doctrine of the Faith in 1984. *Time* magazine's coverage of this event proves illuminating:

> Book burning by censors of the Roman Catholic Church sputtered out long ago. The Index of Prohibited Books, and other means of limiting what the faithful were permitted to read, faded away during and after the Second Vatican Council. Now, however, there are small signs that the pendulum is swinging back slightly. No flames of outright censorship are visible, but a purifying heat seems to be coming out of Rome. For the first time in 17 years, two books, one of them the bestselling adult catechism in English and the other a lesser-known theological work used mainly in seminaries, have had their ecclesiastical stamp of approval revoked. . . . The Paulist Press is . . . responsible for issuing *Christ Among Us,* a catechism by Anthony Wilhelm, a former priest. Since it was first printed in 1967, more than 1.6 million copies have been sold — 166,000 of them last year — and for many of the nation's 52 million Catholics, the catechism had become an indispensable guide to applying church teachings to contemporary problems. Two months ago, however, the Congregation for the Doctrine of the Faith decided that *Christ Among Us* "was unsuitable as a catechetical text" and could not be made otherwise even with 'substantial revisions." The Congregation's head, Joseph Cardinal Ratzinger,

formally requested Archbishop Peter Gerety of Newark to remove his imprimatur. Without it the book cannot be used in Catholic catechism classes; two weeks ago the Paulist Press bowed to the inevitable and stopped distributing it.[302]

Following the New York Times' coverage of the removal, Harper and Row decided to immediately republish the book without the *Imprimatur,* much to *Commonweal's* satisfaction. The CDF's action did not stop the text's use among religious educators in my archdiocese. It was easy to locate the source of the CDF's concern for the orthodoxy of *Christ Among Us,* namely the influence of both Fr. Rahner's Kantian idealism and the *Dutch Catechism* in Wilhelm's text.

Space affords us a look at only one among many examples.[303] In 1966, Fr. Rahner argued over and against St. Thomas and the Council of Trent that the substance of a thing did not contain its material and physical reality, but instead contained its meaning and purpose. Thus Rahner re-explained Trent's term transubstantiation to signify that, after the consecration the bread remained physical bread but now had the fresh meaning of spiritual food, as it was now a symbol of Our Lord.[304] The Dutch Catechism's Fr. Schillebeeckx agreed with Rahner, averring further that the real presence of Christ in the Eucharist was not the consecrated bread and wine, but the presence of Christ in the assembled community.

This novel theory of the Eucharist was well received by some theologians in the United States, notably Marquette's Fr. Tad W. Guzie, S.J., Georgetown professor Monika K. Hellwig,[305] and Wilhelm in *Christ Among Us:* "When we say that the bread and wine 'become Christ' we are not saying that bread and wine are Christ. . . . What we mean is that the bread and wine are a sign of Christ present, here and now, in a special way—not in a mere physical way, as if condensed into a wafer."[306] It shouldn't surprise us that at present 42% of Catholics aged 20–39 believe that the Real Presence is not an "essential of the Faith."[307]

Such neomodernist speculations left academia, filtering down into religious education programs via those Ph.D. and M.A., Religious Education recipients seeking professional careers in dioceses throughout the United States in the 1970s. The ideology remains alive and well in the various religious education conferences held annually, the largest and most notorious of which is the Los Angeles Religious Education Conference.[308] A quick foray *via* a wonderful means of social communication, the Internet, shows that many victims of such theories are featured at the conference today.[309] The Congress originated in the 1950s to educate catechists to teach the Faith more effectively, but by 1987 the influence of neomodernism on presenters at the Congress had produced a creedless, experiential catechesis under the auspices of Sister Edith

Prendergast, yet another of our influential circle of religious education experts.[310]

Perusal of both the Congress's website and links to its speakers divulge ample evidence of the neomodernist tenet that catechesis no longer means passing on received doctrine because the Church can no longer say it possesses revealed truth from God. Participants were taught to discover truth for themselves by reflecting on their experience, the role of the catechist being to facilitate such reflection. And so it was that doctrine increasingly disappeared from the nation's largest religious education conference much as it had from catechetical programs throughout the country, producing a veritable epidemic of doctrinal illiteracy in the United States. The author presumes that many reading this book could add many comparable accounts of this disappearance.

What efforts were made by the Bishops in the U.S. in the face of this crisis of faith? The English edition of the *General Catechetical Directory* was published by the United States Catholic Conference in December, 1971. By November 1972, the Bishops' conference had released *To Teach as Jesus Did: A Pastoral Message on Catholic Education*, distinctive as the first pastoral in the history of the Catholic Church in the United States solely directed at religious education, building on Vatican II's *Declaration on Christian Education* and on the *General Catechetical Directory*. The Bishops' *Basic Teachings for Catholic*

Religious Education (1973) was intended as an implementation in the United States of the *General Catechetical Directory.*

These publications were wonderfully orthodox in their presentation of Catholic instruction in the faith. The important question was why they were never required by the bishops in a methodical way to be incorporated into local catechisms, the religion texts and instructional materials then being published. The answer quite simply is that the bishops did little in these years to compel compliance with magisterial Catholic teaching when the religious education establishment refused to accept this teaching as authoritative. In retrospect it was a sad day for the Church when she decided against a universal catechism as a foundational document for catechesis after Vatican II.

Unable to disregard criticism of their anemic response, the bishops began preparation of their own National Catechetical Directory, *Sharing the Light of Faith,* to strengthen their catechetical ministry. Unfortunately this was not scheduled for publication until 1979, my second year in the classroom. Orthodox in its presentation of doctrine, it was not well-received by the professionals, the religious education establishment, and so did not have the intended effect. Throughout my professional development, I distinctly remember that in my diocese these documents went unassigned and thus unread; had I studied them on my own I would have recognized the discrepancy between what Vatican II had to say on catechesis and what the religion education professionals were maintaining the council had taught.

Fr. McBride, as NCEA's religion director in 1976, put together a team of religious educational leaders to fashion a questionnaire in order to survey the religious beliefs, attitudes, and practices of students in Catholic schools and CCD programs. By 1978, the Religious Education Outcomes Inventory, as it was commonly known, had been administered to 100,000 eighth graders in 2,000 institutions in over 100 dioceses. Fr. McBride's goal was to awaken catechists to the need for a more effective catechesis, as he reported two years later:

> For the second year in a row, students appear to falter when faced with religious code words (eternal life, ecumenism, grace). . . . Here I wish to draw your attention to the matter of what some call a religious 'illiteracy' among our young Catholics. One cannot conclude from REOI that a working vocabulary for young Catholics is not being taught. But one could infer that many of them are not learning it. Frankly, they are not learning the words, let alone the content and meaning of the terms. Such competence ought to be a sign of a trained, informed and literate Catholic.[311]

Such a state of catechesis inspired Fr. McBride to begin his battle against Catholic doctrinal illiteracy, now fully aware of the false assumptions of the religious "experts," which he summarized as follows:

- Human nature is intrinsically good. This erodes Catholic teaching about original and actual sin and makes Christ's sacrificial act of salvation irrelevant.
- There are two magisteriums. This introduces a second magisterium of some theologians and opinion-makers and results in undermining the revelation-based Magisterium of the pope and bishops.
- Concentrate exclusively on a human experience–based method in teaching. This eliminates the pedagogy of faith and revelation which argues that there is a knowledge of our relationship to God which cannot be known from reason or human experience alone; it must be revealed.

Fr. McBride's analysis of the second and third of these assumptions is most edifying, and warrants full consideration:

. . . . How did their approach work in practice? When there is a teaching of the Church Magisterium that certain theologians and catechists wanted to disregard, they took three steps in presenting their viewpoint:

- First, quote the Church's teaching.
- Second, relativize the teaching by making it sound ambiguous.
- Third, introduce a new teaching.

A catechist, for example, could begin by asserting that Jesus is our redeemer. Then the catechist could render the teaching ambiguous, asserting that God seems to be absent from our world, so we are left on our own and must use our personal powers to save ourselves. Lastly, the catechist argues that there is no divine salvation and claims that even God himself tells us we can get along without him.

The third assumption is the so-called human experience-based method of catechesis, one that is widely used in many textbooks. It is a method that follows these steps: 1) Begin with the human experience of the student and see what aspect of God shines through. 2) Refer to Scripture and see how it speaks this truth about God. 3) Ask the student to compare the two results. 4) From that discussion, move the student to apply this in his or her personal and social life.[312]

The fundamental deficiency in this method is its failure to see that as a result of concupiscence, the effect of original sin, human experience is limited in what it can know about God apart from revelation.

It would take nearly twenty years for the renewal of Vatican II to even begin to bear fruit in the vital area of catechesis, in spite of the efforts by U.S. Bishops to fulfill their role as catechists in publishing both *Basic Teachings for Catholic Religious Education* (1973) and the national Catechetical Directory, *Sharing the Light of Faith* (1977). As his last effort as regards catechesis, Paul VI auspiciously decided it should be the main focus or the fourth synod of bishops meeting in Rome in the fall of 1977, attended by Krakow's Archbishop Wojtyla, who, when he acceded to Peter's throne in 1978 turned to the documents produced by the synod in composing his *Catechesi Tradendae.*

In this Apostolic Exhortation, John Paul noted that the synod fathers had detected "not only an undeniable advance in the vitality of catechetical activity and promising initiatives, *but also the limitations or even 'deficiencies'* in what has been achieved to date."[313] While space disallows a thorough study of the document (I strongly recommend reading the entire thing), John Paul II pointed to concerns deserving of the Church's attention. The first condemned the integrity of the content of local catechisms, where he warned that the disciple of Christ has the right to receive "the word of faith" not in mutilated, falsified, or diminished form but whole and entire, in all its rigor and vigor. A lack of faithfulness on this point would result in a "dangerous weakening of catechesis and putting at risk the results that Christ and the ecclesial community have a right to expect from it," adding:

What kind of catechesis would it be that failed to give their full place to man's creation and sin; to God's plan of redemption and its long, loving preparation and realization; to the incarnation of the Son of God; to Mary, the Immaculate One, the Mother of God, ever Virgin, raised body and soul to the glory of heaven, and to her role in the mystery of salvation; to time *mystery of lawlessness* at work in our lives—and the power of God freeing us from it; to the need for penance and asceticism; to the sacramental and liturgical actions: to the reality of the Eucharistic Presence; to participation in divine life here and hereafter, and so on? Thus, no true catechist can lawfully, on his own initiative, make a selection of what he considers important in the deposit of faith as opposed to what he considers unimportant, so as to teach the one and reject the other.[314]

In his discussion of catechetical literature, the Pope concluded by citing what I have tried to show is neomodernism's ignorance of the transcendent in catechesis:

Numerous very successful works have been produced and are a real treasure in the service of catechetical instruction. But it must be humbly and honestly recognized that this rich flowering has brought with it articles and publications which are ambiguous and harmful to young people and to the life of the Church. In certain places, the desire to find the best forms of expression or to keep up with fashions in pedagogical methods has often enough resulted in certain catechetical works which bewilder the young and even adults, either by deliberately or unconsciously omitting elements essential to the Church's faith, or by attributing excessive importance to certain themes at the expense of others, or, chiefly, *by a rather horizontalist overall view out of keeping with the teaching of the Church's magisterium.*[315]

John Paul II went on to expose the red herring in pitting orthopraxis against orthodoxy, which our study of the American catechetical movement clearly shows is precisely what religious educators had done since Vatican II:

> It is useless to play off orthopraxis against orthodoxy: Christianity is inseparably both. Firm and well-thought-out convictions lead to courageous and upright action; the endeavor to educate the faithful to live as disciples of Christ today calls for and facilitates a discovery in depth of the mystery of Christ in the history of salvation. . . . It is also quite useless to campaign for the abandonment of serious and orderly study of the message of Christ in the name of a method concentrating on life experience. No one can arrive at this whole truth on die basis solely of some simple private experience . . . without an adequate explanation of the message of Christ, who is "the way, and the truth, and the life."[316]

On the sophistic contention that *Catechesi Tradendae* was advocating a return to rote-memorization of catechisms, the Holy Father counseled, "The blossoms, if we may call them that, of faith and piety do not grow in the desert places of a memory-less catechesis," contending that in addition to mere memorization the texts "must at the same time be taken in and gradually understood in depth, in order to become a source of Christian life on the personal level and the community level."[317] Nor would they sprout from a "creedless, doctrine-less catechesis which refused to be guided by the Church," a *sine qua non* if catechesis was to be faithful to Christ's command to the Apostles.[318]

In my late twenties I underwent reconversion to the Faith, and chose to respond to God's grace acting in my life by volunteering as a CCD teacher, preparing 8th graders for Confirmation in 1977. I cannot say at that time that I was certain about what Catholics believed after Vatican II, but my heart was in the right place. It was not until later that the Holy Spirit led me to Catholic apologetics summer conferences at Franciscan University in the early 1990s, where I began to relearn in greater depth all that I had been taught as a boy. Years later, in the course of research for this book, I ran across an editorial piece written by an English professor at Notre Dame which concisely summarized the fruitlessness of my efforts as a catechist prior to the 1990s in attempting to employ what I believed was the new catechesis:

> I am continuality struck by the irony that in the years since the Second Vatican Council, the Catholic Church has done everything possible to make Catholicism more "attractive" to young people. Gone is the emphasis on sin and hell. Gone is harsh, proscriptive moral teaching—especially about sex. Gone is Mass in Latin. Gone are "silent" retreats where we listened to sermons, read devotional books, said the rosary (on our knees), and went to confession. Instead, we have continual reminders of God's love; an emphasis on peace and joy; folksy, casual Masses with peppy contemporary songs; and "noisy retreats," where we sit on the

floor and have discussion groups, sing along with the guitar, and celebrate who we are. Yet I don't think there has ever been a time in time history of the Church when there such a wholesale rejection of the Church by the young. Does anyone really care?[319]

In the twenty years which lapsed between the close of Vatican II and the call by the world's bishops for a universal catechism, we have seen that, contrary to the neomodernists' claims that the new catechetics would make the faith more relevant to the lives of young people, it has resulted in widespread religious illiteracy and alienation from Jesus and His teachings. This neomodernist effort to redefine the faith and divine revelation in terms of experience coincides with the era of dissent from the teachings of Vatican II, the National Catechetical Directory and *Catechesi Tradendae*. But Our Lord does most intimately care for souls, and in the power of the Holy Spirit did move His Church to call for a universal catechism.

III

Concern for the handing on of the Catholic Faith was strongly in evidence among the college of bishops in calling for a universal catechism at the 1985 Extraordinary Synod, convened to celebrate the twentieth anniversary of Vatican II. The intent of the synod was to come up with sound guidelines for the proper interpretation of the council. The bishops correctly felt the need to interpret the council in terms of the entire Catholic tradition, for which a universal catechism would serve nicely as a point of reference for subsequent compendiums and catechisms in the various regions in which the bishops served.

Cardinal Ratzinger was of a mind that the need for the Catechism arose from "the problematic situation of catechesis in the seventies and early eighties, when enduring content had in many instances become distasteful and anthropocentrism was the order of the day."[320] John Paul II accepted the idea, convening in the following year a commission of cardinals and bishops from around the globe to prepare the draft version toward the goal of an accurate transmission of the Deposit of Faith for Catholics. The Church, while recognizing the sterility of doctrine without experience, in her greater wisdom recognized that any attempt to commit the whole person to Jesus Christ without attention to doctrine would invariably result in confusion. This universal catechism would provide a much-needed point of reference for bishops, catechists, publishers, and priests and religious, as well as laity in the preparation of catechetical material in the exercise of their ministries. It would supply a rule (or canon) heretofore lacking in postconciliar catechesis with regard to the Deposit of Faith, which had resulted in doctrinal division.

Serving as a point of reference for the commission drafting the catechism was the teaching of the Second Vatican Council together with the preceding magisterium of the Church. The Catechism was to serve as a guide for subsequent textbooks, which would present doctrine geared to the appropriate age levels and with sound analysis and context.

The Catechism of the Catholic Church was presented to the bishops in October, 1992; by 1995 it had sold more than eight million copies. In his Apostolic Constitution marking its publication, *Fidel Depositum,* Pope John Paul II asked pastors and the faithful "to receive this catechism in a spirit of communion," stating that it was intended to assist in the composition of new local catechisms which should preserve both the unity of faith and fidelity to the Deposit of Faith. Not surprisingly, the catechism initially was not accorded a warm reception by the religious education establishment wedded to the new catechetics. No doubt this was because its publication presented the greatest challenge to the cultural relativism inherent in neomodernism — their belief that past theological declarations are suspect, having been formulated in an age manifestly different from our own, which reexperiences divine revelation and gives it expression in age-appropriate terms.

In their response to the Church's call for a universal catechism, neomodernists belittled the teaching that revelation can in part be given expression in universally true creeds and doctrines.[321] Doctrine remained for them the enemy of lived faith, and so they persevered in insisting that Vatican II had steered catechesis away from doctrinal literacy toward making Christ present through a variety of experiences — word, worship, community service, and so forth. Of course authentic catechesis in Church teaching does specifically concern handing on the word — the Word who is Life, done by teaching doctrine in keeping with her universal mission to bring the Gospel to all mankind, still far from completion. Why this opposition? A reading of neomodernist literature gives the reader ample evidence of the apostasy of these professionals. Put simply, they no longer firmly believe that "in the mystery of Jesus Christ, the Incarnate Son of God, who is 'the way, the truth, and the life,' the full revelation of divine truth is given."[322] They do not firmly believe with the Church, faithful to God's revelation, that Jesus Christ is the universal redeemer of man.

While it is now true that the neomodernist positions that have blurred the truth of Catholic teaching for generations have been corrected by the catechism, the faithful are not fully aware of this. The oft-heard sentiment by those in the religious education bureaucracy that "we don't teach like that anymore" still competes in the catechetical field, disregarding the Church's assertion to the contrary:

> The law of God entrusted to the Church is taught to the faithful as the way of life and truth. The faithful therefore have the right to be instructed in the divine saving precepts that purify judgment and, with grace, heal wounded human reason.[323]

With the arrival of the catechism, the debate about what is Catholic teaching in general and on catechesis specifically had ended. Inquiring Catholics now had a sure point of reference for that teaching. The remaining question was whether or not the shepherds of the flock would assert their authority in overseeing the proper implementation of the catechism. Archbishop Edward Hughes admitted as much in his address as chairman of the newly-established subcommittee of the Committee on Education at the spring bishops meeting in 1992. In his remarks to the bishops Hughes articulated "concerns most of us have had about our somewhat limited role in the catechetical procedure," touting the publication of the catechism as "a time when the tradition handed down to us and through us can be renewed, enriched and enlivened . . . a time for us to draw ever closer to our brother bishop, who is Christ's Vicar on earth."[324]

Prior to publication of the Catechism, many bishops were anxious over the neomodernist lobby at work at all levels of diocesan bureaucracies, with good reason. The devotees of the new catechetics greeted the catechism with a negative media campaign, fearing a return to what they contended was a preconciliar mode; most likely they were afraid the catechism would bring order to the confused doctrinal atmosphere in which their experts were free to impose their ideas in the absence of episcopal discipline.[325] Nevertheless, given its best-seller status, the catechism was welcomed by most bishops and by millions of Catholics, necessitating a change in tactics on the part of the religious education establishment.

The change was evident in the theme of a workshop held at the Catholic University of America in May, 1993. Their new approach stressed the need to make local adaptations of the catechism, emphasizing inculturation, that is, the adaptation of the catechism to different or local cultures.[326] The presenters at the workshop argued further that the catechism could not be used as a text for catechetics, as it lacked the basic up-to-date pedagogy. Long-familiar neomodernist speakers, Frs. Sloyan and Marthaler among them, reiterated that religious educators must adapt the catechism to produce inculturated local catechisms, employing experiential catechesis to denude the texts of doctrinal content. In this the presenters completely ignored John Paul II's admonition that:

> This catechism is not intended to replace the local catechisms duly approved by the ecclesiastical authorities, the diocesan Bishops and the Episcopal Conferences, especially if they have been approved by the Apostolic See. It is meant to encourage and assist in the writing of new local catechisms, which must take

into account various situations and cultures, while carefully pre-serving the unity of faith and fidelity to Catholic doctrine.[327]

Nevertheless, from the time of its publication in the United States, the leaders of the new catechetics moved quickly to "Americanize" the catechism, assigning themselves as the professionals qualified to take control of its implementation. In doing so they displayed no effort to maintain unity of faith and fidelity to doctrine, as we shall see. Indeed, in a spring workshop held at the Catholic University of America in 1993, Fr. Marthaler's resentment at lobbying on behalf of the cat-echism was on display. To Marthaler's chagrin, it appeared that the lobbyists perceived what they called a "crisis in the Church!"[328] That the neomodernists' inculturation continued to harvest subjectivity and aversion to doctrine in catechesis is seen in numerous data compiled from the time of the Catechism's publication down to the present:

- In a September 1995 poll conducted by *Time* and CNN, 76 percent of Catholics disagree that using artificial means of birth control is wrong. Seventy-nine percent say it possible for Catholics to make up their own minds about these issues, and 80 percent believe it is possible to disagree with the pope on official positions on morality and still be a good Catholic, only 15 percent of Catholics say a Catholic should always obey official church teachings on such moral issues as contraception and abortion, A *U.S. News & World Report* survey reports similar findings—81 percent of Catholics dis-approve or strongly disapprove of the statement that using artificial birth control, such as condoms or birth control pills, is morally wrong.[329]

- The percentage of Catholics who believe the Eucharist is merely a "symbolic reminder" of Jesus broke down as follows:

    Catholics age 65 and older: 45 percent

    Catholics age 45–65: 58 percent

    Catholics age 18–44: 70 percent

    Catholics who attend Mass every Sunday:

    51 percent[330]

- Despite clear and repeated statement from the magisterium indicating that women cannot be ordained to the priesthood, a majority of Catholics dissent on that issue . . . with 42 percent saying that they 'strongly disagree' with the Church teaching, and another 16 percent that they 'mildly disagree.' Only 20 percent strongly agreed.[331]

- In a 1998 survey conducted by *US Catholic*, 81 percent of Catholics believe a married couple has the right to follow their own conscience on the decision to use birth control. Forty percent say *Humanae Vitae* was a mistake.[332]

- The results of a 2001 Roper poll show that 39 percent of the Catholic Americans 'strongly disagree' with the statement that 'abortion is never justified,' while another 20% 'mildly disagree.' Only 26 percent strongly embraced the Church's unequivocal pro-life position.[333]

Given the above data, the task of handing on Catholic teaching, to which Catholics owe the obedience of faith, will not be effective in the absence of faithful episcopal oversight of religious education in the United States. Ongoing oversight will be a tremendous challenge, for in 1993, just one year prior to the reception of the catechism in the United States, as the bishops gathered for their annual meeting in June, they were faced with a crisis without parallel in modern times. In our first chapter, I alluded to a direct correlation between a failure to uphold and live the Church's sexual moral teaching and the present phenomenon of the sexual abuse of minors by homosexual Catholic priests and inattentive bishops running interference for them. I will never understand how one could fail to see this as anything other than the fruits of a protracted failure to uphold and live the Church's sexual moral teaching in the United States since Vatican II.

The first effective step in authentic catechetical reform was the publication of the Catechism of the Catholic Church. In 1995, the bishops in the U.S. wisely established their Ad Hoc Committee under Archbishop Daniel Buechlein to oversee the process of examining the texts submitted by publishers seeking the Church's declaration that their texts were in doctrinal agreement with the Catechism. The assessment process does not concern itself with pedagogy, or making recommendations — it simply finds the text in conformity, or, informs the publisher of the changes necessary to bring it into conformity with the catechism. Any text making use of quotations from the catechism greater than 1,000 words necessitates permission from the bishop's conference and the Ad Hoc committee. I am happy to report that there is reason for optimism for those grief-stricken by the state of catechesis discussed in this chapter. In June, 1997, Archbishop Buechlein reported a "pattern of doctrinal deficiencies" in ten points of Catholic doctrine extant in catechetical texts under review by the committee:

1. Failure to present the mystery of the Trinity, often by avoiding use of the word "Father."
2. Insufficient clarity about the divinity of Christ and his centrality in salvation history.
3. Failure to present the Church as established by Christ, with magisterial authority, unity of doctrine, and an apostolic mission.
4. Failure to identify man as inherently spiritual, made in the image and likeness of God, an image disfigured by sin but restored to us by Christ. The impression is too often given that man is the first principle and final end of his own existence.
5. Insufficient emphasis on human action as subordinate to God's initiative in the world.
6. Inadequate understanding of grace.
7. Inadequate treatment of the sacraments as effective signs of the outpouring of the Holy Spirit.

8. Failure to teach correctly the doctrine of original sin and its necessary relation to the doctrines of grace, baptism, sin, and redemption.

9. Faulty conscience formation and "meager exposition" of the Church's moral teaching.

10. Inadequate presentation of the transcendent kingdom of God and of Catholic eschatology.[334]

Will the Ad Hoc Committee use its authority firmly enough to restore authentic doctrine to catechesis? I have noted instances where neomodernist catechetical publications attempt an end run around the review process by publishing works which do not employ quotes longer than 1,000 words, or merely do not advertise conformity, as seen in the following three texts selected from an online list of resources in one diocese:

- *Introducing the Catechism of the Catholic Church:*
  Traditional Themes and Contemporary Issues
  Edited by Berard L. Marthaler Paulist Press, 1994
  The articles in this book originated as talks from a meeting of nearly a dozen scholars invited by the Catholic University of America to reflect on the process that brought the catechism into being and assess its likely impact on the church in the years to come.

- *Essentials of the Faith: A Guide to Catechism of the Catholic Church*
  By: Alfred McBride, *O. Praem.* Our Sunday Visitor Inc., 1994

Like the Catechism, Essentials . . . is built on four pillars. The Creed, the Sacraments, the Commandments and Prayer. Essentials . . . puts the complex theological concepts into easy-to-understand, everyday English. Ideal for personal or group study, each chapter consists of a short essay on a topic from the Catechism, a practical life application, thoughtful reflection questions, prayer and a glossary of terms.

- *Understanding the Catechism: Creed*
  By: James Hogan Resources for Christian Learning, 1998
  Found to be in conformity by the Ad Hoc Committee to oversee the use of Catechism of the Catholic Church. Effective lesson plans, prayer ideas, classroom and parish activities, including use of the Creed video segments. A multimedia series for 9th-12th graders which breaks open the pillars of the Catechism in one quarter-length course. Written by current teachers who know how to teach the Catechism to high school youth.[335]

The first two texts, published by major Catholic publishing houses, do not give evidence of conformity, though one is edited by a notorious dissident, the other by one of the premier orthodox Catholic catechetical authorities in the United States. Absent years of experience in the field, the well-intentioned novice catechist, unaware of either Frs. Marthaler or McBride, nevertheless could rest assured in ordering the third text, whose author is not well known.[336] To date there is reason for optimism that the bishops are serious about insuring the integrity of the work of the Ad Hoc Committee.[337] Indeed, it will take a long time, but the bishops' committee reviews mark the first step of a long journey to restore sound catechesis begun by the propitious publication of the Catechism of the Catholic Church.

Another surprising sign of hope is an acknowledgement by the religious education establishment that Catholics today are doctrinally illiterate. The religious education establishment is perplexed as to exactly why, assigning blame to a self-indulgent society, apathy on the part of parents, rapid social change, indeed anything but defective catechesis on their part.

An additional hopeful development is the bishops' Education and Catechesis committees' *National Directory for Catechesis*, which has received the *recognitio* of the Vatican. It is documentary evidence of the American bishops beginning to exercise their proper role as the principle catechists in their dioceses at the expense of the established experts who have brought on the present crisis—indeed, the *National Directory* was compiled without input from the religious education professionals. The text draws abundantly from Vatican II, Sacred Scripture, the Catechism, papal and magisterial documents, and the bishops' own publications in catechesis. It is a first-rate document and a solid guide for the catechist and parents as primary catechizers of their children. The reaction of the experts was predictable; representative of their sentiments was religious education Professor Michael Horan's, lamentation at a workshop on the *National Directory* in 2004:

> He [Horan] held up a clandestine copy of the draft, and described his dismay upon realizing that the USCCB staff and the relevant committee of bishops have composed it without consulting NCCL. Bishops have offered more than 1,000 amendments, amounting to nearly a third of the text, and every one is automatically accepted unless it duplicates an earlier one. Sixty-four of the first 215 amendments were submitted by just two bishops, he said: Fabian Bruskewitz of Lincoln and Raymond Burke of St Louis. Four other bishops, including Thomas Doran of Rockford and Cardinal Bernard Law, late of Boston, accounted for most of the rest. Listing the changes that trouble him most, Horan noted that the term "ecclesial community" was amended to "Church." References to "deacons and their wives" became simply "deacons," and "lay ecclesial ministers" became "seminarians." Archbishop Burke restored one paragraph previously cut in the consultation process, and replaced a reference to "the Holy Spirit working through the people" with time phrase "magisterial truth."

> "In other words," sighed Horan, "we'll be back to discussing the problem of 'eternal' truth." The workshop audience groaned along with him.[338]

It is stirring to see the bishops "bishoping," though we must remember Fr. McBride's caution that the return to sound catechesis will take a long time. One Director of Religious Education, after hearing Professor Horan remind his listeners that "... the document [the *National Directory*] comes through *us,* the catechists" remained hopeful, exclaiming in conversation with Horan, "We are the ones who do the interpreting ..." to which the Professor acknowledged, "That's an ideological struggle we will be having for many years."[339] A reading of the National Directory registers the bishops' awareness that they have not been well served by religious education professionals; it now remains to be seen what oversight they will conduct to ensure sound catechesis in their dioceses. After six years in existence, the Committee to Oversee the Use of the Catechism, as of this writing under Archbishop Alfred Hughes, was still questioning religious education materials, as seen in his report to the November, 2004 meeting on secondary school religion texts. The Archbishop highlighted the following concerns:

- Some of the texts found to be inadequate are relativistic in their approach to the Church and to faith ...
- Our young people are not learning what we know and believe is based on objective truth revealed to us by God. . . .
- The sacramental theology which our young people are being taught is also often seriously flawed. . . .

- Moreover, moral teaching, like faith teaching, may be presented using tentative language, implying that morality is a matter of opinion and personal choice. . . .

- Other problems which commonly recur include a studied avoidance of revealed proper names or personal pronouns for the Persons in the Blessed Trinity. . . .

- The Christology in tests may be unbalanced with an overemphasis on the humanity of Jesus at the expense of His divinity. Sometimes the treatment of the Holy Spirit is either missing or flawed. . . .

- The interpretation of Sacred Scripture tends to rely almost exclusively on the historical-critical method and does not generally draw on the rich patristic and spiritual interpretation in the Church. . . .

- The approach to the Church often overemphasizes the role of the community. . . .

- In general, the high school texts are strong in their emphasis on the social mission of the Church and the moral responsibility that Catholics have in this area. The social teaching, however, is not always grounded in the divine initiative of the Holy Spirit related to personal moral teaching or to eschatological realities. . . . [340]

The need for greater episcopal oversight stems from the fact that the publishers of high school catechetical materials are not required to present their publications for review; submission is on a voluntary basis. Nor is there a requirement for bishops or pastors to use the texts in conformity with the Catechism. It should not surprise us that texts published prior to the initiation of the review process remain in use, and some publishers do not submit their texts. The results set down in the Hughes' report show that many remain problematic. At present, the catechist or DRE who wishes to use materials which conform to Catholic teaching must select from texts posted on the committee's website.

The bottom line in all of this is that should there come a day when a majority of bishops, pastors, DRE's, and parents demand authentic religion texts, market forces would respond to insure that publishers, interested in selling books, would give precedence the orthodox over the ideological.

While the situation is improving, problems in catechesis and knowledge of the faith remain colossal. The bishops must continue to exercise courage in demanding fidelity to Catholic doctrine, lest theological discourse acquire new meanings totally foreign to the tradition of the Church, with the subsequent danger to souls. My final observation on the subject is to remind the reader of Paul VI's teaching, echoed by John Paul II, that the crisis of faith we face is not merely the result of poor catechesis, but is also born of the absence of widespread evangelization (more of which appears later). *Catechesi Tradendae* reminds us that catechesis has as its objectives both the maturation of initial faith and educating the disciple of Christ to a deeper, more systematic knowledge of the person and the message of our Lord. The document also alludes to the reality that baptized Catholics too often are presented for catechetical instruction without any personal attachment to

Jesus Christ, but with the potential for genuine discipleship instilled by baptismal grace and the Holy Spirit.

Thus evangelization remains an integral part of catechesis in arousing initial faith, a truth to which many in the religious education bureaucracy have been blinded by the smoke of Satan. Catechesis also is about "educating *the true disciple of Christ* by means of a deeper and more systematic knowledge of the Person and the message of our Lord Jesus Christ."[341] We have the cart before the horse in assuming that all baptized Catholics have been made disciples of Christ; John Paul II's admonition was that baptized Catholic Christians must live in an environment which fosters a personal relationship with Our Savior and His Church. Where this not the case, catechesis is often not assimilated and subjects one to so-called "cafeteria Catholicism," which is fodder for neomodernist catechistical experts. Leon Suprenant has said it best:

> Trying to teach the faith to those who have not in some meaningful measure committed themselves as Christian disciples is like reading the owner's manual to a new PC to someone who hasn't yet decided that he wants a computer. The information will come in handy at some point, but the timing is not right.[342]

In the realm of catechesis, this phenomenon has gone far to bring about the crisis of faith upon us today. Those responsible for catechesis for the most part have not challenged Catholics to conversion, to repentance in light of God's Kingdom, for true discipleship means a radical commitment of one's life to Jesus Christ, around whom all catechesis is centered. An environment that is favorable to one's personal acceptance of Jesus' reign over their lives presupposes ongoing conversion in the lives of parents, pastors, catechists — all those responsible for catechesis. This environment makes fertile soil in which catechesis can take root and flourish. When baptismal grace kicks in and the timing is right, a true reference for the faith is finally at hand in the Catechism, a surefire weapon in the Church's arsenal against positivism and experience-based catechesis, the work of the Holy Spirit in guiding the Church to truth.

CHAPTER SEVEN

Episkopoi

As he went ashore he saw a great throng, and he had compassion on them, because they were like sheep without a shepherd; and he began to teach them many things.

Mark 6:34

Though already present in his Church, Christ's reign is nevertheless yet to be fulfilled "with power and great glory" by the King's return to earth. This reign is still under attack by the evil powers, even though they have been defeated definitively by Christ's Passover. Until everything is subject to him, "until there be realized new heavens and a new earth in which justice dwells, the pilgrim Church, in her sacraments and institutions, which belong to this present age, carries the mark of this world which will pass, and she herself takes her place among the creatures which groan and travail yet and await the revelation of the sons of God." That is why Christians pray, above all in the Eucharist, to hasten Christ's return by saying to him: *Maranatha!* "Our Lord, come!"

Catechism of the Catholic Church, No. 671.

I

I began the present study by taking note that many Catholics after Vatican II were told by pastors, curates, religious, or theologians that the sacred council had changed certain aspects of Catholic theology or practice, and consequently had never read the documents of Vatican II for themselves. It is therefore appropriate to begin our final chapter with a quick overview of conciliar teaching on the office of bishop, before offering a final concluding reflection concerning the present crisis of faith.

As the Father sent the Son, the Son in turn entrusted His Apostles with their mission of evangelization, willing that their successors, the bishops, should continue their mission "until the end of the world."[343] To maintain unity in the episcopate, Jesus placed Peter at the head of what He intended to be a permanent assembly (college). If one was to attempt a job description for the bishop as successor to the Apostles, it would comprise above all "to be with Him," that He might send them to preach, and that he might have authority.[344] The Holy Spirit at Pentecost marked the confirmation of this apostolic/episcopal mission of the universal (catholic) Church.

It is in the person of the bishop that Our Lord is present in the midst of the Church community, wherein through his service Christ preaches the Word of God, administers the sacraments, incorporates new members into His Body and guides the faithful to their eternal destiny, the Beatific vision.[345] The bishops have no less than the responsibility of taking "the place of Christ Himself, teacher, shepherd, priest and to act as his representatives (*in eius persona*).[346] In carrying out their mission, the college of bishops has no authority save that which comes from being in unity with the Pope, Peter's successor, who has "full, supreme and universal power over the whole church," which can be exercised unilaterally.[347] The college of bishops, too, has supreme and full authority over the Church, power exercised *always in agreement with Peter*, "the Rock," all strengthened by the perpetual influence of the Holy Spirit.

All bishops are bound to foster and safeguard the unity of the Catholic faith and safeguard and teach with a love for the Body of Christ, especially the poor, the suffering, and those persecuted.[348] Primacy is given to the preaching of the gospel, warding off whatever errors might threaten their flocks. Bishops are to be revered by their sheep, who must give assent to their bishops' decisions in matters of faith and morals, and especially to the Pope's authority, even when he is not speaking "from the chair of Peter."[349] The worldwide college of bishops infallibly proclaims Christ's doctrine when, preserving communion among themselves and with Peter's successor, "in their authoritative teaching concerning matters of faith and morals, they are in agreement that a particular teaching is to be held definitively and absolutely."[350] Their decisions must be adhered to with the loyal, obedient assent of faith on the part of Catholics. Thus, the infallibility promised the Church is present in the college of bishops when, with the Holy Father, they exercise the Church's Magisterium. When the Holy Father (or bishops united with him) defines a doctrine, they do so in conformity with divine revelation, to which the faithful must also give assent of faith (though this does not indicate new public revelation as concerns the Deposit of Faith).

The bishop is furthermore the servant of the grace of the absolute priesthood in the Eucharist, the lifeblood of the Body of Christ. Each bishop is given a diocese to shepherd with the help of his priests, a local particular church which subsists in the one, holy, catholic, apostolic Church. In his diocese, a good bishop must witness Christ to all, in the role of chief catechist to the baptized, and in evangelizing wayward souls and those who do not know the Savior. As chief shepherd, Christ charges him with proclaiming the Gospel to all men, proclaiming "the whole mystery of Christ, that is, all those truths ignorance of which means ignorance of Christ."[351] He must teach his flock that worldly things and institutions are ordered by the Father toward our salvation. By example the bishop leads his own to focus on "things that are above," safeguarding the doctrine of Our Lord and equipping his flock to defend and spread it with particular attention given to the unevangelized.[352]

The prime weapons at his disposal in fulfilling this charge are preaching and catechetical instruction based on Sacred Scripture, tradition, the Mass, and the Magisterium, along with doctrinal education in schools, universities, and conferences. As evidenced in our last chapter, ensuring that his catechists are competent in church doctrine is also paramount, as is his responsibility to control and promote the liturgy in his diocese. By his example the bishop should be fervent in fostering holiness in his priests, religious, and laity, along with nurturing vocations and missionary evangelical apostolates.[353] In each diocese, under the shepherd's ministry, the charity and unity of the Church should be manifest, because without it, "there can be no salvation. . . . For the sharing in the body and blood of Christ has no other effect than to accomplish our transformation into that which we receive."[354] Taking as his model the Good Shepherd, the bishop is servant to the point of being willing to lay down his life for his sheep,[355] and one day must render account for the souls in his charge.[356] The faithful in turn are to be as attached to their bishop as the Body is to the Head, that true communion is achieved.

One further topic remains in our summary of the Second Vatican Council's teaching on the episcopacy must be mentioned, that of the role of episcopal conferences. Since Pentecost, bishops in the have Church shared resources and universal hopes in advancing both the common good and the good of their local churches. Thus following Vatican II synods of bishops, provincial councils and plenary councils were adopted to expedite the mission of the bishop. The council Fathers hoped that these institutions would thrive, that local churches would experience the "growth of religion and the maintenance of discipline."[357] The decisions of these episcopal conferences, with a two-thirds vote of active participants and the approval of the Holy See, were to have force of law.[358] Tragically, the episcopal conference in the U.S. since the council has in many cases usurped the canonical responsibility of the bishop as chief teacher of the faith in his diocese as prescribed in *Lumen Gentium* and *Christus Dominus*. The rapid decentralization of the traditional machinery of church government in the episcopal conference has proven imprudent in opening the door to neomodernist-inspired forces operant in the work of their committees, commissions, and experts.[359] The writings of these theologians, priests, sisters and laity began to appear in the syllabi of major seminary professors and on the reading lists of religious and those training to be catechists, myself included. Of this a distinguished Catholic journalist and former spokesman for the U.S. bishops' conference has written:

That what is involved here can be called a culture [of dissent] is apparent in the fact that dissent has had — and even now continues to have — the support of a powerful infrastructure of organizations, schools, periodicals, and publishing houses. Its weapons include propaganda, mockery, the suppression of opposing views, and the tried-and-true practice of rewarding friends and punishing enemies. It has enjoyed the toleration, and sometimes the patronage, of a substantial number of bishops, though fewer now than in the past. It has been a contributing factor, or worse, to the sex-abuse scandal, the religious illiteracy of young (and not-so-young) American Catholics, and the sharp drop both in priestly and religious vocations and Mass attendance in the post-conciliar years.

And although morality is not the only sphere where dissent has been operative, it is the one where dissent has been most obvious and has had the greatest immediate impact.[360]

So it was that many bishops, psychologically ill-prepared to do battle in this direct challenge to their divinely-assigned role as shepherds, permitted the smoke from these forces to seep into their dioceses. As we have witnessed, more often than not this has rendered the Body of Christ hostage to those attempting to prevail against Peter and his successors, in no small way through use of the media. Space allows us to recount only one example — the document *Always Our Children: A Pastoral Message to Parents of Homosexual Children,* issued by the Committee on Marriage and Family of the USCCB. An

American bishop has provided the background to this document which makes my point here:

> As almost always happens when such procedures are used by committees of the conference, the illusion is given, perhaps deliberately, and carried forth by the media, to the effect that this is something the US bishops have published, rather than the correct information being conveyed to the public; namely, that most bishops had nothing to do with this undertaking. I believe one would be justified in asserting that in this case, flawed and defective procedures, badly in need of correction and reform, resulted in a very flawed and defective document.

> The majority of America's Catholic bishops were allowed nothing to say about this document. Still less were they permitted any suggestions or comments about the "advisers" and consultants used by the committee, who, by their own boasting and the ordinary "rumor mill," have been detected to be people whose qualifications in this area of moral conduct are highly questionable. The document, in a view which is shared by many, is founded on bad advice, mistaken theology, erroneous science and skewed sociology. It is pastorally helpful in no perceptible way. Does this committee intend to issue documents to parents of drug addicts, promiscuous teenagers, adult children involved in canonically invalid marriages, and the like? These are far more numerous than parents of homosexuals. The occasion and the motivation for this document's birth remain hidden in the murky arrangements which brought it forth.

Not only does this document fail to take into account the latest revision in the authentic Latin version of The Catechism of the Catholic Church regarding homosexuality, but it juxtaposes several quotes from the Catechism in order to pretend falsely and preposterously that the Catechism says homosexuality is a gift from God and should be accepted as a fixed and permanent identity. Of course, the document, in order to support the incorrect views it contains, totally neglects to cite the Catholic doctrine set forth by the Holy See which teaches that the homosexual orientation is "objectively disordered." Also, the document's definition of the virtue and practice of chastity is inadequate and distorted.[361]

As we have seen, many bishops in the face of this neo-modernist threat have proven incapable of willingness to lay down his life for his sheep. The bureaucracies operating on all levels in the Church were staffed with neomodernist activists and intellectuals who established an entrenched elite committed to the "spirit of Vatican II' in advancing their agenda of radical change. A noted orthodox Thomist and scholar has written, "Today it is the rare bishop who is in charge of the bureaucracy that has metastasized around him."[362] That this presented a major obstacle to furthering Vatican II's call to individual holiness is also evident in John Paul II's response to this phenomenon in his Apostolic Letter of May, 1998, *Apostolos Suos*. Here the Pope urgently reminded the Church of the limited authority of the national episcopal conferences and their bureaucracies, which were to be run by, and speak only for the bishops and not their staffs and commissions. He also instructed bishops that the purpose of each national conference "require[s] that an excessively bureaucratic development of offices and commissions operating between plenary sessions be avoided," and that "commissions and offices exist to be of help to bishops and not a substitute for them."[363]

II

Throughout history there have arisen certain rifts in the Church that disrupted her unity, separating whole communities from full communion with the Body of Christ. One of the Fathers of the Church sees this as a result of sin: "Where there are sins, there are also divisions, schisms, heresies, and disputes. Where there is virtue, however, there also is harmony and unity, from which arise the one heart and one soul of all believers."[364] In examining the causes of these divisions, Canon law distinguishes between *heresy,* the obstinate denial or obstinate doubt after the reception of baptism of some truth which is to be believed by divine and Catholic faith; *apostasy,* the total repudiation of the Christian faith, and *schism,* the refusal of submission to the Supreme Pontiff or of communion with the members of the Church subject to him.[365] Since Pentecost, the Catholic Church's doctrine has clearly been stated such that she expects those who become members of

Christ's body do so in agreement with the binding force of her doctrine.

I have tried to show that the neomodernist heresy borders in some cases on apostasy on the part of Catholic theologians, religious, and intellectuals.[366] Given Catholic teaching on Satan and his *modus operandi,* such spiritual combat is in evidence arrayed against what orthodox scholars have termed a "culture of dissent" since Vatican II — comprised of a so-called alternative magisterium, dissident religious, (especially the Jesuits) and finally, intellectuals operating in Catholic higher education.[367] As we have seen, this culture after Vatican II infiltrated a significant portion of the diocesan bureaucracies through which the bishops were expected to make disciples of men, the results of which were noted by Monsignor Kelly in 1979:

> Teaching priests and diocesan officials recently seem doubtful about any academic arrangement that confines itself to Catholic doctrine. Catholic universities, Catholic theologians, Catholic canon lawyers weekly declare independence of bishops and the Pope. A large segment of the Church's middle management — teachers, editors, administrators — has come to have suspicion of teaching effort that appears to be narrowly Catholic. Indeed, concentration on Catholic doctrine is no longer greeted in some Catholic circles, even as a pluralistic option.[368]

We have seen also that when the hierarchy began to interpret the meaning or application of the documents of Vatican II, many among her knowledge class dissented from magisterial teaching, effecting a controversy over the legitimacy of Church decisions and thus a crisis of authority, the net result of their heresy. In the face of what amounts to episcopal lethargy, such false, pernicious teachings were permitted an audience in high places within the hierarchy, several bishops themselves having been seduced by such opinions.[369] *De facto*, the audience granted the culture of dissent, divided the sheep, thus sinking the credibility and viability of the Gospel message for much of the modern world, in Paul VI's thinking a sign of the diabolic.[370]

Such accommodation to protestant neomodernist sentiments rendered the failure of the American bishops in safeguarding the flock so great that by 1994, the distinguished Jesuit philosopher Fr. James Shall mournfully wondered whether or not Catholicism still existed in the United States.[371] In corroboration, I share a remarkable document which has not received the attention it deserves, given its heartfelt transparency. In May, 1976, their appeared in a national Catholic newspaper an anonymous "Open Letter to Our Beloved Bishops," the work of an orthodox Catholic parish priest in a major U.S. Diocese. The priest asked aloud why it was that the U.S. Bishops routinely awarded key positions to men of questionable orthodoxy, while silencing those of unquestion-able piety, devotion and orthodoxy. The anonymous priest wondered why it appeared that the bishops did not want the loyal services of such priests in defense of the Church in time of grave crisis; indeed, he wondered why they refused even to acknowledge that the there *was* a crisis of faith in the Church. From the letter:

> Dear bishops, your silence is ominous. Your failure to teach, to correct and to admonish. . . . your unwillingness to welcome, transmit, and enforce papal teachings and directives — even of the most essential nature — isolates us from the lifeline of Rome. . . . All around us, voices contradict the orthodox Catholic position. . . . Since you are the one who has either chosen or kept these people, we obviously cannot appeal to you, successors of the apostles, living silently and ambiguously in our midst. . . .

> . . . we dare not even come to you for support or encouragement. You would chide us for our presumption, caution us for our lack of prudence, our "inflexibility," our lack of openness to change. . . .

> If the bishops do not uphold the authority of the pope, who will respect the authority of the bishops? . . .

> Often, we see bishops insist on loyalty and obedience to them-selves, while they in practice, if not in deeds, show no visible loy-alty and obedience to the Holy Father. . . .

. . . . Many priests are completely alienated from the Pope and, indeed *from the supernatural.* They are ordained social workers who insist that the kingdom is of this world. . . .

It is excruciating for the loyal priest, who knows these others are in *de facto* schism. . . .

When an orthodox priest attempts to maintain the purity of Catholic doctrine . . . he runs into the power, prestige, and financial clout of the diocesan religious education establishment. . . . And the conscientious priest is in for the struggle of his life.

And beyond the officially sanctioned heterodoxy, there is the continuing barrage of false teaching given by neighboring priests, assaulting the very essentials of Catholic doctrine. (Are they essentials? Indeed they are, for you bishops have given us the *Basic Teachings*,[372] and these are the doctrines that those in the pulpits and seminars openly attack in whole or part). . . .

And in the face of all this, what do we get from bishops? Silence, or at most an ambiguous, benign, private remark that has absolutely no effect. . . .

. . . "Will there be some way to continue to function as faithful priests if our bishops discard us or consign us to the wolves?"[373]

As we have seen, bountiful evidence exists of the bishops' failure to exercise responsibly their role in exercising the authority granted them (in union with the successor of St. Peter) by Jesus to teach and discipline those who, under the guise of *aggiornamento,* and ecumenism have worked to make what is something other than Christ's Church a reality. The "Open Letter" corroborates what Monsignor Kelly has termed the institutionalization of the debasement of the role of the bishop. We may thus summarize five factors to which many bishops, and indeed many Catholics succumbed, giving rise to our crisis of faith:

1. The powerful attraction that secularity has come to have for Catholic intellectuals.
2. The contemporary disdain of authority at all levels of the Church.
3. Confusing signals from Catholic chanceries almost everywhere.
4. Respectability given to dissent under the nomenclature "pluralism."
5. Conflict of bishops with each other and with Rome.[374]

The results of this condition in the Church were mass confusion among the faithful in many if not all areas of Catholic life and worship, a recurrent theme in these pages. The developing rift between the Vatican and the American culture of dissent precluded the bishops from presenting a united doctrinal front in their dioceses, with the anticipated moral lapses in the lives of the faithful. By their silence, the bishops in the postconciliar years were to consent to heterodox local catechisms, sterilizations at Catholic hospitals, education in contraceptive methods at pre-Cana conferences, and acceptance of the practice of the divorced remarrying without an annulment. As the bishops continued to shy away from exerting the righteous anger needed to drive the neomodernist wolves from the Temple, the second magisterium effectively persisted in influencing other bishops, priests, and religious in their heresy.

In the last chapter we saw evidence of the bishops' misplaced trust in the neomodernist religious education professionals. The contest of wills between the episcopacy and the religious education establishment did not cease with publication of the national Catechetical Directory, as we have seen, nor did the decline in the doctrinal literacy of the offspring of parents raised in the immediate post-Vatican II years, given lax episcopal oversight. The culture of dissent has also enjoyed the toleration, and sometimes the patronage, of a substantial number of bishops.

It has also been a contributing factor to the 2003 sex-abuse scandal. Recall the words of Pope John Paul II in a letter of March, 2002 to the world's priests: "As priests we are personally and profoundly afflicted by the sins of some of our brothers who have betrayed the grace of ordination in succumbing even to the most grievous forms of the *'myste-*

rium iniquitatis' (mystery of evil) at work in the world." As one among many possible illustrations, in the course of my research I received an email concerning developments in the homosexual priest crisis of 2003 which serves rather nicely as a frame of reference for our discussion concerning the U.S. bishops. It proved a disconcerting read:

> This morning, the Boston Globe dropped a bombshell of a story . . . though they seem to have little idea just how major it is. The title was "Bishops seek out opinions, in private: conference focus is church future," and began by explaining that some top bishops "met secretly with a group of prominent Catholic business executives, academics, and journalists to discuss the future of the church." The gathering was convened by former Boston College trustee Geoffrey Boisi and was called "The Church in America: The Way Forward in the 21st Century." Cardinal McCarrick hosted the event at the John Paul II Cultural Center in Washington, DC. The fact that any bishops were involved in a "secret meeting" is strange . . . but it gets a whole lot worse. Reading through the article, the author refers over and over to the "prominent" Catholics—men and women, both lay and religious—who were called to the secret meeting. Just look at a few of these names . . . and make sure you're sitting down:
>
> • Monika Hellwig—director of the Association of Catholic Colleges and Universities. Dr. Hellwig needs little introduction. Most people by now are familiar with her infamous statement calling

Humanae Vitae Pope Paul VI's "personal opinion" and her questioning whether Jesus is the only savior.

- R. Scott Appleby — left-leaning professor at Notre Dame and media darling who has been critical of Church conservatives for not being open to women priests and a married priesthood.

- John Sweeny — president of the AFL-CIO and open supporter of abortion.

- Kathleen Kennedy Townsend — former lieutenant governor of Maryland and an infamous and enthusiastic pro-abortion "Catholic."

- Peggy Steinfels — the former editor of Commonweal magazine, Steinfels is very open about her dissenting views. In fact, she laid them out in an article called "Holy Mother Church's Loyal Opposition: Disagreeing with official Catholic teaching on birth control and other issues should not cut us off." As you probably guessed, one of those tiresome "other issues" is abortion. [Steinfels is Pro-Life]

- Kathleen McChesney — executive director of the Office for Child and Youth Protection under the USCCB. McChesney has been reprimanded by some bishops for her willingness to meet with such dissident groups as Call to Action and Voice of the Faithful (VOTF), calling into question her impartiality when working for the lay review board. Her presence at this secret meeting certainly doesn't help.

- Mary Jo Bane — professor of public policy at Harvard. Also intimately involved with VOTF, she laid out her "personally opposed but publicly supportive" position regarding abortion rights in a paper presented at a Commonweal colloquium. . . .

The sender's analysis of this conference makes clear the all-too-common response of many bishops in the United States in the face of scandal:

> Why on earth would high-ranking bishops — including the president of the USCCB, Bishop Wilton Gregory — entertain a meeting with such known liberals and dissenters . . . and do it in private? Frankly, I[375] find it ironic that the same people who lambaste the bishops for being "secretive," the same people who want openness and transparency in the chancery, are now sneaking around behind the scenes, trying to escape the public eye.
>
> In addition, these are the PRECISE questions about the future of the Church that liberals claim the laity has a right to address. (Predictably, the issues of women's ordination and priestly celibacy came up in some of the meeting's breakout sessions.) But how can we be a part of the great dialogue they champion when it's held in secret?
>
> This says nothing of the fact that there isn't a single person on the list known for his or her stand in support of faithfulness to the Magisterium, the pope, and the teachings of the Church. If this was a meeting of "prominent Catholics," where are the prominent orthodox representatives? Where are George Weigel, Michael Novak, and Father Neuhaus? Why fly in representatives from little-known colleges in Boston when the orthodox president of Catholic University in DC, Rev. David O'Connell, has his office literally right across the street?. . . .

> When the pope called on bishops to crack down on dissent after the sex abuse scandal, I doubt this is what he had in mind. One final irony to top off this nonsense is the fact that the meeting was held at the John Paul II Cultural Center — the Institute constructed in his honor as a testament to his life and dedication to the Truth.[376]

My research was to turn up that not a few of the "prominent Catholics" mentioned in the *Crisis* E-letter have given evidence of neomodernist leanings in their writings, and serves in support of the points made in the "Open Letter" just discussed. The E-Letter's analysis is on the mark—the fact that the bishops met with these dissenting Catholics underscores the seriousness of the movement's ongoing attempt to prevail in combat for the soul of the Church in the United States. It is important to remember that most bishops are true shepherds, but it appears many are not. The Church applies here the Judas principle—recognizing that throughout history some of her apostles have betrayed her.[377] How was it, exactly, that we arrived at this juncture?

The identity crisis of American bishops under discussion, while perhaps undetected by the majority of Catholics after Vatican II, was well known to the more discerning in the Church, those who were aware that the bishops took a managerial approach to the exercise of their office after Vatican II. These bishops saw their basic functions as bureaucratic, not as teaching, governing, and sanctifying in the vision of Vatican

II. They understood the government of their dioceses to be one of mediation between contentious factions within the Body of Christ, not one of the pastoral care and catechesis of the faithful, thoroughly misreading what the Council taught regarding the office of bishop. Too many bishops became mangers, downplaying their role as successors to the Apostles.

The underlying reason for such episcopal failure, as for failure in any Christian vocation, was and is inadequate conversion to Jesus Christ, of true discipleship in the face of the mystery of iniquity. Genuine conversion requires that one "put on the Lord Jesus Christ," such that "it is no longer I who live, but Christ who lives in me."[378] It is not a task that we can accomplish on our own, but requires the gift of God's grace working in one whose heart is open to it. Have all bishops consecrated since Vatican II, indeed, have all Catholics been sufficiently converted to Our Savior Jesus Christ, and do they continue to undergo lifelong conversion, placing all of their trust in Him? It is an examination of conscience we all must make, but especially the shepherds. Thus I shall argue that the present crisis facing the Church is one of conversion, of seeking first God's reign over our hearts, and will be ended only by fidelity to Jesus Christ and His teachings. It is truly that simple, and yet that hard in the face of the seductions of the ever-growing secularity working in the world.

In an earlier chapter we noted the ambiguous position of many bishops in response to the culture of dissent's New York Times statement on *Humanae Vitae*. We now may examine why maintaining unity in doctrine was so difficult during the papacy of Paul VI, concomitant with the sexual revolution. We have seen that following promulgation of *Humanae Vitae*, the neomodernist culture of dissent under the headship of Fr. Curran launched a propaganda crusade against the encyclical which very few bishops openly opposed. Bishops who attempted a defense of Church teaching, notably Cardinal Patrick O'Boyle of Washington, D. C., received next to no support from their brother bishops.

O'Boyle had disciplined nineteen of his priests, who appealed their sentences to the Vatican. Rome's response was to recommend that the cardinal remove his sanctions, as Paul VI was fearful that to sustain them would produce schism in the Church in the United States. The Holy Father was of a mind that temporary tolerance of dissent would open the door to a more verdant atmosphere in which the reception of the totality of the teaching would be possible.

Thus was born the infamous "Truce of 1968," which served only to encourage further unfaithfulness, and which sheds light on Paul VI's remark that "We have perhaps been too weak and imprudent" in the face of Satan's invasion of the temple of God, for he had expected that after the Council a sunny day awaited the history of the Church. Of course what did dawn was "a day of clouds and storms, of darkness, of searching and uncertainties," in Church teaching telltale signs of Satan, "the deceiver of the whole world,"[379] of all his works and empty promises.

The 1968 truce taught orthodox bishops that in the absence of clear guidance from Rome, they should refrain from governing in the matter of dissent if doing so would produce widespread public opposition. It was this lesson which marked beginning of the American bishops' transformation to crisis managers rather than true shepherds in the mold of Vatican II. Bishops assigned themselves the role of facilitating perpetual dialogue between the white and black sheep among their flocks, in hopes of finding common ground. Heterodox bishops, priests, theologians, and religious learned that the advancement of neomodernneomodernist ideas entailed no fraternal correction from Rome. Thus it should not surprise us that the faithful came to think that norms of licit dissent were consistent with the teaching of Vatican II, and that all in the Church's 2,000 year history could be called into question.

In my third chapter, I mentioned that the bulk of dissent from authoritative Catholic teaching centered on Catholic sexual morality, beginning with the neomodernists' claim that *Humanae Vitae* was leading the Body of Christ into error. Inevitably, scandal resulted from these distortions of Catholic moral teaching, another attempt by the gates of hell to triumph over the Church, keeping authentic conciliar teaching from its intended results. These seminarians, postulants, priests, sisters, and laity were thus to fall out of full communion with the Mystical Body of Christ over sex-related issues: contraception, abortion, auto-eroticism, and homosexuality.

Paul VI averred that human *libido* was a fissure through which the Father of Lies might penetrate human hearts, minds and souls. This was especially evident in the infamous 1977 study by the Catholic Theological Society of America: *Human Sexuality: New Directions in American Catholic Thought,* a text found in many seminaries and on catechists' recommended reading lists during the 1980s and 1990s. The book's prominence explains in part the reluctance among many clergy to preach on God's plan for marriage and spousal love, given the role played by *Human Sexuality* in their formation during these years.

Its presentation of sexual morality is at great variance with what the Church teaches in her major documents. The study's heterodox authors and their sponsors, Fr. Curran among them, found the teaching given in *Humanae Vitae* to be too rigid and oppressive, focusing on procreation, natural law, and the physical contours of sexual acts, instead of the overall intentions indicated by one's choices and acts. Instead of using *Humanae Vitae's* norm for the spousal act—the unitive and procreative, the work substituted a more vague, elastic norm—creative growth, to be fostered by liberating, other-enriching, honest, faithful, socially responsible, life-serving, and joyous sexual expressions, the marks of a gospel ethic of love. Such elasticity was used to justify deviations from just about all of the norms of traditional Catholic sexual morality, including acts of contraception, sterilization, adultery, fornication, homosexual acts, and bestiality. The study's thesis, that sex is simply bodily and that the body is subhuman, a matter of sheer facticity, is, of course, Gnostic and Manichean in its roots, and has produced disastrous long-term consequences.

Human Sexuality also put forth a neomodernist-inspired interpretation of Sacred Scripture, claiming that Scripture was silent on the subject of homosexuality and that biblical moral teachings are so culture-bound as to be no longer applicable to modern life. This contradicts authoritative Catholic teaching—that there is a clear consistency in Sacred Scripture on the moral issue of homosexual behavior based on the solid foundation of a constant biblical testimony: the creation of man as male and female, meant to cooperate with God in giving life to new human persons; the fall and resulting concupiscence; the judgments on homosexual behavior found in the Sodom and Gomorrah story;[380] Leviticus 18:22 and 20:13; the teaching of St. Paul in 1 Corinthians 6:9 and Romans 1: 18–32, and finally in 1 Timothy 1:10.

The authors of *Human Sexuality* also failed to embrace Vatican II's Dogmatic Constitution on Divine Revelation, *Dei Verbum,* which states that "sacred Tradition, Sacred Scripture, and the magisterium of the Church are so connected and associated that one of them cannot stand without the others."[381] The Church gave us the Bible; only She has the competence to give an authoritative interpretation of Scripture, and does indeed take into account the way Sacred Scripture has been understood throughout Catholic tradition. But then, arguments based on Scripture are not very persuasive to neomodernists who do not accept its authority, as we have seen.

Because the American bishops did little by way of admonishing the authors of *Human Sexuality* (or, for that matter, the entire culture of dissent), clergy in teaching positions were quite successful in portraying the oxymoronic notion of faithful dissent as consistent with Catholic teaching, with disastrous consequences for priestly formation. This was seen in the loss of the sense of sexual sin, a tremendous decrease in reception of the Sacrament of Reconciliation, and the eventual emergence of an homosexual subculture in major seminaries in the United States.[382] The diabolical element in this is that neomodernist, intellectual self-deception helped prepare the ground for behavioral deceit and self-deception after ordination—especially in matters of sexual behavior.[383] The self-deception was in the heterodox view that the cause of the scandal was retarded psychosexual development and not personal sin brought about by the discrediting of the truth of Catholic teaching. What irony is there in that the Truce of 1968 brought about the very schism that it was intended to avoid, though it must be said that the schism planted by neomodernist ideology was primarily in the souls of the said bishops and their predator priests, thereby wounding the body of Christ.

The spiritual crisis confronting Christ's Church today will be ended when and only when the successors to the Apostles believe, with life-changing power, the truth of what Vatican II teaches they are—those who take the place of Our Lord Himself—teacher, shepherd and priest, witnessing Him with their very lives, evangelizing wayward souls and those totally ignorant of Him. It is a spiritual crisis the answer to which lies in a deeper, more radical conversion to Jesus Christ, with the shepherds in the lead in sounding and living the clarion call to holiness of Vatican II.

Shepherds must recover, with the help of God's grace, a passion for proclaiming the truth of the deposit of the faith. This will require the virtue of fortitude in the face of the culture of dissent, a virtue which, when in one's possession, enables one to conquer fear, even fear of death, in the face of likely trials and persecutions. Exercising this virtue, even to the point of renouncing their lives in defense of the faith, bishops must admonish the culture of dissent in their dioceses, informing its adherents that they are not in full communion with the Body of Christ. They must teach that the salvation which alone heals and restores, being in full communion with the Church, rests on conversion to Jesus Christ. Then, with the help of divine grace, they may think with the mind of the Church, not with the mind of the theologians. Having examined their own consciences, bishops must take the lead in a renewed call to conversion, to holiness in response to Vatican II.

At present, immersed as we are in a secular culture closed to God's transcendence and the Lordship of Jesus Christ, the late Fr. Richard John Neuhaus has stated succinctly the solution to the present failure of faithful discipleship: *fidelity*. And at this writing there are promising signs of such fidelity on the part of several "John Paul II" bishops, beginning to shepherd their flocks in the light of true conciliar teaching. These shepherds quite often appear in the public square as strong spokesmen for Catholic teaching. By their actions, they are creating anxiety amidst the culture of dissent, refusing to remain silent in the face of repeated offenses against the Body of Christ.[384]

We may take heart at recent developments among the bishops, particularly the atmosphere at the tenth general assembly of the Synod of Bishops in Rome in September, 2001.

The synod, rather than focusing on problems real or imaginary in episcopal governance, asked whether the Church of the early twenty-first century could boast of progress in the sanctity of all her members, of apostolic and missionary zeal and growth in the evangelization of those in secular society.

Cardinal Joachim Meisner of Cologne voiced that the synod bishops must tackle the present "crisis of secularization," and act as "a public witness to the faith" rather than a "moderator among differing views." Cardinal Darlo Castrillon Hoyos, prefect of the Congregation for the Clergy, furthered that the Church wants "bishops who guide us with courage—with the spiritual strength of Ignatius, Irenaeus, Athanasius, Eusebius of Vercelli, Borromeo, Faulhaber, and those who defended and maintained the faith behind the Iron Curtain." And Cardinal Joseph Ratzinger, then Prefect of the Congregation for the Doctrine of the Faith, presciently noted that it is not enough for bishops to offer a general message of hope to the world: "Hope has a face and a name: Jesus Christ," he told the Synod. "A world without God is a world without hope. Being at the service of hope means to proclaim God with his human face, with the face of Christ."[385] I am not surprised that the Holy Spirit moved the College of Cardinals to elect Cardinal Ratzinger to succeed John Paul II, nor that his first encyclical was entitled, *SPE SALVI facti sumus*—in hope we were saved.

CONCLUSION

And you he made alive, when you were dead through the tres-
passes and sins in which you once walked, following the course of
this world, following the prince of the power of the air, the spirit
that is now at work in the sons of disobedience. Among these we
all once lived in the passions of our flesh, following the desires of
body and mind, and so we were by nature children of wrath, like
the rest of mankind.

Ephesians 2: 1–3

In our days, many baptized Christians have not yet made their
faith their own in an adult and conscious way. . . . They call themselves Christians and yet they do not respond in a fully responsible way to the grace they have received; they still do not know
what they want and why they want it. . . .

John Paul II

*A*s a Catholic educator I have observed over the years
that, due to the ever-increasing secularization of

American culture, many baptized Catholics appear not to live the life of discipleship, wherein it is not they who live, but Our Lord who lives in them. Why? As a result of sin, and "its instigator, the devil."[386]

If ever there was one who believed in the devil's existence, it was Our Lord, who called him "the ruler of this world."[387] We must remember, however, that while the spirit of anti-Christ has been with us since the dawn of history, our enemy is no more than a rebel angel whom God permits to test us. The Father never wills evil, but He does permit Satan to tempt us, just as he allowed the passion of His Son, through which He showed that regardless of the demonic action, God always attempts to bring a larger good out of our enemy's apparent conquests.

The primary spiritual combat zone here is the human will; because God always respects our integrity, our free will, He never forces us to do good nor to abandon evil choices. Rather, thru His Church He offer us His grace and truth. As mentioned in our first chapter, it is the enemy who seeks to breach the integrity of the human person and effect the ruin of souls. And it must also be said that the contemporary polarization in the Church discussed in the second chapter is a clear attack by the Evil One. As Basil Cardinal Hume has observed, "I suspect that it is a trick of the devil to divert good people from the task of evangelization by embroiling them in endless controversial issues to the neglect of the Church's essential role, which is mission."[388] Thus, in this spiritual combat, trials will come, but God knows they are edifying for us, for they disclose the nature of the enemy and our own need for salvation and growth in relationship with Him.

Because of the deceits of the world, the flesh, and the Devil, many Catholics do not practice their faith to the point of standing out from those who are ignorant of Christ. In approaching the vexing questions of modern society, too many Catholics take positions based on a liberal-conservative spectrum, rather than on the teachings of Jesus Christ which come to us via His Church. Only genuine conversion, *metanoia*, the fruit of evangelization, will change this reality, allowing Catholics to experience the joy of faithful discipleship. No ideology may substitute for real personal conversion. In essence, *metanoia* means to question one's own way of living, to start to see life through God's eyes, and turn away from conformity to this world.[389] Genuine conversion predisposes us not to see ourselves as the measure of all things, but to a humility that trusts ourselves to God's love, which becomes the measure of all things. This was the central teaching of Vatican II: a renewed call to the faithful to strive after holiness, which means doing the Father's will in all things, empowered by His grace.

Holiness makes us love as the Father loves, and brings the fullness of life to the one who is loved, and so is meant to be communicated to the people of God. The Second Vatican Council teaches that bishops, as Our Lord's chief witnesses, must lead in evangelizing lost souls who do not know the Good Shepherd, proclaiming the whole mystery of Christ to them. Apart from holiness, the fruit of evangelization and conversion, we are "slaves to various passions and pleasures, passing our days in malice and envy, hated by men and hating one another," under the sway of "the prince of the power of the air, the spirit that is now at work in the sons of disobedience."[390]

Unhappily, it has been my experience that many Catholics (I, for many years, among them), were never effectively evangelized, and so never made a personal commitment to Christ and His gospel. Born into a sociological or traditional Catholicism, too many Catholics seem never to have met Our Lord! And, as we have seen, many of the flock since Vatican II are fundamentally ignorant of Christian doctrine, or may have received only nominal instruction, and are alienated from the Body of Christ.

I have witnessed the reality in the United States, where we are conditioned by a spirit of modernity to view religion as a private matter, where far too many Catholics grow uncomfortable with the call to evangelization and deep conversion of mind and heart. This is significant, for only from a personal relationship with Christ can effective evangelization develop. For Catholics like myself, there is a burning need to recover the certainty that we have the Truth urgently needed for the redemption of mankind. Why evangelize? When we evangelize, we act on baptismal grace "to preach to the Gentiles the unsearchable riches of Christ."[391] "To evangelize means: to show this path [toward happiness] — to teach the art of living."[392] If we are serious about our sonship in Christ Jesus then let us be not afraid to make the new evangelization the top priority in our lives.

It is right to give thanks and praise to the Father that He gave us His Son to redeem us from our prideful natures, the original wound. For in the end we are not saved by Our Savior's dynamic words, but by His passion, death, and resurrection. But Christ's obedient self-sacrifice must be responded to by repentance and conversion on our part. As Peter Kreeft has written, this new life in Christ "comes into us by faith, through us by hope, and out of us by the works of love . . . but many Catholics think we're saved by good intentions, or being nice, . . . or doing a sufficient number of good deeds."[393]

And what does true discipleship, our new life in Him, save us from? Hell. Unless we are saved from the kingdom of darkness by faith through grace working in love, this state of hell will become stronger and in time everlasting: "Go into all the world and preach the gospel to the whole creation. He who believes and is baptized will be saved; but he who does not believe will be condemned."[394]

In our day, when some modern theologians tell us that people may find their way even if we fail to announce Jesus as the Way, let us not forget Vatican II's teaching on the conditions necessary for our salvation:

> Those also can attain to salvation who through no fault of their own do not know the Gospel of Christ or His Church, yet sincerely seek God and moved by grace strive by their deeds to do His will as it is known to them through the dictates of conscience. Nor does Divine Providence deny the helps necessary for salvation to those who, without blame on their part, have not yet arrived at an explicit knowledge of God and with His grace strive to live a good life. Whatever good or truth is found amongst them is looked upon by the Church as a preparation for the Gospel. She knows that it is given by Him who enlightens all men so that they may finally have life. *But often men, deceived by the Evil One, have become vain in their reasonings and have exchanged the truth of God for a lie, serving the creature rather than the Creator. Or some there are who, living and dying in this world without God, are exposed to final despair.* Wherefore to promote the glory of God and procure the salvation of all of these, and mindful of the command of the Lord, "Preach the Gospel to every creature," the Church fosters the missions with care and attention.[395]

Being lukewarm in the preaching of the Gospel is thus forbidden, lest there come about a time wherein "although they knew God they did not honor him as God or give thanks to him, but they became futile in their thinking and their senseless minds were darkened. Claiming to be wise, they became fools, and exchanged the glory of the immortal God for images resembling mortal man. . . ."[396] Our Lord spoke often and bluntly about Hell, where we all may drift unless we put on Christ, let Him dwell in our hearts, let His thoughts be our thoughts: "The gate is wide that leads to destruction, and those who enter it are many."[397] In my years in Catholic education, I have witnessed close up a veritable silence on Hell as a reality for those who reject the Good News, rendering the teaching of Jesus Christ false, and eliminating a powerful motive for evangelization.

To remedy this, I believe Pope Benedict XVI has seen the need to recover the inseparable connection between the Mass and evangelization, for we evangelize to bring the sheep into the fold of the living God in the Eucharist, an experience which in turn compels us to accept our mission as disciples and evangelize. Would that an awareness of our present condition would spawn a recovery of the vibrant liturgical and evangelical spirituality of the early Christian disciples, who remarked often of their dependency on the Mass for their existence!

Evangelical proclamation of the Gospel invites the believer to be in relationship with God; hence, the importance of prayer—personal, popular, and above all, liturgical prayer. Only in experience of God's life does the reality of His existence dawn on the believer. Thus, in the Holy Sacrifice of the Mass, the most sublime prayer of the Church, emphasis should be placed on God and His action in the sacrifice, not on ourselves. Pope Benedict has noticed an error with regard to current liturgical celebration, that is, approaching it so as to make ourselves understood, which produces banal liturgy. The Holy Father has also said that it is not the personality of the priest which matters, but his faith, which makes Our Lord transparent. In the Mass, God acts, and we respond to His divine action, and in this way evangelization and liturgical prayer go hand in hand, wherein evangelization is the guide to communion with God, bringing the believer into communion with Him. John Paul II's reflection here is prescient:

> The Church never ceases to relive his death on the Cross and his Resurrection, which constitute the content of the Church's daily life. Indeed, it is by the command of Christ himself, her Master, that the Church unceasingly celebrates the Eucharist, finding in it the "fountain of life and holiness," the efficacious sign of grace and reconciliation with God, and the pledge of eternal life. The Church lives this mystery, draws unwearyingly from it and continually seeks ways of bringing this mystery of her Master and

Lord to humanity—to the peoples, the nations, the succeeding generations, and every individual human being—as if she were ever repeating, as the Apostle did: "For I decided to know nothing among you except Jesus Christ and him crucified." The Church stays within the sphere of the mystery of the Redemption, which has become the fundamental principle of her life and mission.[398]

The Holy Sacrifice of the Mass should be set apart by a spirit of deep gratitude and praise for the unconditional love of God experienced in the reenactment of the sacrifice on Calvary. How can we exemplify this spirit if we do not know we have received the gift of redemption, of salvation from eternal darkness, or if we think that we earn it of our own accord? Does not gratitude on our part presuppose that we know what we have been saved from and saved for?

Recently a noted shepherd of the flock has observed that our culture has "lost the vocabulary to understand humanity's oldest and deepest need: faith in an unseen God"; indeed, that "almost nothing of what we believe as Catholics is affirmed by our culture."[399] The bishop went on to say that the Mass requires a new kind of consciousness, a "readiness toward God, an inward awareness of the unity of the whole person, body and soul, with the spiritual body of the Church, present in heaven and on earth."[400] The purpose of my reflections in this book has been to attempt to show that the spirit of modernity has been undermining the Catholic beliefs that make possible this consciousness.

The Church exists to evangelize, to proclaim Jesus as Lord of all, not to put forth a sociopolitical development or liberation project. In 1983, John Paul II called the Church to a "New Evangelization," new not in content, but in fervor, expression, and method. In his challenge the Pope stated that no believer in Christ, no institution within the Church can ignore the supreme duty to proclaim Christ to all peoples:

> We cannot be content when we consider the millions of our brothers sisters, who like us have been redeemed by the blood of Christ, but who live in ignorance of the love of God. For each believer, as for the entire Church, the missionary task must remain foremost, for it concerns the eternal destiny of humanity and corresponds to God's mysterious and merciful plan.[401]

The Pope also reminded his brother bishops that they are the pillars upon which rests the work of evangelization. It inspires hope to see that Pope Benedict XVI has appointed Archbishop Salvatore Fisichella to lead a new Council for New Evangelization in accepting the challenge of re-evangelizing the "secularized" countries of the world.[402] Happily, as I go to press, the U.S. Bishops' Committee on Evangelization and Catechesis has just promulgated their *Disciples Called to Witness: The New Evangelization*. Bishops bishoping!

Our Lord commanded the Apostle: ". . . . rise and stand upon your feet; for I have appeared to you for this purpose, to appoint you to serve and bear witness to the things in which you have seen me and to those in which I will appear to you, delivering you from the people and from the Gentiles — to whom I send you to open their eyes, that they may turn from darkness to light and from the power of Satan to God, that they may receive forgiveness of sins and a place among those who are sanctified by faith in me."[403] Whatever the less discerning "new theologians" may say, the devil, in Catholic teaching, is a puzzling but real, personal presence Pope Benedict has written:

> He [the Devil] is a powerful reality (the 'prince of this world,' as he is called by the New Testament, which continually reminds us of his existence), a baneful superhuman freedom directed against God's freedom. This is evident if we look realistically at history, with its abyss of ever-new atrocities which cannot be explained by reference to man alone. On his own, man has not the power to oppose Satan, but the devil is not second to God, and united with Jesus we can be certain of vanquishing him. Christ is 'God who is near to us,' willing and able to liberate us: that is why the Gospel really is 'Good News.' And that is why we must go on proclaiming Christ in those realms of fear and unfreedom.[404]

That our world needs to turn from darkness to light and from the power of Satan to God, and receive forgiveness of sins is evident by "the abyss of ever-new atrocities:" world-wide racial and ethnic hate which increases wars of unthinkable, often genocidal violent cruelty; children who, if they are allowed to be born live in danger of abuse and violence, at times even in their homes; large urban streets serving as dormitories for the homeless; human insecurities and depression leading to escapism in drug use and even suicide; global poverty and pollution, over-consumption, and crime; popular loss of faith in global leaders; and scandals in business, government, and the Church. I am sure the reader could add his or her own to this list, and the age-old question is: what is the solution? Who may one trust to provide the solution that may be believed? Jesus Christ, God the Son, the Way, the Truth, and the Life.

And yet in the face of all of this, the Church has been lukewarm, comfortable in providing routine services for the already-baptized. I believe I have shown that what the Church lacks is a more faith-filled response which shows her faith that life's purpose and ultimate success come from being in relationship with Jesus, the convincing response to the question of how to live our lives. As Pope Benedict has written: " . . . evangelizing is not merely a way of speaking, but a form of living: living in the listening and giving voice of the Father."[405]

In Catholic teaching, our opponent the Devil truly "prowls around like a roaring lion, seeking someone to devour."[406]

Thought-provoking are the words of St. John Vianney: "The devil only tempts those souls that wish to abandon sin and those that are in a state of grace. The others belong to him; he has no need to tempt them. The greatest of all evils is not to be tempted, because there are then grounds for believing that the devil looks upon us as his property."[407] As the highest expression of Christian love on the part of the faithful, evangelization is our primary mission, for the value of human life depends upon our reception and implementation of the gospel of Jesus Christ.

We began our study noting the ignorance of Catholics about what the Second Vatican Council really teaches, and so I conclude with one final such teaching:

> . . . a monumental struggle against the powers of darkness pervades the whole history of man. The battle was joined from the very origins of the world and will continue until the last day, as the Lord has attested. Caught in this conflict, man is obliged to wrestle constantly if he is to cling to what is good, nor can he achieve his own integrity without great efforts and the help of God's grace.[408]

Our Lord commands us to "Go therefore and make disciples of all nations, baptizing them in the name of the Father and of the Son and of the Holy Spirit, teaching them to observe all that I have commanded you; and lo, I am with you always, to the close of the age." The slothful Catholic risks a terrible consequence for failure here: "So, because you are lukewarm, and neither cold nor hot, I will spew you out of my mouth."[409] With so many in the world waiting to hear of Jesus, let us go with urgency, unafraid even of death to deliver glad tidings, running the race hard, fighting the good fight to win,[410] looking forward to the finish line, meeting and spending eternity with the Church Triumphant, made perfect by the Lamb's blood. *Maranatha!*

ENDNOTES

1. Kenneth C. Jones, *Index of Leading Catholic Indicators: The Church Since Vatican II* (Fort Collins, Roman Catholic Books, 2003).

2. *i.e.*, 1978–87, originating with the papacy of John Paul II.

3. Hans Kung and Leonard Swidler, eds., *The Church in Anguish: Has the Vatican Betrayed Vatican II?* (N.Y.: Harper and Row, 1987), p. xi.

4. Philip Trower, *The Catholic Church and the Counter-Faith: A Study of the Roots of Modern Secularism, Relativism and de-Christianisation* (Oxford: Family Publications, 2006), p. 18.

5. Pope Paul VI, June 29, 1972. Homily during the Mass for Sts. Peter and Paul.

6. Quoted in Fr. John Parsons, "Examining the Impact of Vatican II After 30 Years," http://www.ad2000.com.au/articles/1996/mar1996p10_781.html

7. Positivism refers to the philosophical and religious thought of Auguste Comte (1798–1857). As a *philosophy,* positivism denies the validity of metaphysical speculations, positing that the data of sense experience were the only object and the supreme criterion of human knowledge; as a *religious* system, it denies the existence of a personal God, taking humanity as the object of its devotion.

8. *Cf.* "Confronting the Devil's Power," General Audience of Pope Paul VI, November 15, 1972.http://www.ewtn.com/library/papaldoc/p6devil.htm

9. See the *Catholic World Report,* July, 2008, p. 7.

10. Throughout the New Testament he is referred to by many other names, including Beelzebul (Mk 3:22; Matt 10:25; 12: 24), Belial/Beliar (2 Cor 6:15), the evil one (Mt 13:19; Jn 17:15; 1 Jn 5:18, 19), the enemy (Mt 13:25, 28, 29; Lk 10:19), the ruler of the demons (Mk 3:22), the ruler of this world (Jn 12:31; 14:30), the great dragon (Rev 12:9), the serpent, or serpent of old (2 Cor 11:3; Rev 12:9, 14, 14; 20:2), and the tempter (Matt 4:3; 1 Thess 3:5). And, of course, he is called "the Devil" (Mt 4:1; 25:41; Lk 4:2; Jn 13:2; Acts 10:38), which derives from the Greek word *diabolos* (Latin, *diabolus*), which means "slanderer" or "accuser."

11. http://www.religioustolerance.org/chr_demo2.htm#pub

12. Cosmology is the branch of philosophy which studies the basic principles of the material universe.

13. *Cf.* 2 Thess 2: 7 (Douay-Rheims trans).

14. *Catechism of the Catholic Church,* No. 407; *Cf.* Nos. 391, 395, 414.

15. *Ibid.* No. 817.

16. I am aware of Michael W. Cuneo's *The Smoke of Satan* (N.Y.: Oxford University Press, 1997). Though inspired by Paul VI's phrase, the author's subject is "Conservative and Traditionalist Dissent in Contemporary American Catholicism."

17. Jn 8:44; *Cf.* Jn 12:31–33; 16:11; 1 Jn 3:8.

18. Rev 20:10; *Cf.* 2 Pet 2:4; Mt 25:41; Job 4:18; 1 Jn 3:8.

19. Here I would suggest that we abstain from using the labels *pre-* and *post-* in speaking of the Church and Vatican II; there is only the One, Holy, Catholic, and Apostolic Church of Jesus Christ, the same yesterday, today, and forever.

20. On this a contemporary Catholic scholar has written, "Those usually identified as 'Catholic reformers' would, in at least some instances, be more accurately described as a wrecking crew for whom nothing short of Catholicism's transformation into a kind of high-church, politically correct American 'denomination' — Catholic Lite — will suffice." See George Weigel, *The Courage to be Catholic: Crisis, Reform and the Future of the Church* (N.Y.: Basic Books, 2002), p. 3.

21. On this later humanism see James Hitchcock, *What is Secular Humanism?: Why Christian Humanism Became Secular and How It Is Changing Our World* (Harrison: RC Books, 1982).

22. Recall the famous *cogito ergo sum,* 'I think, therefore I am."

23. Additional schools of thought adopting the rationalist methodology were Atheism, Materialism, Deism, Pantheism, and Skepticism.

24. Thus Locke set out the case that the human mind at birth is a complete, but receptive, blank slate (*tabula rasa*) upon which experience imprints knowledge.

25. Genesis 3:4–5.

26. I caution the reader to discern between what Catholic "traditionalists" write regarding this modernist influence on the Council Fathers, and what in fact the Vicars of Christ on earth have written on this.

27. See Encyclical Letter of Pope Pius X, On the Doctrine of the Modernists, *Pascendi Dominici Gregis,* Nos. 6–8; Russell Shaw, "Under the Ban: Modernism, Then and Now," *Crisis,* September, 2007, p. 13.

28. Msgr. George A. Kelly, *The Battle for the American Church,* (N.Y.: Doubleday, 1979), pp. 39–40.

29. Pope Pius X, *The Syllabus,* accessed 6/14/08 at http://www.ewtn.com/library/PAPALDOC/P9SYLL.HTM

30. For a most illuminating proof of the neomodernist apostasy of Teilhard, see Malachi Martin, *The Jesuits* (N.Y.: Simon and Schuster, 1987), pp. 285–302; Trower, *op. cit.,* pp. 141–155.

31. See Chapter 4.

32. The most influential Catholic theologian of the latter half of the 20th century, for a generation after Vatican II, Rahner's theology dominated Catholic seminaries. Though Rahner was a devout Catholic, his theological writings were heavily influenced by skepticism and relativism, offshoots of the philosophy of Kant, Hegel and Heidegger, and therefore not true theology as the Church understands it. One would be misled, for example, by Rahner's view that assimilation of the culture of modernity was as central to theology as the Cross; *Cf.* Trower, *op. cit.*, pp. 233–260.

33. On neomodernist elements in Fr. Schillebeeckx, see *Ibid*, pp. 310–314.

34. See Chapter 3.

35. See for example Eugene C. Bianchi and Rosemary Radford Reuther, eds., *A Democratic Catholic Church: The Reconstruction of Roman Catholicism* (NY, Crossroad, 1993).

36. Pope Benedict XVI, *Jesus of Nazareth,* (N.Y.: Doubleday, 2007), p. xi.

37. Shaw, *op. cit.*

38. In contrast to rationalist thinking, sense perception is a principal means by which God reveals to us: "That which was from the beginning, which we have *heard,* which we have *seen* with our eyes, which we have *looked upon* and *touched* with our hands, concerning the word of life—the life was made manifest, and we *saw* it, and *testify* to it, and *proclaim* to you

the eternal life which was with the Father and was made manifest to us—that which we have *seen* and *heard* we proclaim also to you, so that you may have fellowship with us; and our fellowship is with the Father and with his Son Jesus Christ." (1 Jn 1:1–3).

39. *Fides et Ratio,* No. 87.

40. Pastoral Constitution on the Church in the Modern World, *Gaudium et Spes,* No. 7.

41. In his Address to the General Audience of November, 1973; see above, pp. 3–5 [italics mine].

42. Genesis 3:4–5.

43. No. 37.

44. Karol Wojtyla, *Sign of Contradiction,* IV, no. 3. [Emphasis added].

45. My chapter was completed prior to publication of Philip Trower's *The Catholic Church and the Counter-Faith: A Study of the Roots of Modern Secularism, Relativism and de-Christianisation.* Trower corroborates Paul VI's warning that a telltale sign of the reality of the Devil's machinations is a radical denial of God, *i.e.,* Trower's brilliant assessment of post-modern atheism, which he styles a religious belief; *cf.* Trower, *op. cit.,* p. 20, n. 2.

46.   http://www.cnn.com/2003/ALLPOLITICS/10/13/column.shields.opinion.shields/

47. Xavier Rynne, *Vatican Council II* (Maryknoll, Orbis Books, 1968).

48. http://www.rbookshop.com/history/v/Vatican_History /Vatican_Council_II_1570752931.htm. Accessed 7/25/08.

49. For examples of such labeling see Thos. P. Rausch, SJ, *Reconciling Faith and Reason* (Liturgical Press, 2000) Ch. 1.

50. The magisterium is the living, teaching office of the Church which ensures the Church's fidelity to the Apostles' teaching in matters of faith and morals.

51. For samplings of their views *Cf.* http://www.geoci-ties.com/cathtrad/docs.html and http://www.sspx.org/. Prominent in this movement are the sedevacantists, a minority of Traditionalist Catholics who claim that the Papal See has been vacant since either the death of Pope Pius XII in 1958 or Pope John XXIII in 1963.

52. James Hitchcock, *The Decline and Fall of Radical Catholicism,* (NY: Image Books, 1971), pp. 24–25. This thesis is presented in Giuseppe Alberigo, *et. al.* eds., *History of Vatican II,* 5 vols., (N.Y.: Orbis Books, 1995).

53. *i.e.,* changes in the Mass, the Revised Code of Canon Law, ecumenism, reform of the religious, episcopal conferences, etc.

54. Philip Trower, *Turmoil and Truth: The Historical Roots of the Modern Crisis in the Catholic Church* (San Francisco, Ignatius Press, 2003), p. 11.

55. *i.e.*, theologians I have termed neomodernist.

56. *Address of the Holy Father John Paul II to the Conference Studying the Implementation of the Second Vatican Council,* February, 2000, No. 2.

57. Mt 12:25.

58. http://www.concilium.org/english.htm

59. *The Ratzinger Report: An Exclusive Interview on the State of the Church* (San Francisco: Ignatius Press, 1985), p. 19.

60. *Lumen Gentium,* paragraph nos. 39–42.

61. For example, a recovery of the Scriptural and Patristic understanding of the mystical and sacramental nature of the Church.

62. Trower, *op. cit.,* p. 13.

63. http://www.rc.net/rcchurch/vatican2/j23open.txt

64. *Cf.* Austin Flannery, O.P., *Vatican Council II: The Conciliar and Post Conciliar Documents* (Northport: Costello Publishing Co., 1975), pp. xviii-xix.

65. Trower, *op. cit.,* p. 16; *cf.* n.4, p. 17.

66. Thus rejecting the neomodernist notion of *evolution* of doctrine.

67. Trower, p. 20.

68. Canons 750, 751.

69. Quoted in *The Ratzinger Report,* p. 22.

70. Lk 10:16.

71. Trower, *op. cit.,* pp. 22–23, and n.

72. Trower, *Turmoil and Truth,* p. 23.

73. For the layman the most readable accounts are Janet E. Smith, "*Humanae Vitae* at Twenty," in Janet E. Smith, ed., *Why Humanae Vitae Was Right* (San Francisco, Ignatius Press, 1993), Ralph McInerny, *What Went Wrong With Vatican II: The Catholic Crisis Explained* (Sophia Institute Press, 1998) and George Weigel, *The Courage to be Catholic* (Basic Books, 2002), Chapter 3. For a more in-depth discussion see Msgr. George Kelly, *The Battle for the American Church* (Doubleday and Company, 1978), Chapter 6.

74. Mk 7:21–23.

75. Quoted in Kelly, *op.cit.,* p. 110.

76. Christopher West, "Redeeming the Erotic," March 6, 2009, *Theology of the Body Channel.* http://tob.catholicexchange. com/2009/03/06/453/

77. *Humanae Vitae,* nos. 1, 2.

78. *Ibid,* no. 3.

79. *Ibid,* no. 4.

80. See Kelly, *The Battle for the American Church,* pp. 166–172. Within hours of *Humanae Vitae's* promulgation, prominent American theologians had taken an ad in the *New York Times,* rejecting the encyclical.

81. Trower, *op. cit.,* pp. 164–168.

82. Robert Nisbet, quoted in H.W. Crocker III, *Triumph: The Power and the Glory of the Catholic Church* (N.Y.: Three Rivers Press, 2001), p. 416.

83. *Cf.* Philip S. Kaufman, *Why You Can Disagree and Remain a Faithful Catholic* (N.Y.: Crossroads, 1995), pp. 22–25.

84. Thus in so doing Lambruschini thoroughly misrepresented traditional Church teaching; see Kelly, *The Battle for the American Church*, p. 164.

85. National Conference of Catholic Bishops, *Human Life in Our Day*, nos. 49–54. Available at http://www.priestsforlife.org/magisterium/bishops/68-11-15humanlifeinourdaynccb.htm

86. Copy printed in a response to an August 4, 1968 letter in the *Saginaw News by* 18 Priests of the Diocese of Saginaw; *cf.* http://www.users.cloud9.net/~recross/why-not/Humane_Vitae.html

87. The branch of theology dealing with how we should understand the Church.

88. The "nature" in paragraph 6 of this document referred to in natural law is not our biological nature but our human nature as rational, free, relational creatures.

89. See Weigel, *op. cit.*, pp. 68–88. Weigel shows that this was due primarily to the bishops' reluctance in American culture to assert their eternal "binding and loosing" authority granted them by Our Lord.

90. Charles E. Curran, et. al., *Dissent in and for the Church: Theologians and Humanae Vitae* (N.Y.: Sheed and Ward, 1969), p. 63.

91. The Vatican Council, 1869–1870, Ecumenical XX (on Faith and the Church) Session III (April 24, 1870). No. 1792. Dogmatic Constitution concerning the Catholic Faith.92. *Lumen Gentium*, No. 25. The signers of the NYT statement failed to mention this teaching, in effect appealing to Vatican II to refute Vatican II!

93. For a lucid discussion of these documents disproving the dissenters' contention see Russell Shaw, "Contraception, Infallibility and the Ordinary Magisterium," *Homiletic and Pastoral Review*, 78 (1978), pp. 9–19.

94. *Lumen Gentium*, No. 12.

95. The position of the Association for the Rights of Catholics in the Church *Cf.* http://arcc-catholic-rights.net/sensus_fidelium.htm [accessed 7/27/08].

96. *Lumen Gentium*, No. 22.

97. In his homily for April 18, 2005. *Cf.* http://www.vatican.va/gpII/documents/homily-pro-eligendo-pontifice_20050418_en.html

98. *Humanae Vitae*, No. 11.

99. Richard A. McCormick, "*Humanae Vitae* 25 Years Later," *America*, p. 7.

100. *Ibid.*, p. 8.

101. *Humanae Vitae*, nos. 11, 12.

102. Apostolic Exhortation *Familiaris Consortio* of Pope John Paul II, No. 32.

103. Lisa Sowle Cahill, quoted in McCormick, *op. cit.*, p. 10. Professor Sowle Cahill, PhD., University of Chicago Divinity School, has taught at Boston College since 1976, specializing in the History of Christian ethics, feminist theology and sex and gender ethics, bioethics and ethics of war and peace.

104. *Ibid.*

105. Quoted in Smith, *op. cit.*, p. 334, n.2.

106. William E. May, *Sex, Marriage and Chastity*, (Chicago, Franciscan Herald Press, 1981), p. 3. Professor May's work contains a most convincing refutation of the separatist view, based on the Church's integralist understanding of human sexuality set down in *Familiaris Consortio* and in John Paul II's theology of the body.

107. *Cf. Ibid.*, p. 113.

108. No. 51.

109. *Catechism of the Catholic Church* No. 2332.

110. *Cf. Ibid.*, no. 2332; *Familiaris Consortio*, no. 11.

111. *Catechism of the Catholic Church*, no. 2366.

112. *Gaudium et Spes*, no. 51.

113. 1 Cor 1:20.

114. No. 12.

115. *Catechism of the Catholic Church*, nos. 1849–50.

116. *Catechism of the Catholic Church,* No. 409, quoting *Gaudiam et Spes. Cf.* 1 Jn 5:19; 1 Pet 5:8.

117. *Cf.* Gn 3:5.

118. See Ch. 1.

119. *Catechism of the Catholic Church,* Nos. 391, 392.

120. Eph 6:12.

121. Mt 16:22–23.

122. *Cf.* Gn 3:15.

123. 2 Cor 10:5.

124. 2 Thess 2:3.

125. 1 Tim 4:1; 2 Tim 4:3–4. This apostasy seems presently to be moving in the direction of paganism and/or the New Age phenomenon, atheism, agnosticism and hedonism.

126. Three among many samples, short and lively are: Smith, *op. cit.,* pp. 519–531; Mary Eberstadt, "The Vindication of *Humanae Vitae," First Things,* August/September, 2008, and Archbishop Charles J. Chaput, *On Human Life,* July 22, 1998, at http://guweb2.gonzaga.edu/~dewolf/chaput.htm

127. Robert T. Michael, "An Economic Perspective on Sex, Marriage and the Family in Contemporary United States," (July, 2003), available at http://www.spc.uchicago.edu/prc/pdfs/michae03.pdf. For a summary of social scientific research on the fallout from ignorance of *Humanae Vitae* see W. Bradford Wilcox, *Why Marriage Matters: Twenty-Six Conclusions from the Social Sciences* (2nd. Ed., Institute for American Values, 2005).

128. Quoted in Naomi Wolf, "The Porn Myth," *New York,* available at http://nymag.com/nymetro/news/trends/n_9437/

129. Eberstadt, *op. cit.,* p. 39.

130. I am indebted to W. Bradford Wilcox for my summary of recent social scientific research; *cf.* "The Facts of Life and Marriage," *Touchstone,* (Jan.-Feb., 2005).

131. Ceci Connoly, "More Women Opting Against Birth Control, Study Finds," *Washington Post.* January 4, 2005, p. A1.

132. Peter Kreeft, How to Win the Culture War: A Christian Battle Plan for a Society in Crisis (Downers Grove: InterVarsity Press, 2002) pp. 11–31.

133. On this see Denis Crouan, *The History and the Future of the Roman Liturgy,* (San Francisco, Ignatius Press, 2005), p. 138.

134. Jones, *op. cit.,* p. 72.

135. In the year 422 A.D. Pope St. Celestine enunciated the axiom, *"Legem credendi statuit lex orandi."* From the Latin, translated literally it means "the rule of prayer determines the rule of faith." In other words, "the way we pray, shows what we believe."

136. Alcuin Reid, O.S.B., *The Organic Development of the Liturgy* (San Francisco: Ignatius Press, 2005), p. 39. Dom Alcuin has given us the foundation of authority in the reform of the liturgy: 1) faithfulness to the principle of organic development, and 2) the authority emanating from the bishops in union with the Vicar of Christ assembled in an ecumenical council.

137. *Ibid.,* p. 44.

138. *i.e.,* the Renaissance humanists' yearning to return to the liturgy of antiquity, *c.* 65 A.D.—410 A.D.

139. *Ibid.,* p. 36.

140. *Ibid.,* p. 38.

141. *Motu Proprio Tra le Sollecitudini:* Instruction on Sacred Music, Encyclical promulgated on November 22, 1903; *cf.* http://www.adoremus.org/MotuProprio.html

142. Reid, *op. cit.,* p. 21.

143. *Ibid.,* p. 26.

144. We of course are not discussing papal authority in matters of *faith* and *morals, i.e.,* papal infallibility [emphasis mine].

145. *Ibid.,* p. 141.

146. *The Catechism of the Catholic Church,* No. 1125.

147. Quoted in Reid., *op. cit.,* p. 10.

148. http://www.catholicnewsagency.com/document.php?n=66

149. Reid, *op. cit.,* p. 191.

150. *Ibid.,* p. 149.

151. "Pastoral" as understood by the Church means that "the faithful should be formed in liturgical piety so that the people can participate in the Liturgy 'with mind and heart'"— pointing out the *contemplative* nature of participation at Mass, as opposed to Bugnini's activist interpretation belittled at the time by Cardinal Danneels; *cf.* p. 227.

152. *Ibid.*, p. 171.

153. *The Pastoral Constitution on the Church in the Modern World, Gaudium et Spes,* No. 44.

154. Jonathan Robinson, *The Mass and Modernity: Walking to Heaven Backward* (San Francisco: Ignatius Press, 2005), p. 18.

155. Heidi Sclumpf, "For us and for our Salvation? Reconsidering the Crucifixion" *U.S. Catholic,* March, 2005, pp. 13–17.

156. Robinson, *op. cit.,* p. 44.

157. Hans Urs von Bahthasar, "Human Religion and the Religion of Jesus Christ," in *New Elucidations,* trans. Sr. Mary Theresilde Skerry (San Francisco: Ignatius Press, 1986), p. 76.

158. *Ibid.*, p. 53.

159. Eric Voegelin, *From Enlightenment to Revolution,* (Durham: Duke University Press, 1975), p. 3.

160. Robinson, *op. cit.,* p. 77.

161. Kant's influence on the Jesuit Fr. Karl Rahner in particular was significant; see p. 11, n.2.

162. *Ibid,* pp. 82–84.

163. *Ibid.*, pp. 84–85.

164. Trower, *op. cit.,* p. 134.

165. *Ibid.*, p. 99, n.4.

166. Joseph Ratzinger, *Milestones: Memoirs 1927–1977* (San Francisco: Ignatius Press, 1998), p. 44.

167. In this Hegel borders on evolutionary pantheism; *cf.* Trower, *op. cit.*, p. 134.

168. Hegel rejected appeals to universal moral, legal, or religious principles, to a transcendent God and individual conscience as sources of ethics.

169. Robinson, *op. cit.*, p. 130.

170. G. W. F. Hegel, quoted in *ibid.*, p. 131.

171. *Ibid.*, pp. 132–133.

172. *Ibid.*, p. 137.

173. J. Frank Henderson, Stephen Larson, Kathleen Quinn, *Liturgy, Justice and the Reign of God: Integrating Vision and Practice,* accessed at http://www.jfrankhenderson.com/pdf/LJRG.pdf, p. 55.

174. Robinson, *op. cit.*, p. 139.

175. *Ibid.*, p. 142.

176. *Ibid.*, p. 146.

177. *Rite* consists of the manner of performing all services for the worship of God and the sanctification of men, *i.e.*, the administration of sacraments, among which the service of the Holy Eucharist, as being also the Sacrifice, is the most important element of all; the series of psalms, lessons, prayers, etc., divided into "hours," to make up together the Divine Office; and all other religious and ecclesiastical functions, called sacramentals.

178. Ratzinger, *op. cit.*, p. 168.

179. *Sacrosanctum Concilium*, No. 23.

180. Denis Crouan, *The History and Future of the Roman Liturgy* (San Francisco: Ignatius Press, 2005), p.147.

181. Ratzinger, *op. cit.*, pp. 122–123.

182. Thus what is preeminent today is what Dom Alcuin Read has termed "activist" liturgy, having as many people doing as much as possible so as to be actively involved — hardly active participation taught by Vatican II.

183. Apostolic letter *Vicesimus Quintus Annus*, No. 10.

184. *Sacrosanctum Concilium*, No. 4.

185. *Ibid.*, No. 23.

186. Klaus Gamber, *The Reform of the Roman Liturgy*, (San Juan Capistrano: *Una Voce* Press, 1993), p. 61.

187. Michael Davies, *Liturgical Time Bombs in Vatican II*, (Rockford: Tan Books, 2003), pp. 24–27.

188. Apostolic Constitution *Missale Romanum*, http://www.vatican.va/holy_father/paul_vi/apost_constitutions/documents/hf_p-vi_apc_19690403_missale-romanum_en.html

189. It should not then surprise us that in July, 2007 Pope Benedict XVI issued *motu proprio* his Apostolic Letter *Summorum Pontificum*, making it permissible to celebrate the Sacrifice of the Mass following the typical edition of the Roman Missal promulgated by Bl. John XXIII in 1962 and never abrogated, as an extraordinary form of the Liturgy of the Church.

190. Ratzinger, *op. cit.*, p. 147.

191. *i.e.*, "as though there were no God."

192. *Ibid.*, pp. 148–149.

193. *Sacrosanctum Concilium*, No. 10.

194. Joseph Cardinal Ratzinger, *The Spirit of the Liturgy* (San Francisco: Ignatius Press, 2000), pp. 19–20.

195. *Ibid.*, p. 21.

196. No. 7.

197. *Ibid.*, p. 23.

198. Jonathan Robinson, *The Mass and Modernity* (San Francisco: Ignatius Press, 2005), p. 18.

199. Kreeft, *op. cit.*, p. 27.

200. *Ibid.*, p. 29.

201. Robert Royal, "The Council at 35," *Crisis*, December, 2000, pp. 59–60.

202. *Ibid.*

203. *Supra.*, p. 3.

204. Representative samples are: Ann Patrick Ware, ed., *Midwives of the Future: American Sisters Tell Their Story* (Kansas City: Leaven Press, 1985); Sandra M. Schneiders, , *Finding the Treasure: Locating Catholic Religious Life in a New Ecclesial and Cultural Context*, (Mahwah, Paulist Press, 2000); *With Oil in Their Lamps: Faith, Feminism and the Future*, (New York: Paulist, 2000); Anne M. Clifford, *Introducing Feminist Theology*, (Maryknoll, NY: Orbis, 2001); Rosemary Radford

Ruether, Women and Redemption: A Theological History, (Minneapolis: Fortress Press, 1998); Catherine Mowry LaCugna, ed., *Freeing Theology: the Essentials of Theology in Feminist Perspective,* (San Francisco: Harper, 1993), Sallie McFague, *Life Abundant: Rethinking Theology and Economy for a Planet in Peril,* (Minneapolis: Fortress Press, 2001).

205. Mt 13:18.

206. See Ann Carey, *Sisters in Crisis: the Tragic Unraveling of Women's Religious Communities,* (Huntington: Our Sunday Visitor, 1997).

207. Immanentism, it will be recalled, is the belief that God exists in, and extends into the entire created universe, including the individual.

208. Ware, *op. cit.,* p. 10; *cf.* Carey, *op. cit.,* pp. 18–35.

209. Sr. Mary Augustine, O.P.; *Cf.* http://www.ad2000.com.au/articles/2005/feb2005p10_1840.html (accessed 8/1/07).

210. "of his own accord."

211. Mt 5:48.

212. Mt 22:37–39.

213. *Lumen Gentium,* nos. 43, 44.

214. *Evangelica Testificatio,* On the Renewal of the Religious Life According to the Teaching of the Second Vatican Council, no. 7; *cf. Lumen Gentium,* No. 44.

215. *Lumen Gentium,* No. 44.

216. *Ibid.* No. 45.

217. Decree on the Adaptation and Renewal of Religious Life, *Perfectae Caritatis,* No. 2.

218. *Ibid.* No.4.

219. *Ibid.,* No. 17.

220. *Ecclesiae Sanctae,* No. 43.

221. Carey, *op. cit.,* p. 42.

222. Kelly, *op. cit.,* p. 270.

223. *Time,* February 23, 1970. http://www.time.com/time/magazine/article/0,9171,876640-2,00.html (accessed 7/13/2007)

224. *Time,* March 23, 1972. http://www.time.com/time/magazine/article/0,9171,942531,00.html (accessed 7/13/2007)

225. Notables given secular media attention were the School Sisters of St. Francis, under Sr. Francis Borgia Rothluebber, and New York City's Sisters of Charity. Kelly, *op. cit.,* pp. 272–294; *Cf.* Carey, *op. cit.,* pp. 38–46, Ware, *op. cit.*

226. The devastating consequences of this occurrence for catechesis will be examined in the following chapter.

227. Quoted in http://www.rc.net/rcchurch/vatican2/j23open.txt (accessed 7/16/07)

228. *The Ratzinger Report: An Exclusive Interview on the State of the Church,* p. 30.

229. Responding to Vatican Council II, the U.S. Catholic Bishops called laity, priests, religious, and bishops to a two-year consultative process that culminated in a U.S. bicentennial year conference, "With Liberty and Justice for All, A Call

to Action" in Detroit in October, 1976. The bishops inquired of the attendees: what is the charism, what should be the character of the Catholic Church in America? Claiming *Guidance by the Spirit,* the delegates called for a Church of inclusion, justice, and accountability. Cardinal John Dearden closed the conference by imploring, "This weekend we have experienced *a new way of being Church.* Go home and *keep us bishops accountable.*" [emphases added]. *Lumen Gentium* supplied the answers to both of the bishops' questions, though the fact that Dearden asked the laity to keep the bishops accountable can be construed as his fundamental ignorance of the dogmatic constitution some two years hence.

230. Art. IV, Sec. 1 of the CMSW statutes of 1962, quoted in Kelly, *op. cit.,* p. 257.

231. German Redemptorist Fr. Bernard Haring, a *peritus* at Vatican II and author of *The Law of Christ,* in which he wrote, "But what shall we say of an ecclesiastical writer, theologian, or scientist who thinks he has reasons to reject the judgment of the Church's authority, particularly if his own intellectual attitude or position has been affected?. . . . He should first of all carefully study. . . . All further public defense of his position must be studiously and respectfully avoided, unless he is absolutely convinced in conscience that defense of his condemned views is of great importance for the understanding or defense of the faith and for the promotion of Christian

piety." (v. ii., p.52); Ex-Jesuit Bernard Cooke to date is Loyola Professor of Theology Emeritus at the College of the Holy Cross and author of many books, including *Power and the Spirit of God: Toward an Experience-Based Pneumatology* (2004); Fr. Eugene Kennedy received his A.B. from Maryknoll in 1950, and his S.T.B. and M.R.E. from Maryknoll Seminary in 1955. In June, 1955 he was ordained a Maryknoll priest. Kennedy taught at Maryknoll College in 1955-1956 before beginning graduate work in psychology at Catholic University in 1956. He received an M.A.in 1958 and a Ph.D. in 1962, both in psychology. Kennedy then returned to Maryknoll College as a professor of psychology where he remained until 1969. He became professor of psychology at Loyola University of Chicago in 1969, and was laicized in 1977. He is married to Sara Charles.

232. Carey, *op. cit.,* p. 109.

233. *Ibid.* pp. 111–112.

234. *Ibid.* pp. 113–115.

235. *Ibid.* p. 121.

236. *Ibid.* pp. 119–121; *cf.* Kelly, *op. cit.,* p. 270.

237. *Ibid.* p. 121.

238. Hereafter cited as LCWR.

239. From 1965-2002 the populations of sisters declined from 179,954 to 75,500, a 58% decrease. *Cf.* Jones, *op. cit.,* p. 36.

240. Carey, *op. cit.,* pp. 307–310.

241. *Cf.* http://www.cultureshocktv.com/coulson/coulson1. html (accessed 7/14/07)

242. For a convincing study of the part played by dissent from Catholic moral teaching intertwined with psychotherapy and the therapeutic mentality in the homosexual priests' crisis of 2002, see George Weigel, *The Courage to be Catholic: Crisis, Reform and the Future of the Church* (N.Y.: Basic Books, 2002), pp. 73–80.

243. http://www.sistersihmofwichita.org/pages/news. htm. (accessed 7/14/07) The author has had the privilege of meeting the "remnant" sisters of this order, now engaged in teaching in Kansas.

244. For the entire interview, see http://www.ewtn.com/ library/PRIESTS/COULSON.TXT; *Cf.* Philip Trower, *The Catholic Church and the Counter-Faith: A Study of the Roots of Modern Secularism, Relativism and De-Christianisation* (Oxford: Family Publications, 2006), pp. 176–178.

245. Quoted in Carey, *op. cit.*, p. 127.

246. The phrase belongs to Fr. Benedict J. Groeschel, CFR.

247. *Catechism of the Catholic Church*, No. 1850.

248. Hitchcock, *op. cit.*, p. 64.

249. See Chapter 1.

250. Donna Steichen, *Ungodly Rage: The Hidden Face of Catholic Feminism,* (San Francisco, Ignatius Press, 1991). My account

of "Catholic feminism" largely follows her first-hand observance of feminist influence on the Catholic women discussed.

251. *Ibid.* p. 202.

252. *Ibid.,* p. 203.

253. Coven was originally a late medieval Scots word meaning
a gathering of any kind. It derives from the Latin root word
convenire, meaning to come together or to gather. The first
recorded use of it being applied to witches comes from 1662
in a witch-trial which described a coven of thirteen members.
The word *coven* remained largely unused in English until 1921
when Margaret Murray promoted the idea, now much dis-
puted, that all witches across Europe met in groups of thirteen which they called "covens."

254. Radford-Reuther was raised in a devout yet liberal/ecu-
menical Catholic home, from which she acquired a belief that
God is the matriarchal ground of being. For Radford-Reuther
theology must engage human beings through critical dialogue, prayer, and social action in a continuing compassionate
commitment to the healing and liberation of all humans and
the earth. Given her presumption of the patriarchal nature
of traditional theology, she posits three stages of development toward this: a critique of sexism, androcentrism, and
misogyny; a recovery of alternative traditions that affirm the
independence and the full personhood of women; and reconstruction of the whole structure of a pluralistic and ecological

Christian theology with whole personhood of women as its core.

255. Steichen, *op. cit., p.* 30.

256. *Ibid.*

257. Wicca, most probably rooted in pagan religions, was popularized in 1954 by a retired British civil servant named Gerald Gardner, who claimed that the religion was a modern survival of an old witchcraft religion, which had existed in secret for hundreds of years, originating in the pre-Christian Paganism of Europe. For a further discussion, see also Fr. Mitch Pacwa, S.J., *Catholics and the New Age: How Good people Are Being Drawn into Jungian Psychology, The Enneagram, and the Age of Aquarius* (Ann Arbor, Servant Publications, 1992); Brian Clowes, *Call to Action or Call to Apostasy? How Dissenters Plan to Remake the Catholic Church in their Own Image* (Front Royal, Human Life International, 1997); Randy England, *The Unicorn in the Sanctuary: The Impact of the New Age Movement on the Catholic Church* (Rockford, Tan Books, 1990).

258. *Ibid.* p. 63.

259. *Ibid.,* p. 64; *Cf.* http://www.lgbtran.org/Interview.aspx?ID=9 (accessed 8/4/07)

260. *Cf.* Jn 3:18–20; Rom 3:23–25; Col 1:13–14.

261. *Cf.* Steichen, *op. cit.,* pp. 9, 11.

262. Mother Teresa of Calcutta, *A Gift for God: Prayers and Meditations,* (New York: Harper & Row, 1975), pp. 68–69.

263. Carmen Guerra, Letter to Editor, *National Catholic Register*, May 18, 1986.

264. Steichen, *op. cit.*, p. 117.

265. Matthew Fox, *The Coming of the Cosmic Christ* (San Francisco: HarperCollins Publishers, 1988), pp. 41–42; 48. Thus, traditional Catholic doctrine takes an inferior or even irrelevant role in Fox's view, as is the case in most New Age beliefs. In 1993, Fox was dismissed by the Dominicans and became an Episcopal priest in 1994. For a most enlightening biographical account of this apostate, see. Ryan Blitstein, "The Reformation of Matthew Fox," San Francisco Weekly, September 7, 2005 [http://www.sfweekly.com/2005-09-07/news/the-reformation-of-matthew-fox/3 (accessed 8/4/07).

266. From the Greek *gnostikos*, "good at knowing."

267. *Cf.* Steichen, *op. cit.*, pp. 161–163.

268. *Cf.* 1 Cor 7:34.

269. *Cf.* Steichen, *op. cit.*, p. 145. Pneumatology is the study of spiritual beings and phenomena, especially the interactions between humans and God.

270. *Ibid.* p. 124.

271. *Ibid.* pp. 148–149.

272. *Ibid.* p. 151.

273. *Ibid.* p. 169.

274. On these especially *cf. Ibid.* pp.167–77, 182–183, 280–284, 310.

275. Rosemary Radford-Reuther, quoted in *Ibid.* p. 302.

276. See http://religiouslife.com/vocsearch/search.phtml for communities in the United States which adhere to *Perfectae Caritatis.*

277. Benedict Groeschel, CFR, The Life and Death of Religious Life," *First Things,"* June/July 2007, p. 15.

278. Apostolic Exhortation *Vita Consecrata,* On the Consecrated Life and its Mission in the Church and in the World, No. 1.

279. Congregation for Institutes of Consecrated Life and Societies of Apostolic Life, *Starting Afresh From Christ: A Renewed Commitment to Consecrated Life in the Third Millenium,* No. 11.

280. Julia Duin, "Vatican Probes Nuns' Heterodoxy," *Washington Times,* April 20, 2009, accessed 7/6/09 at http://www.washingtontimes.com/news/2009/apr/20/vatican-probes-nuns-lack-of-adherence-to-doctrine/ *Cf.* Ann Carey, "Post-Christian Sisters," *The Catholic World Report,* July, 2009, pp. 17–22.

281. See "Women Religious not Complying With Vatican Study," *National Catholic Reporter,* November 4, 2009 accessed at http://ncronline.org/news/women/women-religious-not-complying-vatican-study

282. See for example, The Dominican Sisters of Mary, Mother of the Eucharist at http://www.sistersofmary.org/ and the

Dominican Sisters of St. Cecelia at http://www.youtube.
com/watch?v=uFFiNRvXBQw&eurl=

283. Jn. 16:33.

284. *Cf.* Acts 8:36–37.

285. Decree Concerning the Pastoral Office of Bishops in the
Church, *Christus Dominus,* No. 44.

286. See the Forward to the Sacred Congregation for the
Clergy, *General Catechetical Directory,* 1971.

287. *Ibid.*

288. *Cf.* Chapter 1, *supra.* Gabriel Moran is Professor in the
department of Humanities and the Social Sciences, New York
University; the relevant writings on the "new catechesis" are
Scripture and Tradition (1963), *Theology of Revelation* (1965) and
Catechesis of Revelation (1966). Other devotees of the new cat-
echesis were Fr. Mario Galli, S.J., Jean Piaget, and Lawrence
Kohlberg.

289. For a detailed analysis see Kelly, *op. cit.,* pp. 360–66.

290. Kelly, *op. cit.,* pp. 237–240.

291. Apostolic Exhortation *Catechesis Tradendae* of Pope John
Paul II, On Catechesis in Our Time, No. 53.

292. Alfred McBride, O. Praem., "Resoring Catechesis," *Crisis,*
October, 1995, pp. 30–32.

293. Printed in Msgr. Eugene Kevane, *Creed and Catechetics:
A Catechetical Commentary on the Credo of the People of God*
(Westminster: Christian Classics, 1978), pp. 181–189.

294. Apostolic Exhortation Announcing the Year of Faith of Pope Paul VI, printed in Kevane, *op. cit.*, p.170.

295. *Ibid.*, pp. 168–169.

296. Apostolic Letter in the Form of *Motu proprio Solemni Hac Liturgica* (Credo of the People of God) of the Supreme Pontiff Paul VI, June 30, 1968, nos. 8–30.

297. Apostolic Exhortation of Pope Paul VI, *Evangelii Nuntiandi*, No. 44. Emphasis added.

298. Printed in Msgr. Michael Wrenn, Catechisms and Controversies: Religious Education in the Postconciliar Years (San Francisco, Ignatius Press, 1991), p. 144, n.7. It was Father Sloyan who hired Fr. Charles Curran to teach at CUA, where he earned notoriety in dissenting from *Humanae Vitae*.

299. Apostolic Exhortation of Pope John Paul II, Catechesis in Our Time, *Catechesis Tradendae*, No. 2.

300. Gabriel Moran served as Professor in the department of Humanities and the Social Sciences, New York University; the relevant writings on the "new catechesis" are his *Scripture and Tradition* (1963), *Theology of Revelation* (1965) and *Catechesis of Revelation* (1966). Other proponents of the new catechesis were Fr. Mario Galli, S.J., Jean Piaget and Lawrence Kohlberg. Printed in Wrenn, *op. cit.*, pp. 118–119.

301. Printed in *Ibid*.

302. *Time* May 7, 1984.

303. For a more elaborate analysis see Wrenn, *op. cit.*, pp. 122–133.

304. See Fr. Regis Scanlon, "Is Christ Really Among Us Today?" *Homiletic and Pastoral Review,* October, 1995, accessed 7/31/08 at http://www.cfpeople.org/Apologetics/page51a043.html

305. Hellwig's *Understanding Catholicism* maintains that the words of the consecration more probably meant that Jesus' action of blessing, breaking, sharing and eating in such an assembly in His Name and memory was to be seen as the embodiment of the presence end Spirit and power of Jesus in the community.

306. See Reverend Regis Scanlon, O.F.M. Cap., "Modern Misconceptions about the Eucharist," accessed at http://www.ewtn.com/library/DOCTRINE/MODMISC.TXT This in spite of the *Credo of the People of God,* No. 6, reaffirming transubstantiation.

307. Jones, *op. cit.*, p. 78.

308. Visit http://www.recongress.org/ Speakers rotate through the various conferences; in addition, the National Conference of Catechetical Leadership, the National Catholic Education Conference, the National Conference on Pastoral Leadership's East Coast Conference to the North American Forum on the Catechumenate to the Call to Action Conference. For ecclesiastical cover, conference organizers do invite

orthodox speakers; Fr. Benedict Groeschel, Janet Smith, and Peter Kreeft have presented at the LA Congress.

309. Cf. http://www.qdomine.com/Morality_pages/lareled-congress06.htm (accessed 7/4/08).

310. Together with ex-Brother Gabriel Moran, his late wife, Maria (an ex-Sister of St. Joseph), ex-priest Sloyan of Catholic University; and ex-Sister the late Monica Hellwig of Georgetown among others.

311. McBride, *op. cit., p. 32.*

312. *Ibid.*

313. *Catechesi Tradendae,* No. 17 (emphasis added).

314. *Ibid.* No. 30. (Italics denote Douay-Rheims's translation of this Pauline phrase which is translated as "mystery of iniquity).

315. *Ibid.,* No. 49 (emphasis mine).

316. *Ibid.,* No. 22. For an illuminating account of how one veteran religious came to realize the truth of John Paul's insight, *cf.* Sr. Mary Augustine, O.P., *"Why the New Catechetics is Flawed,"* accessed 7/8/08 at http://www.ad2000.com.au/articles/1991/may1991p8_704.html

317. *Catechesis Tradendae,* No. 55.

318. Wrenn, *op. cit.,* p. 206.

319. Marian E. Crowe, "Why the Younger Generation May Be Lost to the Church," *New Oxford Review,* June, 1997, p. 10.

320. Joseph Cardinal Ratzinger, Christoph von Cardinal Schonborn, *Introduction to the Catechism of the Catholic Church* (San Francisco, Ignatius Press, 1994), p. 14.

321. A Rahnerian disciple, Herbert Vorgrimler, in a 1989 article in *Concilium* assailed the Church's teaching on the transcendent Deposit of Faith; two years later Concilium devoted an entire issue edited by Frs. Johan Baptist Metz and Edward Schillebeeckx in sympathy with Vorgrimler's argument. On the neomodernist challenge *cf.* Avery Cardinal Dulles, "The Challenge of the Catechism," *First Things*, January, 1995, pp. 46–53.

322. Congregation for the Doctrine of the Faith, Declaration *Dominus Jesus*, On the Unicity and Salvific Universality of Jesus Christ and the Church, No. 5. As a representative example, *cf.* Gabriel Moran, "Revelation: A Continuing Problem," in Catherine Dooley and Mary Collins, eds., *The Echo Within: Emerging Issues in Religious Education — A Tribute to Berard Marthaler, O.F.M., Conv.* (Allen: Thomas More, 1997), pp. 17–28.

323. *Catechism of the Catholic Church*, Nos. 11, 2037.

324. Quoted in *Anon.* "Catholicus," *DOA: The Ambush of the Universal Catechism* (Notre Dame: Crisis Books, 1993), p. 69.

325. *Cf.* Msgr. Michael Wrenn and Kenneth D. Whitehead, *Flawed Expectations: The Reception of the Catechism of the*

Catholic Church, (San Francisco: Ignatius Press, 1996), pp. 101-128,164–203.

326. "Catholicus," *op. cit.,* pp. 86*ff.*

327. Apostolic Constitution *Fidei Depositum,* On the Publication of the Catechism of the Catholic Church, No. 3.

328. "Catholicus," *op. cit.,* p. 101.

329. Meghan Hartman, *"Humanae Vitae:* Thirty Years of Discord and Dissent," *Conscience,* Autumn, 1999.

330. *New York Times/CBS* Poll, 1994.

331. *Catholic World Report/Roper* Poll, 1997.

332. Hartman, *op. cit.*

333. *Catholic World Report/Roper* Poll, 1997.

334. *Catholic World Report,* May, 1998, p. 42.

335.   http://www.romancatholic.kingston.on.ca/WEB%20 SITE%20-%20ATTACHMENTS/catechism.pdf   (Accessed 7/17/08)

336. For the up to date conformity listing of texts see http:// www.usccb.org/catechism/document/Currentlist.pdf

337. See Robert McClory, "Trials of publisher who ran afoul of Catechism," National Catholic Reporter, March 11, 1997. Available at http://findarticles.com/p/articles/mi_m1141/ is_n20_v33/ai_19264236?tag=artBody;col1

338. Printed at Catholic Culture website, http:www.catholic-culture.org/library/view.cfm?recnum=6470   (Accessed 7/11/2008).

339. *Ibid.*

340. Thomas Szyszkiewicz, "Questioning the Texts," *Catholic World Report* August/September, 2004, pp. 34–35.

341. *Catechesi Tradendae,* No. 19 (emphasis mine).

342. Leon Suprenant, "Catechizing for Conversion," Catholics United for the Faith Blog, May 28, 2008 Accessed 7/21/08 at http://www.cufblog.org/?p=362

343. *Lumen Gentium,* No. 18; *Cf.* Jn 20: 21–23, Decree on the Pastoral Office of Bishops in the Church, *Christus Dominus,* No. 1.

344. *Cf.* Mk. 3: 14–15.

345. *Lumen Gentium,* No. 21.

346. *Ibid.*

347. *Lumen Gentium,* No. 22.

348. *Ibid.,* No. 23.

349. *Ibid.,* No. 25.

350. *Ibid.*

351. *Christus Dominus,* No. 12.

352. Col 3: 1–2; *Christus Dominus,* No. 13.

353. *Ibid.,* Nos. 14–16.

354. *Lumen Gentium,* No. 26.

355. *Cf.* Jn 10:11.

356. *Lumen Gentium,* No. 27.

357. *Christus Dominus,* Nos. 36, 38.

358. *Ibid.,* No. 38.

359. In 1917 the American bishops formed the National Catholic War Council to make it possible for Catholics to contribute aid to servicemen during World War I. In 1919 Pope Benedict XV urged the episcopate to join him in working for peace and social justice. In response, the bishops organized the National Catholic Welfare Council in 1919; "Conference" soon replaced "Council" in the organization's title, and by 1922 the Conference was overseeing education, immigration and social action concerns. This model continued until 1966 when the National Conference of Catholic Bishops (NCCB) and the United States Catholic Conference (USCC) were established. The NCCB attended to the Church's own affairs in this country, while in the USCC the bishops collaborate with other Catholics to address issues that concern the Church as part of the larger society. Its committees included lay people, clergy and religious in addition to the bishops. he NCCB and the USCC were combined in 2001 to form the United States Conference of Catholic Bishops (USCCB). USCCB continues all of the work formerly done by the NCCB and the USCC with the same staff. *Cf.* http://www.usccb.org/whoweare. shtml#history

360. Russell Shaw, "Vatican II and the Culture of Dissent," *Crisis*, February/March 2006, p. 30; *Cf.* Weigel, *op. cit.*, p. 67. For an analysis of the grave nature of this reality, see Brian K.

O'Neel, "Is the Vatican Being Ignored?" *Catholic World Report*, August/September, 1999, pp. 50–59.

361. Bishop Fabian W. Bruskewitz, "On Always Our Children," *Voices* Online Edition, Winter 1997-Spring 1998 Volume XIII, No. 1–2 accessed 6/24/09 at http://www.wf-f.org/alway-sourchldspr98.html

362. Ralph M. McInerny, *What Went Wrong With Vatican II: The Catholic Crisis Explained,* (Manchester, Sophia Institute Press, 1998), p. 126.

363. Apostolic Letter of Pope John Paul II issued *Motu proprio,* On the Theological and Juridical Nature of Episcopal Conferences, *Apostolos Suos,* No. 18.

364. Origen of Alexandria, quoted in the *Catechism of the Catholic Church,* No. 817. Major occurrences were Arianism, Monophysitism, Nestorianism, Docetism, Pelagianism, the Abligensian and Waldensian heresies, the Great Western Schism, the Protestant revolt, Gallicanism and Jansenism.

365. *Codex Juris Canonici,* can. 751.

366. For a concise summary of neomodernist notions, see the Appendix in Hitchcock, *op. cit.,* pp. 187–89, "Twenty-six Heretical Notions Characterizing Radical Catholicism."

367. Especially following the infamous 1967 Land O' Lakes Conference under the leadership of Fr. Theodore Hesburgh of Notre Dame.

368. Kelly, *op. cit.,* p. *viii.*

369. To recount only one among examples that are legion: a staffer at the United States Conference of Catholic Bishops, Fr. Tom Kramer opposed the excellent RCIA preparation text, *The Teaching of Christ: A Catholic Catechism for Adults* for its assertion that Catholic teaching is identifiable with the teachings of Christ! *Cf. Ibid.*, pp. 372–379 for equally compelling evidence.

370. "We can presume that his sinister action is at work . . . where the spirit of the Gospel is watered down and rejected. . . ."

371. James. V. Schall, S.J., *Does Catholicism Still Exist?* (Staten Island: Alba House, 1994). I used the term "protestant" here in its most literal sense to denote the exercise of private judgment.

372. *i.e.*, the USCCB's *Basic Teachings for Catholic Religious Education*, cited in Chapter 6 *supra.* (emphasis mine).

373. Fr. Richard W. Gilsdorf, *The Signs of the Times: Understanding the Church Since Vatican II*, ed. Patrick F. Beno (Green Bay: Star of the Bay Press, 2008), pp. 127–138; *Cf.* Philip F. Lawler, *The Faithful Departed: The Collapse of Boston's Catholic Culture* (N.Y.: Encounter Books, 2008). pp. 92–93.

374. Kelly, *op. cit.*, p. 353.

375. The author is then *Crisis Magazine* editor Deal Hudson.

376. "The Dissenters' Secret Meeting," *Crisis Magazine* E-Letter of July 11, 2003.

377. For an insightful analysis of how orthodox bishops in the United States failed to gain hegemony over the post-conciliar education process, and thus of genuine reform following the teachings of Vatican II, as well as for the techniques of neo-modernist bishops in pushing "the spirit of Vatican II," *cf.* James Hitchcock, "Conservative Bishops, Liberal Results," http://www.wf-f.org/JFH-ConservativeBishops.html

378. Rom 13:14; Gal 2:20.

379. See Chapter 1.

380. Gn 19.

381. No. 10.

382. Weigel, *op. cit.*, pp. 76–78.

383. *Ibid.*, p. 78.

384. For recent evidence of Episcopal fulfilling the true Vatican Council II, see "U.S. Bishops Praised for Courageous Words," http://www.zenit.org/article-24147?l=english; "Bishop Expands on Why a Bishop 'Would Consider it a Privilege to Die to End Abortion;" http://www.lifesitenews.com/ldn/2009/jan/09011608.html: "Dissenters from Catholic Teaching Not Being Fired Enough from Seminary Posts: Vatican Report," http://www.usccb.org/cclv/final_report.pdf; "Texas Bishop Apologizes for Catholic Hospitals' Unethical Sterilizations;"" http://www.catholicnewsagency.com/new.php?n=14427; "AP Exclusive: Dolan to Fight ant-Catholic Bias," http://www.usatoday.com/news/religion/2009-04-13-dolan-

catholic_N.htm; "Nine More Bishops Make 42 against ND Scandal," http://www.catholic.org/politics/story. php?id=33252; "Bishops Chaput, Finn Slam Fr. Jenkins Speech at ND Commencement: 'Intellectual Vanity;'" http://catholicexchange.com/2009/05/20/118754/; Cardinal: "Obama Election 'Apocalyptic,'" http://ncronline.org/node/2588; "Burkean bishops," *Catholic World Report,* July, 2007, pp. 25–27; "Burke to Fellow Bishops: Stop Ignoring Canon Law," *Catholic World Report,* November, 2007, pp. 26–27, Russell Shaw, "Was 2009 a Turning Point?" accessed 8/14/2010 at http://catholicexchange.com/2009/12/31/125622/

385. For all of this see, The Catholic World Report Staff, "The Bishop as Bishop," *The Catholic World Report,* November, 2001, p. 21.

386. *Catechism of the Catholic Church,* No. 1237. On truths to consider when it comes to the reality and work of the Devil see "Christian Faith and Demonology," in Austin Flannery, Ed., *More Post Conciliar Documents* (Liturgical Press, 1982).

387. Jn 12:31.

388. Quoted at http://www.zenit.org/article-5745?l=english Accessed 8/14/2010.

389. *Cf.* Rom 12:2.

390. Titus 3:3; Ephesians 2:2.

391. Ephesians 3:8.

392. Joseph Cardinal Ratzinger, *Address to Catechists and Religion Teachers*, December 2000. Accessed 7/9/2010 at http://www.ewtn.com/new_evangelization/Ratzinger.htm

393. Peter Kreeft, "Luther, Faith and Good Works," *National Catholic Register*, November 10, 1991, p. 8.

394. Mk 16:15–16.

395. *Lumen Gentium*, No. 16. (Emphasis added).

396. Rom 1:21–22.

397. Mt 7:13.

398. John Paul II, *Redemptor Hominis*, No. 7.

399. Archbishop Charles J. Chaput, OFM Cap., Address of June 24, 2010 to the Liturgical Institute in Chicago, "Evangelization and the Renewal of the Liturgy," accessed 7/3/2010 at http://www.archden.org/index.cfm/ID/4113

400. *Ibid.*

401. John Paul II, *Redemptoris missio*, On the permanent validity of the Church's missionary mandate, No. 86.

402. http://www.catholic.org/international/international_story.php?id=37190 Accessed 7/4/2010.

403. Acts 26: 16–18.

404. Quoted in Vittorio Messori, ed., *The Ratzinger Report*, pp. 138–139.

405. Joseph Cardinal Ratzinger, *Address to Catechists and Religion Teachers*, December 2000.

406. 1 Peter 5:8.

407. Quoted at http://www.catholicbible101.com/spiritual-warfare.htm#504072496 Accessed 7/1/2010

408. Pastoral Constitution on the Church in the Modern World, *Gaudium et Spes,* No. 37.

409. Rev 3:16.

410. *Cf.* 2 Tim 4:7.

CPSIA information can be obtained at www.ICGtesting.com
Printed in the USA
BVOW080147120313

315276BV00003B/3/P